AF505970

Financial Regulation after the Global Recession

Also by Carlos M. Peláez and Carlos A. Peláez

INTERNATIONAL FINANCIAL ARCHITECTURE: G7, IMF, BIS, Debtors and Creditors

THE GLOBAL RECESSION RISK: Dollar Devaluation and the World Economy

GLOBALIZATION AND THE STATE: Volume I

GLOBALIZATION AND THE STATE: Volume II

GOVERNMENT INTERVENTION IN GLOBALIZATION: Regulation, Trade and Devaluation Wars

REGULATION OF BANKS AND FINANCE: Theory and Policy after the Credit Crisis

Financial Regulation after the Global Recession

Carlos M. Peláez and Carlos A. Peláez

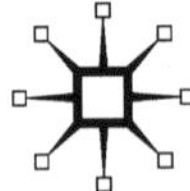

First published 2009 by
PALGRAVE MACMILLAN

Palgrave Macmillan in the UK is an imprint of Macmillan Publishers Limited, registered in England, company number 785998, of Houndmills, Basingstoke, Hampshire RG21 6XS.

Palgrave Macmillan in the US is a division of St Martin's Press LLC, 175 Fifth Avenue, New York, NY 10010.

Palgrave Macmillan is the global academic imprint of the above companies and has companies and representatives throughout the world.

Palgrave® and Macmillan® are registered trademarks in the United States, the United Kingdom, Europe and other countries.

ISBN: 978-0-230-23902-9 hardback

This book is printed on paper suitable for recycling and made from fully managed and sustained forest sources. Logging, pulping and manufacturing processes are expected to conform to the environmental regulations of the country of origin.

A catalogue record for this book is available from the British Library.

A catalog record for this book is available from the Library of Congress.

Printed and bound in Great Britain by
CPI Antony Rowe, Chippenham and Eastbourne

To Magnolia and Penelope

Contents

Tables

Abbreviations

ABCP	Asset backed commercial paper
ABS	Asset backed security
AIG	American International Group
ATM	Automatic teller machine
BCBS	Basel Committee on Banking Supervision
BHC	Bank holding company
BLS	Bureau of Labor Statistics
BOE	Bank of England
BOJ	Bank of Japan
BP	Basis point
CAP	Capital Assistance Program
CD	Certificate of deposit
CDS	Credit default swap
CDO	Collateralized debt obligation
CFTC	Commodities Futures Trading Commission
CLO	Collateralized loan obligation
CLOF	Chief legal officer
COP	Congressional Oversight Board
D&O	Directors and officers
DGP	Debt Guarantee Program
EC	European Commission
ECB	European Central Bank
EESA	Emergency Economic Stabilization Act of 2008
EMU	European Monetary Union
ERM	Enterprise risk management
ESCB	European System of Central Banks
EU	European Union
EUC	European Union Council
FCPA	Foreign Corrupt Practices Act of 1976
FDIC	Federal Deposit Insurance Corporation
FDICIA	FDIC Improvement Act
FHA	Federal Housing Administration
FHC	Financial holding company
FHLB	Federal Home Loan Bank
FIRREA	Financial Institutions Reform, Recovery and Enforcement Act of 1989

FOHF	Fund of hedge funds
FOMC	Federal Open Market Committee
FRB	Federal Reserve Bank
FRBO	Board of Governors of the Federal Reserve System
FRBNY	Federal Reserve Bank of New York
FRS	Federal Reserve System
FSA	Financial Services Authority
FSF	Functional structural finance
FSLIC	Federal Savings and Loan Insurance Corporation
FSMA	Financial Services and Market Act of 2000
FSOB	Financial Stability Oversight Board
FSP	Financial Stability Plan
G7	Group of Seven
G30	Group of Thirty
FX	Foreign exchange
GAADP	Generally accepted auditing principles
GAAP	Generally accepted accounting principles
GAO	US General Accounting Office
GSE	Government-sponsored enterprise
HICP	Harmonized index of consumer prices
HUD	US Department of Housing and Urban Development
IBF	International banking facility
IMES	Institute of Monetary and Economic Studies
IMF	International Monetary Fund
IOLTA	Interest on lawyers trust accounts
IRA	Individual retirement account
IRB	Internal-ratings based
IT	Information technology
LBO	Leveraged buyout
LCR	Least-cost resolution
LGD	Loss given default
LOLR	Lender of last resort
LSE	London Stock Exchange
M&A	Mergers and acquisitions
MBO	Management buyout
MBS	Mortgage-backed security
MPC	Monetary Policy Committee
MTM	Mark to market accounting
NCB	National central banks
NCUA	National Credit Union Administration
NCUSIF	National Credit Union Share Insurance Fund

NIE	New institutional economics
NIRA	National Industrial Recovery Act
NLRA	National Labor Relations Act
NOW	Negotiable order of withdrawal accounts
NPV	Net present value
NYS	New York State
NYSBD	New York State Banking Department
OCC	Office of the Comptroller of the Currency
OECD	Organization for Economic Cooperation and Development
OFHEO	Office of Federal Housing Enterprise Oversight
OPSR	Official prudential and systemic regulation
OTC	Over-the-counter
OTS	Office of Thrift Supervision
PCA	Prompt corrective action
PCAOB	Public Company Accounting Oversight Board
PPIP	Public-Private Investment Program
PPIPF	Public-Private Investment Program Funds
QLCC	Qualified legal compliance committee
REPIX	Retail price index excluding mortgage payments
RSRP	Reverse sale and repurchase agreement
RTC	Resolution Trust Corporation
S&L	Savings and loan
SAIF	Savings Association Insurance Fund
SLHC	Savings and loan holding companies
SME	Small and medium enterprises
SEC	Securities and Exchange Commission
SEIR	Structured early intervention resolution
SIV	Structured investment vehicle
SOX	Sarbanes-Oxley Act of 2002
SPV	Special purpose vehicle
SRO	Self-regulatory organization
SRP	Sale and repurchase agreement
TAF	Term Auction Facility
TAGP	Transactions Account Guarantee Program
TALF	Term Asset-Backed Securities Loan Facility
TARP	Troubled Assets Relief Program
TLGP	Temporary Liquidity Guarantee Program
VA	Veterans Administration
WPA	Works Progress Administration
WTO	World Trade Organization

Acknowledgments

This book provides an accessible review of financial regulation in the light of the global recession. We are very grateful to Taiba Batool, Economics Editor of Palgrave Macmillan, for the encouragement of the project and for important improvements. We are most grateful to Gemma Papageorgiou at Palgrave Macmillan for steering the manuscript to publication. The team at Newgen Imaging Systems revised the manuscript with highly useful suggestions and competent typesetting for final publication.

We are grateful to many friends who helped us in this effort. A partial list includes Professor Antonio Delfim Netto, Ambassador Richard T. McCormack, Senator Heráclito Fortes, Professor Paulo Yokota, and Eduardo Mendez. Magnolia Maciel Peláez, DDS, and Penelope Solis, JD, reviewed the manuscript providing many suggestions deriving from their long experience of health regulation, which is the subject of a new joint project.

In writing this book we remembered dear friends and colleagues who helped and motivated in the interest on scholarly work and international affairs, Clay and Rondo Cameron and Otilia and Nicholas Georgescu-Roegen. We are solely responsible for the shortcomings and errors in this work.

CARLOS M. PELÁEZ AND CARLOS A. PELÁEZ
ATLANTIC CITY AND NEW YORK CITY

Introduction, Scope, and Content

One of the most cited legal scholars observes the regulatory environment of the credit/dollar crisis as:[1]

> A natural response is to tighten up regulation. In the case of commercial banks, this would not require new legislation. The bank regulators have virtually plenary control over banks: thus the crack "what does a bank say when a regulator tells it to jump?" Answer: "How high?"

The fact is that there is an ambitious, extensive, and heavy agenda for regulation of banks and financial institutions. This book provides an accessible review of the principles and experience of banking and financial regulation. Regulation must be based on clear analysis of the origins and resolution of the credit/dollar crisis that has culminated in the global recession to avoid overregulation that can frustrate economic growth. Finance is one of the most technically forbidding fields in economics. This book provides access to financial principles while maintaining the original technical purity with which to analyze the credit/dollar crisis and regulation proposals. Regulatory reform will affect the strength of the recovery of the economy and, thus, future prosperity.

Chapter 1 consists of a systematic review of the economic theory of the state. The difficulty of resolving economic issues by appeal to data in contrast with science results in a collection of approaches or models instead of a unified theory. Economists have constructed a first best allocation of scarce resources, such as capital, labor, and natural resources, to producing competing goods and services, whose consumption provide satisfaction to society. The breakdown of the abstract assumptions of this first best is termed "market failure," which is used to propose government intervention. This is the *public-interest view* by which government intervention consists of collective action to improve the well-being of society as a whole. For example, a lending bank knows less well the actual financial/economic situation of a potential borrower than the borrower herself. This imperfect information is called asymmetry of information. Investors ceased to finance assets of banks because of the uncertainty of their quality or likelihood of default. In fact, banks themselves were uncertain about the actual quality of their own assets. Consumer loans, such as for purchasing autos, credit cards, and others, are bundled into securities sold to investors that in turn finance them with short-term loans from other investors. The collective action in this case has consisted of loans by central banks, such as the US Federal Reserve System (FRS), to finance the securities, reducing uncertainty, and restoring credit. Another regulatory measure is to eliminate asymmetry of information by mandating strict standards on loans, inspected and enforced by the financial authorities, such as the FRS. The *private interest view* argues that the regulators, politicians, and government officials, promote their self-interest instead of those of the public by exchanging regulation for political contributions from the regulated industries. That is, the industry captures the political process, influencing regulation to obtain excess profits. For example, incumbent banks obtained restrictions on the establishment of new banks from out of state or within states to maintain local monopolies that allowed them to charge higher interest rates to borrowers and pay lower interest rates to depositors. The major approaches to regulation are analyzed in Chapter 1 to provide a unified framework for issues that recur throughout the text.

The approaches to banking and financial regulation are divided into two general arguments in Chapter 2. Most of the agenda originating in official sources follows the approach of official prudential and systemic regulation (OPSR). Market failures, such as lax credit standards in nonprime mortgages, require strong regulation to prevent future crises. The functional structural finance (FSF) view departs from the need of innovation in functions performed by banks and financial institutions in a structure that includes also government regulation, thus being free of ideology. The FSF view balances regulation with the need to provide credit in financing progress. The functions of banks are reviewed because they are basic to understanding regulation. The chapter also considers two basic types of regulation of banks: minimum capital requirements as a buffer for unforeseen losses and deposit insurance to prevent bank runs. The United States has a complex, monumental system of housing finance around Fannie Mae and Freddie Mac and the Federal Housing Administration (FHA), which is reviewed in detail.

Chapter 3 considers the issues of monopoly in banking markets and central banking. The elimination of restrictions on interstate and intrastate banking and the technological revolution of online banking and automatic teller machines (ATM) have eroded the power of banks in local markets. The US FRS and the major central banks of the world are analyzed exhaustively. Supervisors inspect banks' operations and regulators create and implement rules for their conduct. The US system has multiple federal and state regulatory agencies but its simplification is not in the agenda perhaps because of political factors and complexity. The system of inflation targets of the Bank of England (BOE) is carefully analyzed because it was considered the paradigm of central banking but it has been eroded by the credit/dollar crisis. The chapter also provides the basic principles for understanding the policies followed by central banks.

The experience with recession regulation during the Great Depression is analyzed in Chapter 4 by means of the Glass-Steagall Act of 1933 that prohibited investment banking at commercial banks. There is evidence that elite investment banks influenced securities legislation to prevent the competition in their markets by the national retail distribution of securities created during the financing of World War I. Glass Steagall was not repealed until 1999, distorting banking in the United States during almost 70 years. There were no effects on the credit/dollar crisis from repealing Glass Steagall. Hedge funds are analyzed not because they have been important in the credit/dollar crisis or earlier crises but because they are in nearly every regulatory proposal perhaps just for the sake of completeness. A critical issue in finance is corporate governance or the solution to the conflict of managers promoting their self-interest at the expense of shareholders. Incentive remuneration of executives has attracted attention from the general public to the President and the principles of analysis are provided. The United States has created an effective system of corporate law crafted by the Delaware courts over many decisions.

Chapter 5 considers regulation of capital markets or the issue and trading of equity of corporations. There are two major approaches to securities regulation: rules and principles. The Securities Exchange Act of 1934 created the Securities and Exchange Commission (SEC) entrusted with protecting investors and the general public from abuse. The SEC regulates by rulemaking and more aggressive litigation. The Financial Services Authority (FSA) of the United Kingdom followed principles and lighter touch of regulation. The credit/dollar crisis has eroded both approaches, with the SEC and the FSA proposing more intrusive and aggressive regulation. The best example of rush of regulation is the Sarbanes-Oxley Act of 2002 (SOX), which created onerous compliance on US corporations with hardly concrete new benefits. There are no proposals in the agenda to modify SOX. There is active debate on whether SOX caused erosion of the competitiveness of US securities markets similar to the loss to London of banking and foreign exchange following Regulation Q interest rates ceilings that was part of the Glass-Steagall Act of 1933.

The tools and material developed in the first five chapters are used in Chapter 6 in analyzing the causes and resolution of the credit/dollar crisis. The public interest/OPSR view argues that the crisis was created by lax standards of credit and risk management in banks. Banks lent to nonprime borrowers with careless evaluation and documentation, bundled the mortgages in securities, sold them to investors, and kept a part for high profits. The essence of regulatory proposals is the creation of a systemic regulator to prevent contagion of the crisis among large and complex banks. Supervision would be tightened to control the risks of these large institutions.

The private interest/FSF view finds the origin of the credit/dollar crisis in the reduction by the Fed of interest rates among banks to nearly zero in 2003–4 in fear of deflation that never occurred. The United States provides a yearly housing subsidy of $221 billion. In addition, Fannie Mae and Freddie Mac guaranteed or acquired $1.6 trillion nonprime mortgages for a total 10.5 million unsustainable nonprime loans using reckless leverage of 75 to 1. Fannie Mae and Freddie Mac were rightly perceived as free of risk of insolvency because of the implicit guarantee by the full faith and credit of the US government. The low interest rates, the housing subsidy, and the endorsement of nonprime loans by the US government through Fannie Mae and Freddie Mac created the massive default of loans by borrowers that were not creditworthy. The financial innovation of bundling loans to finance them in markets was merely the vehicle that processed the primary adverse shock of low interest rates and guarantees to nonprime loans.

Chapter 6 reviews the policies followed by the Fed and Treasury in the attempt of resolving the credit/dollar crisis. There is also extended discussion of the current resolution efforts of separating good and bad assets in banks and of the similar Swedish workout program. The Conclusion summarizes views on the credit/dollar crisis. The notes to the extensive literature are at the end followed by an index of subjects.

1
Government Intervention and Finance

Introduction

There is significant government intervention in financial markets. The economic theory of the state or regulation does not provide unique and generally accepted principles. There are many approaches. Finance is singled out for regulation because financial entities provide services instead of goods for final consumption, creating the impression that financial institutions are merely intermediaries that do not add to output. In addition, financial crises have been accompanied by declines in production and rising unemployment. This chapter provides a comprehensive review of these approaches to regulation that helps to understand the issues relating to financial regulation. The final sections elaborate the reasons for existence of financial markets and their role in economic growth. An appendix introduces present value concepts.

The first best of efficiency and satisfaction

Adam Smith launched economics in 1776 with his *Wealth of Nations*. This book is rich in analysis of the interactions of humans in economic affairs. It would be interesting to learn what Adam Smith would think of the contemporary interpretation of his concept of the invisible hand. The proposition is that individuals in seeking their self-interest promote the public good.[2] Perhaps it would be more appropriate to relate the ideas of Smith to the reaction during his times to mercantilism and excessive intervention by the state in economic affairs. The main concern of Smith was on how specialization of tasks in the modern industrial factory expanded the market; this economic growth increased the "national dividend" or goods and services produced by a nation.

Increasing amounts of goods and services, or a growing pie, increased economic welfare.[3] Economists have concentrated in analyzing the conditions under which the allocation of resources in markets, without intervention by the state, would result on its own in maximum efficiency in the production of goods and services and optimum welfare or satisfaction. It took two centuries after Adam Smith to rigorously prove this proposition.

Individuals derive satisfaction or welfare from the consumption of goods and services. An objective of an economic system is to attain optimum satisfaction, that is, that individuals feel the happiest possible in the consumption of goods, such as automobiles, and the use of services, such as health care. Production consists of using the available technology to combine inputs or resources of production—capital, labor, and natural resources—in producing goods and services. In a steel mill, capital consists of the installed machinery and equipment and bank balances to pay for production; workers provide labor; and coal and iron ore are the natural resources. The task of the economic system is to attain efficiency, which consists of combining technology and resources or inputs to obtain the maximum output possible subject to costs.

All theory is merely an attempt to explain reality with a simplified set of assumptions. The application of logic to these assumptions provides a compact or shorthand explanation and prediction of reality. The theory of the first best departs from ideal or simplified conditions that permit the derivation of simple but powerful principles. The basic assumption of the first best is the perfectly competitive model or the lack of "frictions," which violate the assumptions. Some of the assumptions are as follows. There is no "market power" by buyers or sellers of goods and services, which means that no individual buyer or seller is large enough to influence market prices as in a region with only one public electricity company. Goods and services are perfectly divisible in small quantities, such that huge investments are not required to establish production in certain goods, which would prevent entry of producers. If investment is indivisible, such as an auto factory or an electricity plant that require large minimum investment in a factory, the first producer to enter can gain market or monopoly power to set prices because of the huge investment required by competitors. There are no "externalities." For example, the increase in output of a steel factory does not cause pollution that soils the production of the nearby laundry. Buyers and sellers of goods and services have perfect information. For example, bankers know exactly the economic/financial conditions of borrowers such that there is no adverse selection, which means that banks finance the projects that result in economic efficiency. Under perfect information the borrower could not use the loan in activities with higher risk without knowledge by the lender or bank. For example, under less than perfect competition the borrower could invest in real estate speculation instead of in the agreed project of producing goods and services. This use of the loan in higher-risk speculative activities than in the agreed loan project is called moral hazard, which could cause unexpected default. A significant part of the text in this volume consists of relaxing these assumptions to explore the rationale for government intervention.

The proof of the first-best outcome requires the concept of "Pareto optimality," named after its originator Vilfredo Pareto. There is Pareto optimality in consumption when it is not possible to improve the satisfaction of one consumer without reducing that of another. There is Pareto optimality in production when it is not possible to improve the output of a good or service without reducing that of another. There is overall Pareto optimality when it occurs both in consumption and production.

There are two fundamental welfare theorems in economics.[4] The first theorem states that the allocation of inputs under perfect competition results in an optimum of satisfaction and maximum efficiency, that is, in overall Pareto optimality. The second theorem states that every state of overall Pareto optimality can be converted into a perfectly competitive allocation of resources by "lump sum" transfers of resources. The economics of welfare explores alternative economic states. A state differs from another one, for example, in the conditions or not of perfect competition, taxes, subsidies, and so on. Welfare in economics is well-being or efficiency in consumption and production. It does not have the connotation of the welfare programs such as social security, health benefits, and others. However, those programs can be analyzed with welfare economics: the comparison of the "welfare" or well-being of the society in the states of having or not having those programs.

The theory of second best

The first best is unlikely to occur in reality if judged by the unrealistic assumptions. The theory of second best throws cold comfort on economics. In general, it states that if one of the conditions for the first best is not attained, it does not necessarily improve welfare (in the well-being sense) to try to enforce the other conditions. It becomes nearly impossible to assess in theory or practice what is the second-best solution.[5]

An example serves to illustrate the theory. Under perfect competition price is equal to marginal cost. This is a basic condition for attaining economic efficiency in the long run. Marginal cost is the addition to cost of increasing production by an extra or marginal unit. The costs include "normal profits," or those minimum profits that the producer must receive to engage in production. Economic profits, or those in excess of normal profits, are zero. Producing an extra unit brings in revenue in its price and increases costs by marginal cost. If price were higher than marginal cost, the producer would gain by producing an extra unit because it would bring more, price, than what it costs, marginal cost. If price were lower than marginal cost, producing an extra unit would lose money. Thus, the perfectly competitive producer would produce exactly the output corresponding to price equal to marginal cost. Under Pareto optimality, prices equal marginal cost in all activities.

Under market power, the monopolist produces an output corresponding to a price higher than marginal cost, earning excess profits. The theory of second best states that when one condition is violated in the first best, such as equality of price and marginal cost, it is nearly impossible to evaluate, theoretically or empirically, the second best allocation of resources. Complying with marginal conditions of the first best does not necessarily improve economic well-being or welfare.

The public interest view

Market failure occurs when the market on its own cannot attain the first best of efficiency and welfare. The public interest view recommends policies of ameliorating market failures to obtain Pareto improvements over a free-market allocation. That is, public policy may increase satisfaction of some agents without reducing the satisfaction of others. The coercion powers of the government may be used to tax and subsidize economic activities to obtain results that are superior to those occurring under free markets. The public interest view focuses on identification of market failures and policies that can ameliorate their effects. Moreover, the public interest view predicts that government intervention occurs in response to market failures.

There are two classical cases of market failure in "neoclassical economics."[6] There could be positive or negative externalities in production. A second set of market failures originates in the occurrence of "market power," as, for example, the existence of only one source of spring water in a community, such that the owner can set the price to obtain excess profits.

There is a negative externality or nuisance when the output of one factory increases the cost of another factory. Suppose there is a laundry shop in a community that dries the clothing with the heat of the sun. A new steel factory is then established such that its pollution soils the laundry. In this case

> Marginal cost of steel producer = private marginal cost < marginal social cost = marginal cost of steel producer plus cost of pollution

The decision of the polluter ignores the cost of pollution. The solution is a per unit tax on the price of steel to make output lower, corresponding to marginal social cost. The production of greenhouse gases is an externality of modern economic activity that pollutes the atmosphere, causing potential global warming with harmful effects. The proposed solution is a price of carbon to reduce output to slow the increase in the stock of greenhouse gases.

There is a positive externality when the output of one good or service reduces the cost of others. Education increases the efficiency of most other economic activities, lowering their costs. However, education provided by a free market without government intervention may not be sufficient for attaining Pareto optimality. Intervention could be in the form of a subsidy to increase education to the socially desirable level.

In the case of market power, output is lower than under perfect competition because price exceeds marginal cost. The solution in terms of government intervention would be regulation to administer the prices of monopolies in a way that output is at the socially desirable level. However, the second-best theory creeps in the analysis. Higher output by the monopolist could result in higher pollution, constituting a simple example of how restoring a marginal condition of the first best need not result in an improvement of welfare. Unfortunately, there is no comprehensive model in economics including all frictions, or violations of assumptions, that can be used in practical policy problems. The first best does not exist in the real world, which is plagued by frictions.

Imperfect information

The model of perfect competition requires perfect information. All agents have the same information on prices, technology, credit, and so on. Several economists writing after 1970 focus on incorporating in models asymmetry of information, consisting of the assumption that some agents have information that others do not possess.[7] These efforts prove that in case of imperfect information, the free market does not attain Pareto optimality on its own. Thus, there is the possibility that collective action in the form of government intervention may implement Pareto-improving policies.

The initial intention in analyzing asymmetry of information was to explain the illiquidity or lack of a market for used cars because sellers had better knowledge of the vehicle than potential buyers.[8] Imperfect information could result in extremely thin markets. This illiquidity could explain the fluctuations in output and sales of new cars that were important determinants of economic activity in the first decades after World War II. Asymmetric information had solutions in some markets by means of repeat sale and reputation. However, there were other markets, such as insurance and credit that could experience serious breakdowns. Important examples were the difficulty of the elderly in obtaining health insurance and small business in receiving credit. Underdevelopment is significantly caused by the failure of credit markets.

The interpretation is that the incorporation of asymmetric information in price theory constituted part of a revolution to derive postulates from more realistic assumptions than in the first best. In standard economics, markets are Pareto efficient unless there are market failures. Thus, Pareto efficiency is not attained under imperfect information.[9] In this view, asymmetry of information requires a new paradigm of economics as well as new avenues of political economy. Asymmetry of information is widespread in the economy. It consists of the proposition that knowledge differs among people.[10] For example, the individual buying insurance has knowledge of her health habits, such as regular exercise, which are not available to the insurance company. The borrower knows more about her financial situation and the viability of a project than the lender and the owner of the firm knows more than the potential investor. Market equilibrium with imperfect information may have undesirable characteristics. In the credit market, there may be credit rationing, as lenders do not lend to borrowers above a certain interest rate because of the uncertainty that borrowers will default. This uncertainty is caused by the lack of information on the creditworthiness of those borrowers. In the labor market, the wage rate may be above the rate at which demand and supply of labor are equal, resulting in unemployment.

The information paradigm affirms that asymmetry of information is more important in financial markets than in those of goods.[11] Thus, the government should provide information that would be missing under free financial markets. Information on the soundness of financial institutions is indispensable for investors and depositors to make their best decisions. There are positive externalities in monitoring of debtors by financial institutions that could encourage lending by other lenders. There are negative externalities by unsound creditors that may prevent raising capital by healthier institutions. The failure of a bank or its perceived insolvency may spread to other financial institutions, preventing availability of credit to potential borrowers with sound projects. Imperfect information may cause the choice of unsound debtors or adverse selection and the use of funds for higher risk or moral hazard. Perfect competition breaks when information is not perfectly available. The breakdown of the assumption of perfect information prevents Pareto optimality. Government-enforced disclosure of information may improve choices by investors.

Government failure

The correction of market failures by designing policies that attain efficient allocation appears quite difficult. Once the economy is in the world of second best, policy design may be frustrating. The authorities would themselves need perfect information, that is, the regulators must be omniscient, knowing everything, and omnipotent, capable of doing everything, similar to the "benevolent dictator" in the theory of welfare economics. The possibility of government failure is actively debated in the technical and policy literature.

The proponents of the public interest view may be excessively enthusiastic in comparing intervention by a government that never makes mistakes with a "blackboard" or textbook case of market failure. This is the "Nirvana Fallacy," comparing theoretical markets that have imperfections with flawless government intervention.[12] If the markets fail because of imperfect information, government intervention will also fail for the same reason. There is no superiority of information by the government in intervention. For example, there is no reason why government-owned banks would give fewer loans to defaulting companies than privately owned banks. In fact the traffic of political influence may result in more bad loans in government-owned banks because the need of avoiding bankruptcy creates disincentives to provide bad loans in privately managed banks. Government-owned banks are more likely to provide loans to socially unrewarding projects of vested interests that have political connections and power passing on the burden to the general public in the form of taxes, higher product prices, and an inefficient economy.

The estimate of the cost of inefficiencies caused by the government in intervention to ameliorate market failures is in the hundreds of billions of dollars.[13] In cases of actual existence of market failures, there were successes at the expense of diminishing significant benefits and there were reductions of welfare or economic well-being in various instances. Government failures occur because policies are erroneous or ineffectively implemented, being subject to influence by interest groups against the general social interest. There are cases when there is evidence favoring government measures, but politics and ineffectiveness of the relevant agencies prevent sound policy and implementation.

Transactions costs and property rights

Neoclassical or mainstream economics and the theory and policy of market failures ignored the existence of transaction costs. This is not uncommon when developing theories from abstract assumptions; a change in assumptions leads to a different proposition. The fact is that transaction costs are significantly large and cannot be ignored in the analysis of the firm and in their relation to property rights.

An important turning point in the debate is that the conventional approach to externalities identifies a perpetrator and a victim and takes actions to make the perpetrator compensate the victim.[14] This approach is wrong because of the essentially reciprocal nature of externalities. The principle should be preventing the most serious harm.

The *first case* considered is that of the pricing or market system working effectively *with liability for damage and without costs.*[15] In this case, the damaging business has to pay for the cost of the damage and there is the explicit assumption of no costs of transactions. It is important to incorporate these costs in the decision by firms, revealing their implications for allocation and public policy. The costs consist of almost everything that is not included in the costs of physical production and transportation. They include the costs of negotiation, legal counsel, litigation, and enforcement of judgments, among many. If there are no such costs, the party that is liable would bargain with the other party and enter into an agreement that would internalize the externalities. For example, internalizing by the steel factory would take into account the price of clean air, which would allow measurement of marginal social cost, determining output at the socially desirable level at which price equals marginal social cost. This is basically the idea in climate change: finding a price for carbon that would signal companies output that slows global warming.

Thus, transaction costs are the expenses incurred in bargaining the effects of externalities or could be considered as the costs of internalizing the externalities. Internalizing means that the output is equivalent to that with taxes or subsidies. The discovery in this case of liability and no transactions costs is that if property rights are well-defined and there are no transaction costs the perfectly competitive market would attain efficient allocation without any need of government intervention. There is no claim that this case occurs in reality, but it simply brings in relief the neglect of the costs by neoclassical economics and the derived market failure analysis and how they affect property rights and a solution to the problem. It qualifies an important proposition of neoclassical economics.

The *second case* maintains the assumption of no transaction costs.[16] However, in this case there is no rule of liability for damages. The pricing system has no liability for damage and no transaction costs. In this case, there may still be bargaining between the parties in the externality but a solution is uncertain. The competitive pricing system may or may not internalize the externalities, that is, take into consideration the price of carbon in the greenhouse gas example.

The approach uses the assumption of no transaction costs in the first two cases, which is considered to be very unrealistic.[17] The third case describes the types of transaction costs. These costs include discovering the party for the transaction, communicating the desire to bargain, and the terms of bargaining, engaging in the negotiations to reach a settlement, drafting the contract, ascertaining by inspection that there is compliance with the terms of the contract and many other transaction activities. These transaction costs are quite high in the real world, close to one half of GDP in the United States,[18] such that they would preclude the transactions hypothesized in the model with no transaction costs. In cases of high costs the government may use its coercion powers to force a solution. However, such a solution is not costless because the government also faces costs, which in some cases may be extremely high. The arrangements to find a solution may differ from case to case. The theory of second best resurfaces in the analysis. In the greenhouse gas example the government would levy a carbon price on producers.

The new institutional economics

There are two distinguishing characteristics in the new institutional economics (NIE), the claims that institutions are important and that they can be analyzed by economic theory. The second characteristic distinguishes the NIE from the initial US institutionalists.[19] The focus is not the traditional economic concerns of allocation but the use of economic tools to analyze how institutions developed the way they did.

Table 1.1 shows the stages of institutional development that require different forms of social analysis.[20] Institutional research is concerned with the two intermediate stages, institutional environment and governance. The final stage is the subject of the theory of choice or mainstream economics.

The research on the economics of property rights focuses on the issues of the second stage of institutional environment. According to a strand of thought, the system of private enterprise needs property rights to function adequately.[21] The user of a resource has to remunerate the owner. There must be definition of property rights and a process of arbitration of disputes for optimum allocation of resources.

An important characteristic of the NIE is the criticism of ideals based on omniscience, benevolence, nil transaction costs, and similar assumptions. Various works challenged the proposition of omniscient and benevolent governments that could ameliorate all market failures.[22] All forms of organization are subject to failures, including markets and the government.[23]

The analysis of transactions costs[24] leads to the concept of the firm as a governance structure.[25] Governance is the set of rules and vehicles by which a firm obtains optimum results from its operations. It can consist of checks and balances such as the role of independent directors in

Table 1.1   Stages of economic institutions

Stage	Institutional Characteristics
I Embeddedness	Informal institutions, customs, traditions, norms, religion
II Institutional environment	Game rules: property (polity, judiciary, bureaucracy)
III Governance	Game play: contract, relating governance structures and transactions
IV Allocation/employment	Prices, quantities, incentives

Source: Oliver Williamson, The new institutional economics: taking stock, looking ahead. *Journal of Economic Literature* 38 (3, 2000): 595–613.

the corporate board to enforce the interests of shareholders in the decisions and actions of executives or senior management. Governance and transactions are aligned in accordance with their economies of transaction costs, requiring descriptions of transactions, governance structure, and the process of economizing transaction costs. The fundamental transaction cost is vertical integration. There are multiple consequences for policy arising from labor, capital, corporate governance, regulation/deregulation, multinational, and public sector transactions.

The economic theory of regulation

The economists of the University of Chicago developed what came to be known as the economic theory of regulation. This theory is the essence of the private interest view of regulation with predictions that are different from those of the public view. The public interest view predicts that regulation will occur in response to market failures. The excess profits charged by a monopolist or the externalities of pollution cause government intervention to find an efficient allocation that cannot be obtained in a free market. The private interest view claims that the regulated industrialists, politicians, and government officials interact to create regulatory agencies and measures to optimize their self-interests. It is common for regulation to have outcomes that are different from those intended by regulation.[26]

The departing point for what came to be known as the economic theory of regulation is that the state has the power to help or harm many industries.[27] The theory intends to analyze the parties receiving the benefits or costs of regulation, the shape of regulation and its impact on efficiency or resource allocation. The main proposition is that the regulated industry manipulates the government agency for its benefit. This aspect of the theory became known as regulatory capture or the control of the regulatory body by the regulated industry for its self-interest.

The state has unique strength in its power to coerce.[28] Taxation permits the government to seize money. The state does not require the consent of individuals and companies to organize resources and take decisions of households and companies. Thus, an industry can capture the state to increase its profits. The industry may obtain four different types of favors from the government:[29] direct subsidy of money; restriction of entry in the industry by a rival to create market power, obtaining excess profits; interference with substitute and complementary goods to enhance market power; and fixing advantageous prices by regulatory agencies.

The objective function for maximization of self-interest by political actors includes attaining and maintaining political power.[30] The representative politician has the power of deciding the variables in regulation such as prices, numbers of firms and others. Votes and money are the two objects of choice of politicians. Groups may vote for or against the representative politician depending on the effects of a regulatory measure. The politician prefers decisions that result in favorable votes because her goal is obtaining and maintaining power. There are multiple forms by which regulatory decisions can secure campaign funding, free efforts to get out the vote, bribes, or well-remunerated political appointments.

The representative politician values wealth and knows that the successful election bid requires campaigns that have financing and qualified staff. Thus, the politician will focus on the consequences of regulatory measures for obtaining votes as well as money for electoral purposes. The essence of the theory is that the representative politician does not maximize the welfare of the constituency but rather her very own. Optimization of aggregate welfare is important only in increasing the economy to obtain a larger share of its growth. In short, the politicians and regulators exchange regulatory measures for votes and money. The delivery of the benefits requires some form of group organization.[31]

The target of regulation is one or a few producers operating in monopolistic or oligopolistic markets in which they make excess profits. These producers do not have to create costly organizations to raise the funds required to bid for the regulatory measures because they are individually financially strong. The organizations have low costs because they represent only a few producers. The producers will likely win the bidding for regulatory measures because of the strength of their financial position and the ease of organization. Regulatory capture is more likely by producers than consumers.

The original contribution of capture[32] is termed the economic theory of regulation to distinguish it from earlier theories of capture of regulation.[33] The distinguishing characteristic is the formal consideration of demand and supply of regulation. Economists derive formally demand equations from maximization of satisfaction and supply from maximization of net revenue or profits. The link with the earlier capture theories of political science is that economic regulation is designed to promote the interests of groups with effective political pressure.

There are two important deficiencies of implementing public interest regulation.[34] First, regulatory agencies may be assigned unfeasible tasks by the legislature. The regulation of public utilities has required that the regulatory agencies calculate the costs of regulated companies, maintaining prices equal to marginal costs. The agencies do not have the required theoretical knowledge and empirical techniques to measure the costs. The failure of the agencies is explained by the unfeasible tasks specified by legislation. The attempts to regulate prices without knowing marginal costs can distort markets in worst ways than the alleged market failures.[35]

Second, the cost of monitoring regulation by the legislature may be prohibitive.[36] Legislative bodies engage in complex bargaining. That process in large groups could have very high transaction costs. Thus, legislatures operate with majority instead of unanimous voting to conduct business reasonably. There is a sort of "life cycle" theory of administrative regulation. Legislatures approve regulation when there is high interest in the issue, typically after crises. The declining interest after crisis resolution moves attention to other more current affairs. Thus, legislatures may monitor past regulation ineffectively because of growing number of other issues.[37] Growth and exogenous shocks cause administrative failures when legislative monitoring is costly and ineffective.

The critical concept in the extension of the theory of capture or economic regulation is that the regulatory body is not captured by a single economic interest.[38] The maximization of utility or self-interest by the politician derives from the typical marginal conditions of price theory, allocating benefits across groups. There need not be pure producer protection if consumers can provide votes or money. In other words, the politicians allocate favors among groups of consumers and producers so as to maximize their utility. In the extreme of monopoly, price would exceed marginal cost while in perfect competition price would be lower or equal to marginal cost, corresponding to higher output. The inclusion of consumer interests would result in a price by intervention of the politician/regulator that is between the extreme of monopoly, causing a loss to consumers, and the bliss of perfect competition, fully protecting consumers.[39]

An extension of capture theory explicitly considers the impact on the competition for political influence of the distortions caused by taxes and subsidies, known as deadweight costs.[40] The taxed groups are stimulated to lower taxes by deadweight costs while the subsidized groups are discouraged from raising subsidies. The model can also explain traditional government intervention because of market failure. The competition among pressure groups explains government measures that increase efficiency, such as public goods and taxes on pollution, because the groups that benefit from measures that increase efficiency have advantage over those adversely affected by the measures.

Rent-seeking and public choice

The basic idea of rent-seeking is that the monopolist spends resources in seeking the rents from regulation and in maintaining them.[41] These expenditures in rent-seeking are a waste of resources.

Rents are excess profits, that is, profits higher than those that are required for the firm in perfect competition to start production. Monopoly profits are rents. The existence of rents raises the issue of the consequences of their distribution,[42] which does not exist in a situation of no rents. The distribution of rents could occur in the political area, affecting the politics of democracy. Rents also affect the governance of corporations because of their internal distribution. Higher rents increase agency costs for principals. The agency problem is the manipulation of the firms for the interest of management instead of shareholders, causing structures within firms to restrain those costs. Similarly, higher rents increase political struggle to distribute them within the national economy.

The view of disclosure and regulation

There is a highly empirical approach by many writers seeking to find an intermediate position.[43]

There could be an excessive interest on the malevolent, incompetent regulator and the competent, benevolent judicial system. Regulators and judges are government servants, experiencing political pressures, incentives, and limitations. The regulators may not be a solution but that could also be argued about the court system. There are cases in which regulation may be beneficial. For example, investors may prefer the prevention of excesses by issuers of securities obtained through a regulatory body such as the SEC. There is an alternative in blending the Chicago objections to the public interest view with recognition of public intervention in some activities.

Suppose that a country desires to have stable and sound financial and banking markets.[44] There can be reliance on the interests of banks in preserving their reputation by disclosing all information about their operations and guaranteeing its accuracy. There is here the least involvement possible by the government with competition and private agreements determining the outcomes.

The government can rely on the enforcement of laws through the judicial system, with depositors and investors recovering their misappropriated funds in civil litigation.[45] There may be use of custom and common law, resulting in less involvement by the government in dictating laws. However, there is decision authority by judges that are government agents.

The regulatory approach would consist of capital requirements, supervision, regulation, and rules of disclosure, as in Basel II capital requirements for banks, discussed in Chapter 2.[46] Government intervention significantly increases in this strategy. The government writes the rules as in dictating the application of Basel II to local conditions; supervises their implementation (through a central bank or other monetary and securities authorities); and imposes penalties (as provided in local legislation and recommended in Pillar II).

The political economy of the regulatory state

An interpretation of the transaction costs approach is that a market economy that is functioning adequately and has well-defined property rights needs only common law to solve the problem of social harm.[47] In this view, the reasoning followed by the approach of transaction costs does not lead to the superiority of strict private litigation. Efficiency could be attained by multiple regimes: private litigation, regulation, a combination of private litigation and regulation or no form of government intervention. The model is developed to analyze the desirability of alternative regimes and apply it to the analysis of the rise of the regulatory state in the United States in 1877–1917.

The model departs from the assumption that the key goal of economic institutions is to ensure secure property rights, making offenders accountable.[48] This goal is invariant over time. The appropriate institutions for protecting and enforcing property rights may vary over time and across countries. An important characteristic of the model is that there can be subversion of judges and regulators. In real life, subversion extends to legislators, competitors and other industries.

If the cost of subversion is low relative to the scale of economic activity, the system of strict liability or private litigation under common law would be the ideal system. This view proposes that only this system attains the first best of efficiency.[49] The United States around the nineteenth century had conditions that allowed it to rely almost solely on the system of private litigation. More than one half of the population was engaged in agriculture and there were no significantly large companies in industry. Thus, there was no incentive to subvert the system. The damages granted by courts were not significantly large to motivate subversion of the system.

The increase in the fines or costs of social harms increased together with the increases in scale of industries and companies as the United States became more industrialized and integrated in commerce in the second half of the nineteenth century. Liability would incorporate negligence. The progressive movement gained impetus when the fines increased and became more common while the increasing size of industries and companies made attractive the subversion of the judiciary. Regulation became an important part of the progressive movement in the United States. This view distinguishes between high and low costs of social harms. Protection of property rights would be more efficient under regulation if social costs were high. The argument proposes that the costs of regulation and uncertain outcomes would determine no government intervention if the social costs were low. In extreme cases of weak law enforcement, as in some developing countries, the most efficient outcome may simply be no government intervention. In such situations attempts to correct market failures by regulation could have very high costs and results different from those intended.

The theory of capture is extended with asymmetric information to include three actors: the politician (principal), the regulator, and the firm (agent).[50] The firm has information not available to the regulator who in turn may mislead the politician about the actual available information. The costs of capture can be quite high if there is redistribution of income from consumers to firms.

Contrasts of public and private interest views

Maximum legal interest rates, or interest rate ceilings, illustrate the differences between the private and public interest views in financial regulation. The private interest view is illustrated by the analysis of usury laws, or maximum legal interest rates, in US states in the nineteenth century.[51] Usury laws could result from the interest in promoting social welfare by transferring wealth toward households, in the public interest view, or from political influence by incumbent business groups desiring to restrict competition and enjoy high profits, in the private interest view. The issue is whether usury laws protect the poor and disadvantaged or promote the interests of the financially powerful incumbents. There is evidence that usury laws restrained some borrowers in some states at points of time, showing that they were financially important.

The changes of interest ceilings in usury laws across states can be explained by tension of private and public interests. States tightened usury laws when it was less costly, raising the interest rate ceiling when market interest rates increased closer to the maximum legal rate, that is, when interest rates would have risen anyway under free-market determination. States also relaxed their usury laws after similar action by bordering states or during periods of financial hardship. Financial regulation had real or perceived effects on economic development, behavior consistent with both public and private interest views.

The evidence favoring the private interest view is the correlation between financial repressions by tighter usury laws in states with wealth suffrage restrictions in which powerful interest groups decided the outcome of elections. In addition, usury laws were tighter in states restricting entry of new firms. Maximum legal ceilings cause credit rationing. Incumbents were not worried about credit shortage because they had collateral in the form of assets that they could pledge and reputation that ensured they were first served in terms of credit. It was in their interest to prevent the entry of competitors which could cut prices, reducing their excess profits or rents. Credit restrictions by interest rate ceilings of usury laws perpetuated less efficient economic structures, retarding economic progress and change while benefitting established business at the expense of the general public of consumers.

There is a new theory proposing financial restraint to mitigate moral hazard resulting from financial liberalization that illustrates the public interest view.[52] The first stage is financial market liberalization. The motive for liberalization is to increase banking competition that would result in higher volumes of financial assets at lower interest rates, providing the financing of sound projects required to accelerate growth.

In the second stage, the liberalization has the desired result of increasing banking competition. The increased competition causes erosion of bank profits; banks become more fragile and are not remunerating adequately their capital. Bank franchise capital is the present value (see appendix) of future profits, the reason for existence of a capitalized bank. Competition erodes current profits and lowers the expectation of remuneration of capital with future profits. Banks have lower incentives to provide quality loans and moral hazard in choosing unsound loan increases.

Banks are faced with low returns on quality loans because of profit erosion caused by financial liberalization.[53] The typical bank has an incentive to "gamble" by taking high risks. If the bank is successful, it appropriates rents from gambling. If the bank is unsuccessful, it passes on to depositors the realized risks of the failure. In this view, freely determined deposit rates prevent the banking system to reach the Pareto optimum. This view considers two alternative policies: ceilings on deposit rates and increased capital requirements. There is high cost in capital requirements. Deposit-rate ceilings can equally move the banking system toward the Pareto-efficient outcome and are preferable. Financial liberalization increases moral hazard problems, which consist of lending to unsound projects. Other possible policies to mitigate moral hazard include "asset-class restrictions, entry restrictions and enhancing direct supervision."[54]

Applied welfare economics

The practical usefulness of economic advice does not originate in a desire for elegant economic optimum analysis. Economists face in real practice decisions on such things as different choices of agricultural programs, the effects of new taxes and the merits of building a new bridge. The decisions need to recognize the existence of departures from market allocations that cannot be controlled.[55] Typically, the practical question involves ranking alternatives in terms of their potential damage and benefits.

The state of the art in applied welfare economics is as follows.[56] The three following principles are accepted.[57] First, the value of a unit of a good for a demander should be measured by the competitive demand price. Second, the value of a unit for a supplier should be measured by the competitive supply price. Third, the costs and benefits of a group, such as a nation, should be added in the evaluation of projects, programs, or policies without consideration of who receives the benefits. The demand price is a measure of the benefit while the supply price is a measure of the cost. Efficiency considerations dictate that it does not pay to engage in activities where supply price (extra cost) exceeds demand price (extra benefit). Similarly, it pays to expand into activities where extra benefit (demand price) exceeds extra cost (supply price). Economists use technical methods in calculating costs and benefits to determine practically the desirability of multiple projects and policies. The appendix provides introductory technical analysis.

Finance, efficiency, and growth

Adam Smith referred to the role of finance in terms of a parable.[58] Specialization in producing repetitively different tasks in the modern factory system was the driver of economic growth that Smith observed during the industrial revolution. The transition to specialization from a self-sufficient barter economy required a medium of exchange, provided by money. The early characterization of economic development was the movement away from the subsistence to the money economy, which is not far from the parable of Smith.

Another parable focuses on the need for the entrepreneur to escape the constraints of self-generating resources to obtain the appropriate risk, liquidity, intertemporal allocation, and volume of resources provided by financial markets and institutions.[59] External financing is the key opportunity and function provided by financial markets that permits individuals and even large corporations to escape the constraints of self-generated capital. External finance requires financial markets and institutions and makes a significant difference in modern technologically and organizationally driven economic growth. The functions of financial intermediation cannot be considered in isolation, except for specific analysis, but rather must be taken together to identify how they promote the two channels of capital and technological accumulation.[60] This section focuses on the relation of finance to efficiency in the allocation of resources and economic growth.

The perfectly competitive model of the first best of efficiency assumes that there are no frictions or imperfections of information and transaction costs.[61] Financial analysis must add frictions to the standard economic model. Without the frictions there is no role for a financial system engaged in evaluating projects, monitoring managers, developing/applying risk-management systems, and spending on systems to gather information and facilitate transactions.

The synthesis of financial theory begins with the origin of financial markets and institutions to ameliorate the market frictions created by information and transaction costs.[62] Financial markets and intermediaries perform numerous functions that are outlined in Table 1.2. These financial functions operate on two channels of growth: capital accumulation and technological innovation. The consequence of this interaction of financial intermediation with the channels of growth is economic growth itself.

There is no need of financial market intermediaries in the first-best model of perfect competition without market frictions and perfect knowledge.[63] Agents would be able to find optimum investment opportunities for their savings. Under uncertainty, there would still not be need for financial intermediaries because markets would develop that would provide liquidity in one time period in exchange for payment in a future time period.

Table 1.2   Functions of financial intermediation

I. Permitting Economies of Scale
  - Transforming securities from bonds and stocks into demand or savings deposits
  - Mobilizing savings
    - Pooling multiple small funds of investors into the financing of large projects
  - Facilitating risk management
    - Pooling concentrated risks into diversified risk instruments for smaller investors
    - Transferring/trading risks, permitting larger projects that diversify risks among many institutions
  - Allocating resources
    - Facilitating intertemporal allocation: financing presently directly productive activities with long gestation/high return for future repayment
      - Creating liquid markets to securitize directly productive activities
        - Converting long-term, large-scale project financing into short-term liquidity for small investors
    - Screening risks of large projects, providing information at low cost
  - Reducing transaction costs
    - Facilitating vertical integration to reduce transaction costs
II. Bridging Asymmetry of Information and Incomplete Markets
  - Providing instruments that reduce the asymmetry of information
    - Hedging liquidity and credit risk
    - Hedging market risk
  - Exerting corporate control
    - Lowering costs of discipline, enhancing monitoring and control
    - Providing takeover opportunities of inefficiently run companies

---

Source: Zsolt Becsi and Ping Wang, Financial development and growth. *Economic Review— Federal Reserve Bank of Atlanta* 82 (4, 1997): 46–62; Ross Levine, Financial development and economic growth: views and agenda. *Journal of Economic Literature* 35 (2, 1997): 688–726.

There were early contributions to the analysis of the roles of financial intermediaries.[64] The relaxation of the assumptions of perfect competition creates important functions for financial intermediation. Modern technology requires relatively large investments that are indivisible. For example, it is impossible to construct a dam or a railroad with small, incremental investments. Thus, technology makes investments indivisible. As analyzed in monopoly theory, there could be heavy sunk investments and the incumbent firm may produce at low costs relative to potential entrants. The analysis even applies in contestability theory when potential entrants have the resources to make the required heavy investments.[65]

Financial intermediaries provide important services. They can transform the large-volume securities, stocks and bonds, issued by the firm into smaller investments demanded by investors. Thus, firms may have access to a large pool of investors. Underwriting of securities and loan syndications by banks constitute an important form of making large investments accessible to small savers. This technique actually helped in financing the new world as English portfolio investors financed the infrastructure of the United States and many other new countries. Accounting and auditing firms developed in response to the need to monitor and control the investments. Financial intermediation provides bridges of liquidity, risks, and information that are essential to finance large investments. The asymmetry of investors not having sufficient information about borrowers can be bridged by financial intermediaries, providing lower cost monitoring and control in the form of privately issued contracts.

Banks provide monitoring functions as shown in II in Table 1.2. There is an interesting view of delegated monitoring by financial intermediaries.[66] There are two doubts on the rationale for financial intermediaries. First, there is the issue of why investors do not lend directly to borrowers instead of lending to banks. Second, the nature of the financial technology of banks to serve as intermediaries must be clarified. Banks have the incentive of costly liquidation to coerce borrowers to repay their obligations. However, banks can selectively avoid inefficient (costly) liquidation of borrowers by monitoring. The function of monitoring could be extremely expensive if carried out by a multitude of potential inventors but it can be centralized in financial intermediaries such as banks. The nature of the contracts is important: banks issue unmonitored debt (deposits) and monitor loan contracts. The monitoring of loan contracts is required while that of deposits is not required because of the financial engineering technology of financial intermediaries made available by diversification. This financial engineering of diversification permits the mitigation of risk. Thus, banks provide "delegated monitoring." The conclusion is that "debt, monitoring and diversification are the keys to understanding the link between financial intermediation and delegated monitoring."[67] The financial engineering of diversification is essential to institutions such as banks that use leverage of about ten times of capital such that bad loans can bankrupt the institution.

Vast technical literature supports the existence of a strong positive association between long-term economic growth and the functioning of the financial system.[68] There are important qualifications of these results and conflicting views. However, the weight of the evidence supports the view that financial intermediaries are important in explaining growth.[69] An important microeconomic result is the facilitating role of financial development on external finance. It is difficult to conclude from this vast literature that the financial system has a passive role in economic growth, that is, that financial development is simply triggered by economic growth, which is in fact determined by other factors.

Summary

There is a wide spectrum of arguments in favor of and against government intervention. The main analysis for departure is the first best of efficiency. Under ideal conditions, allocation of resources in free markets is a Pareto efficient allocation. With suitable lump-sum transfers every Pareto optimal allocation can become a free-market allocation. There are two cases for government intervention in neoclassical economics. Producers could earn excess profits by using their market power, resulting in lower welfare relative to perfect competition. In addition, negative externalities result in more output than the social optimum and positive externalities in less output than the social optimum. The remedies range from regulation to government ownership and control of industries. The theory of second best illustrates the difficulty of finding an ideal allocation when even one of the conditions for the first best of efficiency is violated in theory or practice.

The public interest view generalizes the case of government intervention by introducing the concept of market failure. The breakdown of the assumptions of the first best of efficiency opens the possibility of Pareto-improving policy. An important development is the extension of the breakdown of competition to cases of imperfect information.

The private interest view affirms that regulation originates and perpetuates itself by the self-interest of politicians, government officials, and the regulated industries. In practice, regulation frequently attains results that are opposite to those intended by policy. The NIE incorporates transaction costs and the role of institutions to explain long-term growth and market organization. Various theories explain the distortions resulting from rent-seeking activities and the promotion and defense of government programs.

Recent research is focusing on a modified private interest view in which institutions play an important role. This new current of analysis emphasizes general contributions on multicountry differences in the rule of law. Theoretical research is accompanied by empirical verification. Disclosure is important for monitoring the financial sector by the market and regulators. Financial markets and institutions are important in allocating resources to dynamic activities that promote growth.

Appendix: Security prices and cost/benefit analysis

Consider a simple example of a one-year security with an interest payment of 10 percent. An investment of $100 in that security now yields $110 in a year, consisting of the principal of $100 and the interest of $10 (10 percent of $100). Thus, the yield is 10 percent. Suppose there is an instantaneous change in the interest rate to 20 percent. What is the new price of the security with principal of $100 paying $10 in a year? The new price requires the use of the new interest rate of 20 percent. To obtain $110 in one year with interest of 20 percent the security would have to be priced at $91.666. The interest of 20 percent on $91.666 is 0.20 times $91.666, which is equal to $18.333. At maturity, the buyer of the security would receive the $91.666 invested plus the interest of $18.333 equal to $109.999. In shorthand calculation, $110 divided by 1.20 equals $91.666. Thus, the original buyer at $100 with 10 percent interest would only be able to sell the security at $91.666 because the interest rate increased to 20 percent. The loss of principal would be $100 less $91.666 divided by $100 equal to 8.3 percent. Thus, the prices of bonds decrease when interest rates increase. If the interest rate were to decrease from 10 percent to 5 percent, the price of the bond, in the shorthand calculation, would be equal to $110 divided by 1.05, which is equal to $104.762. In this case there would be a capital gain of $104.762 divided by $100, which is equal to 4.762 percent.

Consider now a security paying 10 percent in year one and 10 percent in year two when it returns the principal of $100. The price of that security is calculated as:

$$p = \frac{\$10}{(1.10)} + \frac{\$10 + \$100}{(1.10)(1.10)} = \frac{C_1}{(1+r)} + \frac{C_2 + N}{(1+r)^2}$$
$$= \$9.09 + \$90.91 = \$100 \tag{1.1}$$

That is, the price of a security paying two yearly coupons of 10 percent and the principal of $100 would be worth today $100.

Consider a five-year bond paying interest in the form of coupons every month and returning the principal in the sixtieth month. The formula for the price or net present value (NPV) of such a security would be

$$p = \frac{C_1}{(1+r)} + \frac{C_2}{(1+r)^2} + \frac{C_3}{(1+r)^3} + \dots + \frac{C_{59}}{(1+r)^{59}} + \frac{C_{60} + N}{(1+r)^{60}}$$
$$= \sum_{t=1}^{60} \frac{C_t}{(1+r)^t} \tag{1.2}$$

The variables are as follows: P is the price of the security; r is the discount rate or yield in proportion such that 10 percent would be 0.10; C_t is the cash flow at time t, which are from 1 to 60; N is the principal; and Σ is the summation notation that expresses in shorthand the sum of all the discounted individual terms or cash flows from 1 to 60. The denominators of 1.2 are discount factors, bringing to present value the cash flow. The first one, $C_1/(1+r)$, is the same as in the example of \$110/1.10 equal to \$110/ (1+0.1), with the interest rate converted to the equivalent monthly rate The second coupon payment, C2, must be brought to present value by two discounts of (1+r) over two months as in 1.1. The same is true for the remaining cash flows. The discount rate connects present and future cash flows.

Equation 1.2 is one equation with two unknowns, *P* and *r*. Suppose that a broker quotes the discount factor, or yield, *r* as 10 percent. Then equation 1.2 can be used to compute the price to pay for the security. If the dealer quotes the price, then the equation can be solved to obtain the yield or *r*. The discount factors enter the formula in the denominator. Thus, the higher the yield the lower the price or what is the same, the higher the price the lower the yield.

The basic analysis of project evaluation consists of calculating the NPV of the project. Consider a project that begins in time period *0* and ends at *T*, where *t* is the index of time, *B* are the benefits, *C* the costs and *r* the constant social discount rate, then present value is obtained by the formula:[70]

$$NPV = \sum_{t=0}^{T} \frac{B_t - C_t}{(1+r)^t} \tag{1.3}$$

It is possible to rank policies by their *NPV* to make choices. A policy with positive NPV is socially desirable. Net refers to the deduction of costs from benefits and present to the discount to the current period. However, there is a difficult decision as to how positive a project should be. The variables are subject to estimation error, not only the costs and benefits but also the discount rate. This process is typical in private sector companies that are making capital budgeting decisions. There are situations in which there is a maximum capital budget and the present value calculations have to be used to work within the budget. Another complication is the extension of projects over multiple time periods, making comparisons more difficult. Standard practice consists of using current consumption as the measuring rod of costs and benefits. Shadow prices may be used for such things as the cost of labor when there are distortions, which is the typical case.

The calculation of NPV requires adjustments for inflation. For purposes of simplification, assume a constant rate of inflation per period of π. The conversion of nominal to constant benefits and costs is obtained as follows:[71]

$$b_t = B_t/(1+\pi)^t \text{ and } c_t = C_t/(1+\pi)^t \tag{1.4}$$

The nominal interest rate, i, must follow:

$$(1+i) = (1+r)(1+\pi) \tag{1.5}$$

Thus, the net NPV can be rewritten in real terms as

$$NPV = \sum_{t=0}^{T} \frac{b_t - c_t}{(1+i)^t} \tag{1.6}$$

2
Bank Regulation

Introduction

The first few sections in this chapter consider the approaches to bank regulation. The emphasis in policy proposals is on the approach of prudential and systemic regulation, which is based largely on collective or government action to correct market failures, such as the current credit/dollar crisis. The competing approach focuses on the functions of finance allowing structural changes, including regulation, with the objective of facilitating innovation to promote effective financial systems. Bank functions are then analyzed, providing foundations for the analysis of banking crises. Housing finance is overwhelmingly important in the current crisis. The innovations in securitization and credit-risk transfer have been profound, motivating regulatory proposals. Two important regulations of banks, minimum capital requirements and deposit insurance, are also considered. The final section provides an overview of the political economy of banking regulation. A final section briefly summarizes the chapter.

Approaches to bank and financial regulation

It is instructive to provide a framework of general principles of bank and financial regulation. The design and definition of financial systems depends significantly on the approach followed. Part of the analysis has centered on the convenience of basing financial systems on banks versus finance through stock markets. Conventional regulation is designed to ameliorate market failures, using government intervention in attempts to improve outcomes relative to freer markets. A more general principle is to consider functions provided by financial markets and show how institutions adapt in different ways to effectively providing those functions. Another variant is to consider the effectiveness of banking and finance in different legal systems.

Banks versus finance

Protracted debate has attempted to identify the relative performance in promoting growth and efficiency of financial systems based on banks versus financial systems based on markets such as stock exchanges.[72] Much of this effort has centered on the bank-based systems of Germany and Japan and the market-based systems of the United Kingdom and United States.[73]

The banking view argues that the allocation of capital and corporate governance is promoted by the information that banks acquire in their relations with firms and managers.[74] Economic growth and efficiency are promoted by the management of liquidity risk by banks, providing for consumption and investment over time and across sectors and regions. Banks can also provide capital to companies to benefit from economies of scale, or lower costs per unit produced as companies expand output, an opportunity afforded by technology requiring bulky investments. Because of the close relation with their clients, banks can monitor that the funds are invested in the project for which they were lent instead of in different riskier activities, diminishing moral hazard that could cause costly defaults. Banks have been identified as providing an important role in early stages of economic development.[75]

The market view emphasizes the benefits of well-functioning markets for equity or shares in companies.[76] Research activities of investment banks in deep, liquid equity markets reveal valuable information to investors. Corporate governance is enhanced by an active market for corporate control in which inefficiently managed companies are acquired or broken down and sold in parts.[77] Efficient markets for corporate control permit exit of corporations from lines of business made obsolete by technology, allowing the reorganization of companies required for high rates of economic growth.

It is difficult to find strong conclusions on this debate because the evidence is mostly on four countries—Germany, Japan, the United States, and United Kingdom—that have had similar rates of economic growth over the long term even if they have differed in growth performance in some decades. A revealing approach consists of the construction of a sample to test the relationship of financial structure and economic growth for 48 countries in 1980–95.[78] The conclusion of this empirical analysis is that better financial systems promote economic growth but that the form of financial development, bank-based or market-based, is not important in reality in explaining relative growth performance. The experience of financial systems with economic growth leads to the consideration of two major approaches to bank and financial regulation. First, OPSR, followed by government in most countries, is largely based on the knowledge acquired in the practice of regulation over two centuries and the concept of market failure or deviations from the first best. Second, the FSF approach departs from the functions of financial systems and how institutions develop to perform them. A variant of this approach is the law and finance view. These approaches are considered in turn.

Prudential and systemic regulation

This section considers the general principles of OPSR. The conventional approach to bank and financial regulation before the credit crisis focused on protection of depositors, investors, and the general economy from failures in banking and financial markets. Banking and financial crises have occurred that eroded the savings of investors and depositors. Part of the regulation centers on preventing fraud. Significant emphasis is placed on ensuring the soundness and safety of banks and financial markets to prevent losses to depositors. Minimum capital requirements are designed to provide available liquid resources with which banks can compensate losses resulting from bad loans or credit risk. For example, the debtor of the loan could default, which could result in the loss of all or a significant part of the money lent by the bank. Some losses to banks in the slowing economy originate in defaults in loans to consumers, such as credit cards, home equity loans, and so on, and other losses originate in defaults by commercial clients, such as companies.

The appendix to Chapter 1 provides analysis of how an increase in interest rates causes a decline in the price of fixed-income securities such as bonds, which is market risk. For example, in March 2009, a bank could borrow overnight loans, such as fed funds, which are deposits at the Federal Reserve Banks (FRB) that banks lend among themselves in overnight agreements without collateral, with the rate of 0.25 percent. The bank could lend to a company at the fixed prime rate of 3.25 percent for one year, earning a net margin or spread of 3.25 percent less 0.25 percent or 3 percent. However, the fed funds rate would have to remain at 0.25 percent for one year because the bank would have to renew the fed funds borrowing on a daily basis for a year. If the fed funds rate would increase, for example, to 4 percent the following day and stayed at that level the bank would lose roughly 0.25 percent less 4 percent or 3.75 percent. Interest rates rarely jump as widely as in this example. The bank provides the loan to the company and does not receive the principal for one year but must renew the borrowing of fed funds every day. This is called a mismatch of the contractual term of lending for a year funded with daily repeated borrowing. Market risk consists of the losses that banks may experience because of fluctuations of interest rates.

Depositors could run to withdraw deposit in banks not necessarily in lines at bank teller windows as in historical banking panics but as it occurred in the silent run of Washington Mutual in which deposits were withdrawn online. Investors could lose all or a significant part of their investments in equity and/or debt securities of banks and financial institutions, as it happened to the shareholders and creditors of Bear Stearns, Lehman Brothers, Fannie Mae, Freddie Mac, CountryWide, and others. The public loses because pension and savings funds are invested in equity and securities of corporations. Deposit insurance by the government, such as by the Federal Deposit Insurance Corporation (FDIC), is designed to prevent runs on banks by allowing the banks to maintain their deposits while they circumvent a situation in which their cash is temporarily short relative to potential withdrawals, but the loans cannot be converted into cash without a discount even if they are sound at maturity. Another tool of temporary access to cash by liquid but solvent banks is the discount window by which the central bank discounts promissory notes and securities held by banks; the discount window consists of a loan injecting cash by the Fed to the illiquid bank secured by obligations delivered to the bank such as Treasury securities. The fed could recover the disbursement of the loan by selling the promissory notes in case of default by the bank.

The analysis of market failure provides additional types of regulation. Banking markets are typically characterized by less than perfect competition. Regulation can prevent banks from using market power to pay deposit rates that are too low, harming depositors, and charge lending rates that are too high, harming consumers and business. The most important market failure originates in financial crises and is called systemic risk.[79] The failure of one bank, such as Bear Stearns in March 2008 and Lehman Brothers in September 2008, can threaten the existence of other companies, such as American International Group (AIG) and Citigroup, which may lose the ability to finance themselves in the market. The stock prices of affected companies collapsed toward zero, preventing them from raising capital. Systemic crises have been accompanied throughout history by contractions in credit that caused declines in output of goods and services and unemployment. Debates and proposals on regulation focus on systemic risk, both its prevention and resolution when it happens.

Functional and structural finance

The FSF, also known as the "financial view"[80] and the finance view,[81] consists of an articulate framework using functions of finance in "designing and managing the financial systems of countries, regions, firms, households and other entities."[82] An appealing foundation of the FSF is the need for technological progress in finance by the characterization of an "innovation spiral."[83]

It is not feasible to seriously argue in favor of change to increase prosperity with reservations on progress in technology, which is what brings about change in human wellbeing. A brief digression to research in health economics illustrates the need for innovation.[84] There are estimates of various factors of growth of health care costs in the technical literature. The approach followed by the Congressional Budget Office consists of obtaining the various estimates in the technical literature of the contribution of various factors to growth of health care cost: population aging, changes in third-party payments (such as Medicare and Medicaid), growth of personal income, health care prices, administrative costs, and defensive medical practice to avoid law suits. The residual of health care costs after deducting these factors can be considered to be primarily caused by technological progress. The conclusion is that over the past four decades changes in medical technology caused about one half of the growth of health care costs.[85] In four of the case studies of diseases—heart attacks, low-birth-weight babies, and depression—the present value of the benefits exceeds the costs. In the fourth case, breast cancer, benefits and costs are even. It is difficult to conclude on the entire health system from these four cases. However, benefits from lowering infant mortality and improved treatment of heart attacks are approximately equal to the entire costs of cumulative medical care. The conclusion is that benefits from medical spending more than compensate the costs.[86] Investments in innovations in health prolong lives and service in the labor force, reducing the costs of care of acute disease of the aging population. Retarding innovation has costs and lost opportunities in every facet of human efforts to push the frontiers of knowledge, including finance.

The institutional structure of the FSF consists of "financial institutions, financial markets, products, services, organization of operations, and supporting infrastructure such as regulatory rules and the accounting system."[87] The FSF is ideology-free because the financial functions can be provided by the private-sector, government, and family institutions. The financial functions, accompanying discussion, are outlined in Table 1.2. The FSF considers six functions of the financial system or structure:[88]

1. *Clearing and settlement systems.* Various institutions provide these functions. In the United States, the fed wire plays a key role in the transfer of funds in a secure and rapid form among banks. Depository institutions, such as banks, transfer resources worldwide. Technology has made this function extremely efficient, reducing transaction costs and stimulating business.

2. *Mobilization of savings.* Small funds of investors are channeled to finance large-scale projects that are indivisible and the participation of investors is broadened by the subdivision of corporations with productive projects in small shares in the stock.

3. *Intertemporal and spatial transfer of resources.* Households and business can consume and invest now transferring resources across time, such as the returns on investment in education and in research and development that materialize in the future. Capital can be transferred around the world and within nations to the areas of highest marginal productivity.

4. *Risk management.* Change requires the capacity to measure, identify, and mitigate risk to extract optimum opportunities. Financial institutions, markets, and products provide the vehicles and risk management to transfer risks. Risk pooling can make risky transactions feasible.

5. *Information.* The financial system provides information on prices that is used in decentralized sectors throughout the entire economy. Prices of securities, such as equities and debt, reveal the potential of economic activities.

6. *Incentives.* Chapter 1 provides discussion of moral hazard, or the use of loans for riskier activities than those proposed, adverse selection, or the financing of unsound projects to the detriment of sound ones, and information asymmetries, or differences in knowledge of the different borrowers, creditors, depositors, and investors. The financial system creates the incentives to reduce information asymmetries.

The strategy of the FSF paradigm is to treat the functions as exogenous, that is, as given or facts. The analysis treats the institutional forms as endogenous, that is, determined by the functions and interplay in the specific environment.[89] The analysis of changes in the financial system proceeds with the neoclassical paradigm of rational agents operating to optimize their self-interest in markets without frictions. This is the analysis of the first best applied to finance, which has resulted in multiple contributions.[90] The novelty of the FSF is the combination of the neoclassical financial analysis with the NIE and behavioral economics. The NIE argues that the neoclassical model of the first best provides an explanation of efficiency in markets at a specific time but that there is no theory of evolution over time, which requires a framework of how different institutions mold the growth of different nations and regions.[91] Behavioral economics also disputes the universal rationality of economic agents, considering cases of irrational behavior. FSF investigates the reason why in reality institutions and human behavior differ from the neoclassical model by identifying the effects of frictions.

The NIE departs from the contribution that transaction costs are high.[92] This process in finance can be explained by means of a current transaction, trade financing of exports. The exporting firm must find a buyer and a price for the product in overseas markets. This requires the cost of acquiring knowledge of foreign markets in multiple ways. In addition, the firm must find the price at which the product can be sold in various markets and make a choice of selling abroad versus selling at home. These functions require expenditures in financial planning. There is then a complex, costly process of negotiating a contract, likely with several potential customers. Language and cultural skills may be quite important. The drafting of the contract will require expenditures with specialized attorneys, perhaps in more than one jurisdiction or through a law firm with international contacts. There is then the process of negotiating trade finance with an international bank or a domestic bank that acts as a correspondent of a foreign bank. The exporter would then obtain the proceeds of the future sale immediately instead of having to wait for several months until the products are actually exported. The receipt of the funds immediately allows the firm to hire employees, buy inputs and pay all the operational expenses of production. The bank will have to verify the credit and extend credit to the foreign buyer, which results in expenditures that are likely to be charged as fees to the exporter that receives the proceeds immediately. The exporter must be vigilant that the foreign buyer will comply with the agreement. The transaction costs of the NIE are an important part of everyday business, currently and in historical times. They are an important friction in the first-best model.

The progress in technology and the reduction of transaction costs augments the potential for creating innovative products.[93] Transaction costs and irrational individual behavior are frictions that trigger institutional reactions toward better arrangements, in similarity with the "invisible hand" of Adam Smith. The change in the institutional environment can trace future institutional changes or provide normative guidelines for innovation. There is competition of financial intermediaries and markets that generate an innovation spiral.[94] Two important examples are commercial paper and high-yield or "junk" bonds. First, highly rated corporations discovered that they could lower their financing costs by shifting away from bank loans and issuing commercial paper for short terms of a few months tied to their receivables. Money-market mutual funds were able to compete with banks and thrifts by providing immediate liquidity and safety to depositors on the basis of portfolios of highly rated commercial paper. The yield in money-market funds is higher than the yield for bank deposits; the principal is safe as $1 invested is redeemed with at least $1; and funds are managed to provide immediate liquidity. Second, companies with rating below investment grade could only finance their projects with costly banking relations. The creation of the junk bond provided these companies the means with which to finance their expansion. The innovation spiral continued with the financing of market exit and restructuring of companies financed with junk bonds.

Finance facilitates the implementation of projects with technical innovations that drive economic growth and prosperity. The consequences of restricting financial innovation could be quite harmful:[95]

> If financial innovation is stifled for fear that it will reduce the effectiveness of short-run monetary and fiscal policies, the consequences could be a much slower pace of technological progress. Furthermore, long-run policies that focus on domestic saving and capital formation as key determinants of economic growth do not appear to be effective. Policies designed to stimulate innovation in the financial system would thus appear to be more important for long-term economic development.

Design of policies to recover credit and the real economy in the credit/dollar crisis should be forward looking, preserving innovation channels and allowing institutions to correct frictions.

The law and finance view

There are interesting conclusions on investor and creditor rights in relation to families of legal rules.[96] There is much stronger protection of rights of investors in countries where the legal rules originate in the tradition of common law than in that of civil law, with the tradition of French civil law being the worst and those of German-civil-law and Scandinavian countries falling in between. There is strong protection of investors of all types in common-law countries. The evidence supports the hypothesis that shareholders and creditors in different legal jurisdictions have different bundles of rights, which depend on the laws instead of on the securities. The strongest enforcement of laws is in German-civil-law and in Scandinavian countries, followed by common-law countries, with French-civil-law countries being the worst. Enforcement quality is independent of the standards, such as accounting, but is positively associated with income level. Low quality of investor protection generates alternative mechanisms of protection.[97] In some cases, there are provisions in statutes in the form of mandatory dividends or legal reserve requirements. Civil-law countries use these alternative protection mechanisms. Concentration of ownership is another course of protection because of weak rights of shareholders. The three largest shareholders own about one-half of the equity of a public company in the data set. Concentration of ownership is inversely associated with sound accounting standards and shareholder protection, showing that concentration is a reaction to weak protection of investors.

There is research on securities laws in 49 countries in relation to the issue of new securities.[98] The conclusion is that securities laws contribute to improving markets because they facilitate private contracting. The existence of a focused and independent regulatory enforcer does not show statistical significance in developing capital markets. Larger stock markets are positively associated with disclosure requirements and liability standards that allow investors to recover losses. The emphasis on market discipline and private litigation of common law, in the form of private contracts and standard disclosure, explains the stronger development in countries with that legal regime.

There is analysis of external finance in terms of origin of the legal system, strength of legal protection of investor rights and quality of enforcement of laws with a sample of 49 countries.[99] External finance consists of funds that are obtained in capital markets instead of those generated internally from the profits of a firm. The results show that the legal environment is important for developing a country's capital markets. Legal protection of investors by laws and their enforcement encourages them to exchange funds for securities, broadening capital markets. The lowest development of capital markets is in countries with civil-law systems, especially worst in French civil-law systems.

Bank functions

The FSF framework is based on financial functions. These functions differ among institutions in the financial structure. In the case of banks, monitoring and liquidity transformation constitute two key functions that illuminate the fragility of banks and arguments in favor of their regulation. Credit risk transfer, or bundling loans into a security sold to investors, has changed banks but the analysis can be extended to cover this innovation.

Monitoring and diversification

The model of delegated monitoring provides rich insights on the reason of existence of banks.[100] The model abstracts key elements of banking to extract the function of monitoring. There are three types of agents in the economy. First, the entrepreneur has skills in developing a project. The project requires investment now and will deliver high returns in the distant future. In the framework of cost/benefit analysis of the appendix to Chapter 1, the project has positive and significant present value, which means that the cash flows of the projects exceed the costs and is superior to investment in an alternative paying the riskless interest rate. That is, the project is valuable because its future cash flows net of cost in the horizon of investment exceed the interest payments derived from an investment paying interest without risk. The risky project yields more than investment without risk. Second, the saver has excess cash savings that she does not need for immediate consumption and would like to realize a return on the savings with as little possible risk. Third, the banker has expertise in providing loans to entrepreneurs and in taking deposits from savers.

If savers wanted to invest in the project of the entrepreneurs, they would need to evaluate the project and monitor its performance. Evaluation would consist of an analysis of the soundness of the forecasts of cash flows of the project, its costs and a proper interest rate to estimate if the present value of the project merits investment. That is, the saver would not desire to engage in adverse selection, which consists of choosing a project that is not sound and could result in default and loss of her savings. If the saver incurred the costs and evaluated the project correctly, she would still need to monitor the implementation of the project. Monitoring would require periodic evaluation of the progress in the project. The saver would also require a contract to impose conditions and penalties on the entrepreneur if there were deviations from the initial project. There is risk of default in neglecting monitoring if the entrepreneur used the cash provided by the saver to engage in a project with significantly higher risk. This is the risk of moral hazard. For example, the entrepreneur may misinform the saver that the cash would be used in a project to produce parts for computers while actually investing the cash in acquiring high-risk commercial real estate. The entrepreneur would appropriate abnormal profits from the risky project but the saver would absorb all the losses in case of default. The saver would not have the same information as the entrepreneur on the soundness of the project and its execution. Moreover, the cost of evaluating and monitoring the project could be so high as to reduce the interest paid by the entrepreneur to very low levels. The costs and risks would not compensate the saver.

The conceptual framework of the model is that the banker can reduce the asymmetry of information between the saver and the entrepreneur by offering the services of "delegated monitoring."[101] Depositors delegate to banks the monitoring of entrepreneurial projects to which the bank lends the funds of depositors. That is, the bank monitors on behalf of depositors. There are two properties of delegated monitoring. First, bank monitoring can be socially less costly than individual monitoring by many savers. Banks develop the capacity to evaluate and monitor business projects by hiring, training, and developing specialized staff. Assume there is a given cost of evaluating a firm and an additional cost of the bank in evaluating that firm. If there are many savers, each one would have to incur at least the cost of project evaluation of the bank or perhaps more. The bank would be more cost effective than the sum of the costs of individual evaluations by many savers. If the cost of evaluation of the bank plus delegated evaluation were less than the sum of the costs of many savers, which is a likely outcome, the bank would be socially less costly in monitoring. Banks also accumulate knowledge and develop expertise in following up on projects, or monitoring. There is here also the same result that banks are more likely to provide effective and less costly the monitoring of a borrowing company than if many savers conducted monitoring individually.

Banks also have significant advantage in diversification.[102] Banks reduce the exposure in concentration of credit to one or a few clients by lending to many entrepreneurs. A diversified portfolio with many loans that are not highly correlated, that is, in different sectors and types of clients, has significantly less risk than a portfolio concentrated in one or a few clients in the same line of activity. For example, a portfolio of loans to a few clients in commercial real estate has significantly more risk than one diversified in smaller loans to clients in different fields that do not experience difficulties simultaneously. Diversification is the "financial engineering" of banks that permits them to issue unmonitored deposits. If the portfolio of the bank consists of many loans to projects that are independent of each other, an increase in the number of projects decreases the costs of delegation.[103] Monitoring results in banks that are diversified, with funding mostly through deposits and low probability of default.

The bank function can be conceived as the savers or depositors delegating the function of monitoring to the bank.[104] The ubiquitous issue of asymmetry of information creeps in the model. The entrepreneur would know more about the project than the bank and would be tempted to keep a higher share of the return on the project instead of sharing it fairly with the bank. In addition, the bank would know more about the project's return than the saver and could be tempted to pass on a lower than fair return to the saver. Competitive pressures over time would tend to diminish these imperfections. In this simple abstraction, the model is quite powerful in showing how banks provide through delegated monitoring an essential function for the allocation of savings to promising projects that promote growth of the economy and prosperity.

Liquidity transformation

Provision of liquidity is a critical function of banks.[105] The various services of banks are illustrated by a simplified balance sheet in Table 2.1. Assets are revenue-producing services mostly provided to borrowers. In this simplified balance sheet there are only loans. The services are considered above: evaluation to reduce adverse selection, choosing sound loans and rejecting loans with higher probability of default; monitoring to reduce moral hazard or periodic evaluation of the implementation of the project funded by the loan; and approval of the loan with the disbursement of the contracted funds.

The left-hand side contains the liabilities that in this simplified balance sheet are provided by depositors. Banks hold deposits for clients that can be converted into cash immediately in the case of demand deposits. Banks clear transactions on behalf of clients by means of

Table 2.1 Services provided by banks

Assets Provided to Borrowers	Liabilities Provided to Depositors
Loan:	Deposit holding
Evaluation (reduce adverse selection)	Transactions clearing
Monitoring (reduce moral hazard)	Currency inventory
Approval	Payment for goods and services
→Transformation→	
Converting illiquid loans into liquid deposits: liquidity creation	

Source: Douglas W. Diamond and Philip H. Dybvig, Banking theory, deposit insurance and bank regulation. *Journal of Business* 59 (Jan 1, 1986): 55–68.

online banking, wire transfers, automatic payments, and other processes. Banks maintain currency to face withdrawals from clients. Banks also make payments for goods and services as requested by clients.

Liquidity transformation is the most complex service provided by banks because it involves both sides of the balance sheet, assets and liabilities.[106] The loans on the asset side are illiquid; they cannot be sold because the project that they finance would be interrupted before completion. At best, the bank could sell the loan to another financial intermediary at a discount and under pressure would not be able to obtain the full value of the deposits. Demand deposits on the liability side are not monitored. Thus, the bank can be conceptualized as transforming risky, illiquid assets into unmonitored demand deposits that can be converted into cash immediately. The savers would not be able to convert their loans into cash after disbursing the loan to the entrepreneur who in turn would not be able to return the cash to the savers until completion of the project and generation of cash flows.

Housing finance

The United States has a somewhat unique system of housing finance with the structure composed of public, public/private, and purely private entities. This system collapsed during the credit/dollar crisis after 2007. The analysis is crucial because the structure of residential housing finance in the United States provided the first and deepest securitization of loans in the form of mortgage-backed securities (MBS), which financed homeownership during decades. This structure was used after 2003 in financing the subprime and Alt-A loans whose default characterized the beginning of the credit/dollar crisis. This section analyzes the housing finance system of the United States that helps to understand the issues of securitization and credit-risk transfer in the following section. Housing finance and securitization are at the heart of any comprehensive proposal of financial regulation.

The housing finance system of the United States was created during the Great Depression of the 1930s.[107] Congress established the Federal Home Loan Bank (FHLB) system in 1932 with the objective of providing short-term loans to retail mortgage institutions by regional FHLBs in an effort at stabilizing lending in local credit markets.[108] The stronger credit of the government was used to borrow through the FHLB system to provide lower cost financing to private entities in local credit markets. Congress created the FHA in 1934 to provide insurance of home mortgages against default. The FHA currently deposits insurance premiums paid by homeowners to fund the program.[109] The GI bill of 1944 created a mortgage program at the Veterans Administration (VA) providing a guarantee by the federal government of part of the face value of a veteran's mortgage.[110] The government created the Federal National Mortgage Association, known as Fannie Mae, in 1938 to develop a market for FHA-insured mortgages.[111] Fannie Mae became a privately owned company in 1968, operating with its own capital and the authority to buy mortgages other than FHA-insured. The Government National Mortgage Association,[112] or Ginnie Mae, received the portfolio of government-insured mortgages of Fannie Mae, which became a publicly owned company with a federal charter as a government-sponsored enterprise (GSE). In 1970, the federal government chartered the Federal Home Loan Mortgage Corporation, Freddie Mac, to promote the secondary market by bundling mortgages originated by thrift institutions in securities guaranteed by Freddie Mac. This was the origin of the securitization of mortgages that gained impetus in the 1980s.[113] Freddie Mac became a publicly traded company in 1989. In 1992, the federal government created the Office of Federal Housing Enterprise Oversight (OFHEO) at the Department of Housing and Urban Development (HUD) to regulate Fannie Mae and Freddie Mac.[114]

The US federal government provides large and diversified subsidies to housing. There are various types of large federal subsidies to the housing GSE.[115] First, some subsidies to the GSE derive from their federal charters, which result in treatment as federal agencies instead of for profit companies. Thus, the GSE are exempt from state and local income taxes and registration requirements and fees with the SEC. The US Treasury provides the GSE a line of credit of $2.25 billion and they use the Fed as fiscal agent. The debt of the GSE can be purchased by the Fed in open market operations and is eligible as collateral for public deposits and in unlimited investment by federally chartered banks and thrifts. Second, the major part of the federal subsidy originates in the implicit guarantee of their debt and MBS by the federal government. That guarantee materialized in the credit/dollar crisis after 2007 when Fannie Mae and Freddie Mac collapsed, being taken into government conservatorship. The subsidy of the implicit federal guarantee permits the GSE to borrow, by issuing debt, at a lower cost. GSE debt is rated somewhere between AAA and US Treasury debt while the estimated rating would be between AA and A. The subsidy is estimated as a funding benefit of 41 basis points, growing from $4.7 billion in 1995 to $13.7 billion in 2003, measured in constant 2006 dollars. The fast expansion of Fannie Mae and Freddie Mac explains the major part of the tripling of the subsidy. In addition, the implicit federal guarantee of the GSE provides a higher credit rating for the MBS of Fannie Mae and Freddie Mac relative to that of private entities, amounting to $10.1 billion in 2003 measured in 2006 dollars. The combined estimates of the GSE federal subsidies in 2003 amounted to $25 billion of 2006 dollars, increasing by 188 percent in real terms over $8.7 billion in 1995. The total subsidies to housing in the United States amounted in 2006 dollars to $221.1 billion composed of: "$37.9 billion in government outlays for low-income housing assistance, $156.5 billion in federal tax expenditures for housing and $26.7 billion in credit subsidies, including the GSEs and the VA."[116]

The operations and dimensions of Fannie Mae and Freddie Mac can be analyzed by means of the data in Table 2.2. These housing GSE engage in two types of operations with different risks. The first column is the retained portfolio, consisting of acquisitions of MBS by the two housing GSE, which reached $1.5 trillion in the third quarter of 2008. The second column is the insurance of MBS by the housing GSE, reaching $3.7 trillion. The combined assets of the housing GSE reached the gigantic value of $5.2 trillion in the third quarter of 2008, corresponding to 43.5 percent of total mortgages in the United States of $12.1 trillion. The subsidies to the GSE, directly by the charter or indirectly by their lower cost of borrowing implicit in the belief, which actually materialized, that they are a liability of the US government, and the pressure by the government of expanding home ownership propelled the share of the housing GSE from less than 10 percent of total US mortgages in 1980 to 43.5 percent in 2008.

There are three major risks in the operations of Fannie Mae and Freddie Mac. First, there is credit risk in both the retained portfolio and the guaranty portfolio if mortgagors default in their obligations, causing a loss to the housing GSE. Second, there is complex risk in managing the

Table 2.2 Mortgages of Fannie Mae, Freddie Mac, and the United States (in billions of current dollars)

Year	Fannie Mae and Freddie Mac			US Total Mortgages	Fannie Freddie % of Total
	Retained	MBS	Total		
1990	135	604	740	2,911	25.4
1991	153	714	867	2,075	28.2
1992	189	831	1,021	3,227	31.7
1993	246	910	1,156	3,383	34.2
1994	293	947	1,240	3,562	34.8
1995	360	972	1,332	3,736	35.7
1996	424	1,021	1,445	3,972	36.4
1997	481	1,055	1,536	4,219	36.4
1998	671	1,115	1,786	4,609	38.8
1999	846	1,217	2,063	5,076	40.6
2000	993	1,282	2,276	5,533	41.1
2001	1,210	1,516	2,726	6,127	44.5
2002	1,410	1,770	3,180	6,922	45.9
2003	1,580	2,052	3,632	7,796	46.6
2004	1,589	2,260	3,850	8,886	43.3
2005	1,446	2,573	4,019	10,069	39.9
2006	1,426	2,900	4,326	11,199	38.6
2007	1,433	3,500	4,934	12,088	41.1
2008 Q1	1,435	3,642	5,078	12,095	42
2008 Q2	1,541	3,688	5,209	12,103	43
2008 Q3	1,498	3,744	5,243	12,057	43.5

Source: Office of Federal House Enterprise Oversight http://www.ofheo.gov/Research.aspx?Nav=111

immense interest-rate exposure of Fannie Mae and Freddie Mac. Third, there is model risk because the credit-risk and overall risk-management methods used in financial institutions, including Fannie Mae and Freddie Mac, did not prevent the huge losses of financial entities during the credit/dollar crisis. The users of the models excluded the default risk of nonprime securities.

The charter of the national mortgage associations or GSE contains a declaration of purposes for which they are authorized by Congress (12 USC § 1716). The charter requires that the GSE "support the secondary market for residential mortgages, assist mortgage funding for low- and moderate-income families and be attentive to the geographic distribution of mortgage funding, including underserved areas."[117] The retained portfolio of MBS of the GSE is not required to satisfy their charter obligations and its risks resulted in heavy losses to the companies, requiring an expensive bailout with taxpayer funds, and systemic risk to the financial system of the US and the real economy. The net income of Fannie Mae in 2008 was a loss of $58.7 billion and that of Freddie Mac a loss of $50.1 billion. Thus, the GSE constitutes a threat, which materialized in 2007–8, and not a guarantee of the stability of the US residential mortgage market. The technical literature reaches consensus that "affordable housing goals have not substantially increased homeownership among low-income families,"[118] but a study shows gains in neighborhoods.[119]

A former CEO of Fannie Mae argues that the credit risk profile changed after 2004 when the company followed the market in changing its credit-risk appetite because of changing market conditions.[120] In this view, Fannie Mae was a follower of the market in adopting lax credit standards but not a leader. The Alt-A mortgages without sufficient information and documentation, popularly called liar mortgages, acquired by Fannie Mae performed better than that segment of the market. Subprime mortgages constitute only about 1 percent of Fannie Mae's guaranty portfolio. The losses of Fannie Mae in the first three quarters of 2008 amounted to $18 billion of which about $17 billion resulted from the credit losses in the guaranty portfolio. Significant part of the losses, about 70 percent, originates in guaranteeing high-risk Alt-A loans and in lesser magnitude by subprime loans. The losses in the subprime segment are about 2 percent of the losses in single-family credit losses; the subprime segment is about a third of one percent of the single-family portfolio. The increase in Alt-A loans in the guaranty portfolio began in 2005–6. The private label portfolio of MBS held by Fannie Mae in September 2008 reached $117 billion, of which $55 billion were backed by Alt-A or subprime mortgages, causing write down of $2.4 billion. Whether Fannie Mae was a leader in subprime and Alt-A loans is not as important as the endorsement of these loans by what the market has always perceived to be the full faith and credit of the US government.

The former chief credit officer of Fannie Mae depicts the role of the GSE in the housing event as follows:[121]

There are approximately 25 million subprime and Alt-A loans outstanding, with an unpaid principal amount of over $4.5 trillion, about half of them held or guaranteed by Fannie and Freddie. Their high risk activities were allowed to operate at 75:1 leverage ratio. While they may deny it, there can be no doubt that Fannie and Freddie now own or guarantee $1.6 trillion in subprime, Alt-A and other default prone loans and securities. This comprises over 1/3 of their risk portfolios and amounts to 34% of all the subprime loans and 60% of all Alt-A loans outstanding. These 10.5 million unsustainable, non-prime loans are experiencing a default rate 8 times the level of the GSEs' 20 million traditional quality loans. The GSEs will be responsible for a large percentage of an estimated 8.8 million foreclosures expected over the next 4 years, accounting for the failure of about 1 in 6 home mortgages. Fannie and Freddie have subprimed America

The special report of the regulator of Fannie Mae, OFHEO, concludes that the enterprise projected a false image of using best-class world standards of risk management, financial reporting, internal controls, and corporate governance.[122] OFHEO finds that the senior management of Fannie Mae reported false sustained growth of earnings with the objective of meeting quarterly targets of earnings per share. The accounting policies and practices of Fannie Mae did not conform in many cases to the Generally Accepted Accounting Principles (GAAP). Fannie Mae overstated reported income and capital by an estimated $10.6 billion in 1998 to mid-2004. Senior management of Fannie Mae distorted accounting by inflating earnings to meet targets with the intention of maximizing bonuses and other executive compensation. The CEO of Fannie Mae received $90 million in 1998–2003, of which $52 million were tied to attaining targets of earnings per share. Fannie Mae was exposed to significant interest rate risk, losing billions of dollars in the decline of interest rates in 2002. Operational and reputational risk exposures were also significant. The fabrication of earnings and excessive risks were facilitated by the board of directors of Fannie Mae that failed to be adequately informed and did not act independently of the senior management. The senior management of Fannie Mae attempted to interfere with the special examination of the OFHEO by directing its lobbyists to exert pressure on the examination and funding of the OFHEO. Similar practices resulted in a restatement of $5 billion at Freddie Mac.[123] The analysis of the compensation of the CEO and CFO of Fannie Mae concludes that even without assuming wrongdoing there were incentives in compensation packages to harm shareholders.[124]

There are three proposals for the regulation of the GSE.[125] First, the guarantee function of the housing GSE would be relocated to a new, independent agency of the federal government and the retained portfolio of assets would be returned to shareholders without any link to the federal government. Second, the GSE model would be maintained with regulatory changes to prevent unsound balance sheets and systemic risk. Third, the originating financial entities would issue covered bonds collateralized by the cash flows of the mortgages to create incentives for sound origination of mortgages, which may have been weakened by independent layers of origination, servicing and funding or placement of MBS with investors. Fannie Mae and Freddie Mac relaxed credit-risk management and drastic changes are required. The entire program of housing subsidies has to be reconsidered with cost/benefit analysis where possible that may at least reveal the large potential social harm.

Securitization and credit-risk transfer

Securitization is a vehicle by which the originator of a loan transfers its risks of credit, market (interest rate), and liquidity (funding) to investors. That is, the loan or most of it does not remain in the balance sheet of the originating financial entity. For example, a bank would extend a loan to a family for the purchase of a house. It would create a MBS by packaging similar loans in terms of credit rating; the loans provide the interest and principal payments of the MBS. The bank would then sell the MBS to investors. The bank typically services the mortgages in the MBS pool, that is, collects interest and principal that it transfers to the MBS after deducting a servicing fee. In turn, investors would finance the MBS in sale and repurchase agreements (SRP). The SRP is a contract by which the holder of the MBS or any other security, the financed counterparty, enters into a contract to sell the security to another entity, the financing counterparty, with an agreement to repurchase it at a specified time at a specific price plus accrued interest. SRP terms are from overnight to a few months to benefit from paying lower short-term interest rates while the security financed pays higher long-term yields. SRP prices are discounted by a "haircut" from observed market prices to hedge the possibility of decline in price in case the financed counterparty does not honor the contract in which case the financing counterparty has a loss in the form of the lower market price at which it can sell the security less the price financed in the SRP. The transaction is as follows with principal discounted by haircut:

Today

Financed Counterparty sells MBS to Financing Counterparty with agreement to repurchase

Financing Counterparty transfers cash (principal less haircut) to Financed Counterparty

Settlement

Financed Counterparty transfers cash (principal less haircut plus interest) to Financing Counterparty

Financing Counterparty returns the MBS to Financed Counterparty

Securitization has extended to most lending activities. Loans are now packaged in securities known as asset-backed securities (ABS) and collateralized loan obligations (CLO). The funds for consumer credit are largely obtained from securitization of receivables from credit cards, consumer loans, auto loans, and so on. A large market of asset-backed commercial paper (ABCP) is the driver of loans and a favorite investment of money market funds. Short-term financing by SRPs of securitized products, such as MBS, ABS and ABCP, provides the liquidity that is used to extend most loans by banks and other financial institutions. Liquidity risk occurs when the financed party cannot renew the SRP or cannot obtain financing with which to repurchase the security. The fear of decline in the prices of the securities used in SRP financing because of defaults originating initially in underlying nonprime mortgage loans caused sharp reduction in counterparty financing, which propagated throughout all ABS and ABCPs.

This system is "originate to service to funding" because of the three stages of the process. It has significant benefits.[126] Concentrations of large loans to a few debtors or credit segments have been the cause of individual bank failures and financial crises. Securitization affords an opportunity to transfer credit risk from originating financial institutions to investors, diversifying the portfolios of financial institutions, thus reducing their risk, while earning fees from the origination of the securitization and servicing, by collecting principal and interest, to remunerate the costs of the bank's franchise. High rates of economic growth worldwide and of global trade and investment during a new technological revolution after the 1970s created large demand for credit. Securitization has been an important innovation facilitating growth and prosperity through the availability of credit. There have been significant gains in transparency and pricing of credit. Defaults of mortgages in MBS reduced the capacity of financing them with SRP counterparties.

The critique of the system centers on the different incentives in the chain of securitization, in particular of mortgages. In contrast with earlier practice, the originator does not bear any of the default or rate risk of the mortgage, having an incentive to create mortgage agreements without full documentation and income verification. The servicing function is merely collection of cash flows that are transferred to the investor. The ultimate risk of default is with the investor. Rating companies began to derive significant revenue from securitization and relaxed their standards. This is the basic argument for regulation because of imperfections in credit markets. Another argument is that financial institutions did not control liquidity risk in the form of failure to obtain financing from counterparties.

There are two objections to the characterization of securitization. First, the credit problems were concentrated on subprime and Alt-A loans that resulted in the initial defaults observed at the beginning of the credit crisis. Defaults in other segments have occurred after the recession began in December 2007. Second, as elaborated in Chapter 6, there was another regulation failure, the lowering of the fed funds rate by the Fed to nearly zero in 2003–4, which created the impression that housing prices would increase forever. Subprime and Alt-A borrowers demanded credit and financial entities provided it under this mirage caused by government policy in which the only risk was to sell the house at a profit after two years when monthly interest and principal increased such that the mortgagor could not make the contracted mortgage payment. The interest rate shock by the central banks raised leverage and lowered credit standards throughout the entire production chain of loans and the gigantic housing subsidy. The near zero interest rate provoked leverage and illiquidity, compressing savings, which created an unparalleled financial crisis when the Fed rapidly raised interest rates from 1 percent to 5.25 percent after it realized deflation did not occur.

MBS and other ABS were packaged in new derivative securities. The ABS collateralized debt obligation (CDO) gained most of the attraction as the culprit instrument causing write downs that fractured the balance sheets of banks and financial entities.[127] The ABS CDO was offered in three tranches to cater to the risk appetite of investors. The junior or equity tranche provides the highest return because it includes the lowest credit quality of securities, such as subprime mortgages. The manager of the CDO allocates to the junior tranche the first losses until its value is exhausted. The mezzanine tranche has securities with lower return and higher quality, absorbing the losses after the exhaustion of the junior tranche. The senior tranche consists of AAA-rated securities and suffers losses only after the junior and mezzanine tranches have been wiped out by losses.

The problem is that banks incorporated the senior tranches in their balance sheets and in off–balance sheets entities known as structured investment vehicles (SIV). The SIVs were a form of generating returns while consuming less capital. The legal structure was a special purpose vehicle (SPV), which consisted of an entity created to acquire CDOs. The funding for the acquisition was by the SIV issuing ABCP that gained the AAA rating because it was guaranteed by a credit line of the bank. The SIV financed the ABCP in SRPs. With the funds obtained from the SRP of the ABCP, the SIV acquired the CDO portfolio. The spread was very generous, consisting of the difference of the high CDO leveraged long-term interest rate less the low short-term SRP interest rate. In addition, another benefit was that the off–balance sheet SIVs did not use much of the capital or liquidity of the bank. After the first losses of the CDOs caused by defaults of nonprime mortgages, the SIVs were unable to refinance their ABCP with the financing counterparty or obtain new financing from other counterparty to repurchase the ABCP. The SRPs were guaranteed by a line of credit of the bank, which was forced to provide the liquidity to repay the SRP value to the financing counterparty.

CDOs became illiquid after mortgage defaults, that is, they could not be sold even at deep discounts. After procrastination with financing through the rediscount windows of central banks and plans to create a super SIV to finance other SIVs, banks and regulators had to bite the bullet and incorporate the assets of the SIVs in bank balance sheets, beginning with Merrill Lynch. There were no reliable indicators of market prices of CDOs and models differed widely in their calculation of prices. Several hundred billion dollars of bank capital were erased by write downs of mortgage-related structured products. The counterparty distrust spread to other segments of the securitization system, paralyzing credit in most segments. Banks began to deposit excess reserves in the Fed, which used them to finance the markets, without reducing counterparty risk perceptions. The origin was the subprime and Alt-A loans, which in turn originated in the erosion of risk/return calculations caused by the euphoria that interest rates would remain low forever driving increases of asset prices.

The combination of a massive housing subsidy with central bank rates of nearly zero created a shock of major proportions. The recognition of the true origins of the credit/dollar crisis in policy shocks instead of only on the irresponsibility and failure of self-regulation of the financial system should enter into balanced proposals for regulation of financial markets. Markets failed in large part because of regulatory failures. It is not practical or even advisable to regulate away the potential for financial innovation, in accordance with the wisdom of the FSF view. A revised Basel II framework and best principles by the Basel Committee on Banking Supervision (BCBS) should provide new standards for the financial industry in the sound management and transparency of structured products.[128] The process should be guided by the constructive participation and consultation generated by the BCBS, including central banks and market participants, as in earlier reforms of international financial architecture.[129] The process of soft-law enlists participation in regulatory reform throughout the world in government and the private sector.[130]

Bank capital theory and requirements

Banks have limited equity capital of about 10 percent of their assets, significantly lower than more than 50 percent in the nineteenth century. The capital structure of banks combines equity with deposits that can be converted into cash. Demand deposits provide the liquidity or cash for banks to lend to projects of entrepreneurs that are illiquid because they provide cash flows in a relatively distant future. Recalling a loan from a borrower would interrupt the project and could only be sold at deep discount, resulting in realized assets of the bank lower than the face value of deposits. Banks are committed to convert deposits sequentially. In the historical bank run depositors withdraw at the teller's window on a first-come first-served basis. Banks provide liquidity to entrepreneurs with projects in a loan contract, on the asset side of the balance sheet, and provide immediate withdrawal of demand deposits, on the liability side of the balance sheet.[131] The liquidity transformation of banks is the source of the fragility of its capital structure. Loss of confidence on a bank to convert its deposits into cash could trigger a bank run, which currently would occur silently through online withdrawals.[132]

Banks operating under certainty can lend to their maximum capacity in a capital structure that is rigid and fragile because of the possibility of bank runs. The decline of the value of assets below the value of deposits, in conditions of uncertainty, can trigger a loss of confidence that results in a bank run.[133] The management of a bank is a trade-off of credit and liquidity relative to the high costs of a bank run. Capital is a buffer protecting against the decline of asset values.

The model of bank capital is based on abstract concepts such as loans and demand deposits that would exist only in ideal conditions in traditional deposit banks.[134] The complex positions of actual banks, on and off the balance sheet, are captured by the loans in the model. Skills of bankers are required to manage these complex positions. Demand deposits are similar to guarantees of liquidity in financing SIVs with

SRPs of their ABCP. Banks develop expertise in managing complex positions and guaranteeing liquidity, much the same as in providing liquidity to loans and demand deposits in the abstract model. The liquidity creation function of banks is illustrated by the financing of the CDOs. On the strength of their balance sheets, banks issued commercial paper of the SIVs, which were rated AAA because of the credit rating of the guarantor, the bank. The increasing default of mortgages resulted in exacerbated perceptions of counterparty risk. Banks faced increasing difficulty in refinancing maturing SRPs and had to honor the letter of credit issued to the SIVs. Banks experiencing write downs of their assets suffered a liquidity run in the form of failure to refinance SRPs even secured by sound assets. Although defaults in underlying mortgages occurred in subprime and Alt-A tranches, the uncertainty of write downs of bank assets eroding bank capital paralyzed the funding of structured financial products with SRPs. The securitization chain had provided liquidity with SRPs to structured financial products, MBS, which in turn originated in mortgages that passed on the liquidity to mortgagors to buy illiquid physical assets, such as houses. Weak bank balance sheets could no longer provide confidence for financing the securitized financial products.

The fragility of banks can be compensated by two alternatives, deposit insurance and lender of last resort (LOLR) functions by the central bank.[135] Deposit insurance is considered in the balance of this chapter and central banks in Chapter 3. The Banking Acts of 1933 and 1934 affected bank capital investment significantly by the introduction of deposit insurance and regulation through the FDIC. After FDIC no bank desiring to insure capital could escape federal regulation. If deposits are insured by the federal government, a bank may reduce its level of desired capital relative to assets. Capital would not be needed as a buffer to honor deposits that would not be withdrawn in a run because of government insurance. A counterfactual consists in analyzing the conduct of individuals and variables in alternative regimes or policies. The classical empirical counterfactual in deposit insurance is the current effects of regulation on bank capital investment compared with what would have been capital investment without regulation.[136] Appeal to data in economics is partly frustrated by the observation of variables with the effects of regulation, but not without the effects of regulation and other variables. Data for 49 states in 1963, 1964, and 1965 support the proposition that banks substitute deposit insurance for bank capital but do not support the proposition that banks behaved without regulation differently than they actually did under capital regulation. That is, regulation did not change the behavior of banks. A subsequent study with 323 banks drawn randomly from 32 states in 1970 supports the finding that banks substitute deposit insurance for capital and that regulators did not attempt to reduce this substitution effect.[137] However, this subsequent study finds evidence that banks increase their ratios of capital to assets when they fall below what regulators believe to be prudent.

International capital requirements

The BCBS reached on an agreement on Basel II at the May 2004 meeting. Finally, it published Basel II, or Framework, in June 2004.[138]

The BCBS determined that capital be divided in two tiers, 1 and 2.[139] Tier 1 consists of core capital, equity plus disclosed reserves obtained from retained profits after taxes. Tier 2 consists of supplementary capital up to value equal to core capital. Supplementary capital consists of:

- Nondisclosed reserves originating in profit and loss account and approved by supervisors;
- Reserves originating in revaluations;
- General reserves and reserves originating in loan losses;
- Hybrid capital instruments (such as preferred stock);
- Subordinated debt with minimum original term of five years up to 50 percent of core capital.

The dual objective of Basel II is to strengthen domestic and international financial stability while at the same time preventing capital requirements from creating competitive disadvantages among banks in various jurisdictions. Since the Capital Accord in 1988, financial institutions innovated significantly in quantifying and controlling financial risk. Basel II incorporates this reality and intends to promote sounder risk management processes in financial institutions. An important principle in Basel II is to relate capital adequacy regulation to actual financial risks. Basel II can incorporate changes in risk management through its more advanced approaches to credit, following the industry dynamically. However, some features of the 1988 Accord still remain: regulatory capital ratio of 8 percent of risk-weighted assets, the 1996 Market Risk Amendment and the definition of eligible capital. Most of the innovation of Basel II is in the denominator or calculation of risk-weighted assets.

Basel II consists of three pillars:

- *Pillar I*: Minimum Capital Requirements
- *Pillar II*: Process of Review by Supervisors
- *Pillar III*: Market Discipline

A method of menus considers each category of risk:

- Menu of Approaches to Measure Credit Risk
  - Standardized approach (modified version of existing Capital Accord)
    - Foundation approach based on internal ratings
    - Advanced approach based on internal ratings
- Menu of Approaches to Measure Market Risk (unaltered))
  - Standardized approach
  - Approach of internal models
- Menu of Approaches to Measure Operational Risk
  - Approach of basic indicators
  - Standardized approach
  - Internal approach of measurement or Advanced Management Approach

Basel II seeks an appropriate capital approach based on sensitivity standards of risk and internal measurement by banks. New forms to treat credit risk and specification of capital requirements for operational risk constitute the most important changes in capital requirements. The Standardized Approach, the Foundation and Advanced Internal-Ratings Based (IRB) provide avenues for treating credit risk. The objective is to encourage banks to improve management and measurement of risk, to apply the most advanced techniques for risk sensitivity and to determine adequate capital.

The objectives of Basel II consist of:

- Promoting safety and soundness of the financial system, maintaining existing minimum capital requirements;
- Strengthening equality in competition;
- Providing more extensive approach to risk;
- Implementing approaches to capital requirements that incorporate sensitivity to degree of risk and bank activities;
- Focusing on banks with international operations but applicable to different levels of complexity and sophistication.

The BCBS developed an IRB approach that reflects a bank's individual risk profile. It developed IRB for use by more sophisticated banks, but believes that the number and type of qualified institutions will increase. Every category consists of three elements:

- Risk components, for which the bank must use its own estimates or those of supervisors;
- Function of risk weight that transforms risk components in weights to adjust assets;
- Minimum requirements for banks to be eligible for IRB.

The BCBS developed the IRB based on best existing practices in risk control. Banks classify their debtors by risk categories. They estimate a probability of default, with higher precision in some banks. It is more difficult to estimate the percentage of loss given default (LGD).

The BCBS finds that increasing capital requirements during the current world financial crisis would accentuate problems. It intends to strengthen standards and capital resilience after the crisis, perhaps in 2010.[140] Changes in Basel II are considered in Chapter 6.

Deposit insurance

Deposit insurance did not fully prevent bank failures in the United States. In 1983–90, 1150 US commercial and savings banks, about 8 percent of the industry in 1980, failed, almost twice more than between creation of FDIC in 1934 through 1983.[141] In addition, over 900 savings and loans associations (S&L), or about 25 percent of the industry, were closed or merged by the Federal Savings and Loan Insurance Corporation (FSLIC) or placed in conservatorships. The Financial Institutions Reform, Recovery and Enforcement Act of 1989 (FIRREA) abolished the insolvent FSLIC, creating the Resolution Trust Corporation (RTC) and the Savings Association Insurance Fund (SAIF) and providing $150 billion of taxpayer funds to resolve insolvent S&Ls. The threat of banks economically insolvent or close to insolvency prompted Congress to enact the 1991 FDIC Improvement Act (FDICIA). Commercial banks recovered with record profitability by 1995 and few banks were classified as undercapitalized. The recovery of the thrift industry was much slower. FIRREA also introduced the new regulator of S&Ls, the Office of Thrift Supervision (OTS).

FDICIA implemented partially the philosophy of structured early intervention resolution (SEIR) in the form of prompt corrective action

(PCA) and least-cost resolution (LCR).[142] FDICA specified five zones of capital/asset ratios to which regulators quickly assigned percentages. Regulators would take corrective actions when capital/asset ratios entered zones of peril that could indicate possible insolvency. Regulators also moved to resolution at the lowest possible costs. Although the standards of SEIR were not followed in practice, regulation experienced improvement.

The Federal Reserve Act of 1913 imposed limitations on the types of assets that could be discounted by the Fed but the Glass Steagall Act of 1933 authorized advances by FRBs to member banks on any asset.[143] The Banking Act of 1933 prohibited payment of interest on demand deposits and imposed limits on interest rates paid on time deposits issued by commercial banks. These measures were motivated by the belief that the banking panic of the Great Depression originated in unsound banking in the form of high-risk loans by banks trying to obtain sufficient revenue to pay competitive rates on deposits.[144] Decreasing competitive pressure would reduce the occurrence of unsound banking. Subsequently, controls were influenced by the pressure to direct credit to mutual savings banks and savings and loan associations that complained of unfair competition from commercial banks, which prevented them from financing housing. These controls were unimportant when implicit rates on demand deposits were at or below zero percent and when market rates on time deposits were below those imposed by Regulation Q. The interest-rate controls became important already in the 1960s and increasingly during the rise in inflation during the stagflation of the 1970s.

The imposition of controls of interest rates over a long period permitted banks to find ways of evading and avoiding them. Banks avoided the zero interest imposition on demand deposits by providing services to customers and loans at less than market rates.[145] The rise in market rates of certificates of deposits above Regulation Q rates in the second half of the 1960s triggered compensatory reaction by banks. The growth of money market banks occurred through the invention of the large certificate of deposit (CD) that provided the funding for the increasing volume of loan demand. Outstanding CDs declined from $24 billion in mid-December 1968 to less than $12 billion in the beginning of October 1960.[146] There was no decline in banks' total liabilities because of the rise in liabilities on which the banks could pay a market rate in the euro-dollar market. The banks paid market rates on CDs by accounting them as "due from head office" in the balance sheets of their European offices. The head office changed the liability "due to foreign branches" for "due on CDs."[147] The future was predicted:[148]

> The banks have been forced into costly structural readjustments, the European banking system has been given an unnecessary competitive advantage, and London has been artificially strengthened as a financial center at the expense of New York.

The controls were unfair to people with lower incomes and wealth who received rates on their savings below those that would prevail in a free market and had almost no other alternative allocation for their savings.[149] The argument that the poor are net borrowers does not justify the reduction of their real savings and their ability to improve their wealth. There were also effects on the efficiency of the capital markets in the form of erroneous signals.

The credit crunch would consist of a reduction in the supply of loans by banks while keeping constant the riskless interest rates and the quality of potential borrowers.[150] The evidence suggests that there was a "capital crunch" after 1987 concentrated in several states, especially in New England. The real estate collapse in that region was the likely cause of the decline in bank capital and lending. Relaxation of interstate banking restrictions would permit banks to smooth their operations through geographical diversification.

There is evidence of a capital crunch in New England during the early 1990s.[151] Banks may shrink instead of issuing new equity because of asymmetry of information. There are no incentives for bankers to reveal their problems. Potential investors may not buy bank equity at normal economic returns because of the fear of dilution of current equity holders. Because equity cannot be issued at prices that are acceptable to bankers, shrinking is the only alternative to the banks. The sample of New England indicates that some banks in New England chose shrinking to recover capital/asset ratios because of pressures of regulation and financial markets and the preferences of bankers. Banks provide credit to small and medium businesses where information is private. Shrinkage because of capital crunch can reduce bank lending that is not provided by other lenders, or a credit crunch.

Political economy

The approach of political economy attempts to analyze the interests supporting regulation. The contrast with optimal regulatory arrangements would provide evidence on the validity of the various theories of regulation.

The deregulation of interstate branching constitutes an important experience for testing theories of regulation because it occurred gradually across states, providing more significant variation of cross-section and time-series samples than national regulation.[152] Moreover, deregulation at the national level occurred through the Interstate Banking and Branching Efficiency Act of 1994, permitting political economy analysis of whether the same factors determined national and state deregulation. The restriction of the US constitution to the issue of fiat money by states forced them to find financing in banks. States obtained revenue in the form of fees for granting charters, sometimes owned shares in banks or imposed taxes and restricted geographic competition to strengthen these revenues. Branches from banks in other states were restricted because those banks did not contribute to revenue. The number of banks in the United States reached about 30,000 by 1921.[153] Smaller banks, especially in rural areas, lobbied for deposit insurance to obtain protection in times of stress and from competition by larger banks. Political considerations likely influenced the introduction of restrictions on bank branching and federal deposit insurance with the purpose of benefiting small unit banks that could not compete with large banks with many units.[154]

Empirical analysis focuses on the time of deregulation of intrastate branching by means of consolidation in mergers and acquisitions (M&A).[155] Smaller banks would benefit more from the geographical restrictions because of less competition from larger banks. The sample includes 637 observations of 39 states after 1970, 36 of which deregulated branching. In agreement with the private interest view, the empirical results show that higher share in the banking industry by small banks delays regulation; the effect is economically important with one standard deviation (or dispersion) in small bank share increasing time to deregulation by 4.7 years.[156] The positive and significant association of the relative performance of small banks suggests that deregulation is delayed when small banks are financially stronger in relative terms. The result is consistent with the private interest view but also with the public interest view because declining financial strength of small banks could cause failures with high-cost bailouts. Insurance companies could oppose declining profits from the economies of scope of selling insurance by banks. The result is that time to deregulation increases with a relatively large insurance sector. Small companies that are dependent on banks could exert pressure for deregulation. The result is earlier deregulation in states with numerous small companies depending on bank services. The result is consistent with both the private interest and the public interest views. Intervention on behalf of the public interest would ameliorate the lower financing volumes at higher rates resulting from restricted competition.[157]

The analysis at the national-level is conducted by means of the roll-call vote on an amendment to a financial reform package in 1991.[158] The amendment proposed interstate branching and deregulation. Although the bill was defeated, the amendment passed by 210 to 208. The result is that legislators from states with relatively lower share of small banks are more likely to support the deregulation of interstate branching. As in intrastate results, the share of small institutions in banking is the most important explanatory variable of the voting decision of legislators. Legislators from states with strong insurance industry are less likely to support deregulation of interstate branching. The conclusion of this research is that interests in the state legislatures are similar to those in Congress. Important technological innovations, such as credit cards, ATM services, credit scores and transportation/communication improvements, which reduced the value of geographical monopolies, reinforced the strength of the movement toward deregulation.[159]

The FDIC was an important change of the US system of supervision and regulation of financial institutions. Empirical research uses the creation of the law as background for analysis of the various theories of regulation.[160] The competition among interest groups and the struggle among groups are important in explaining the shape of regulation. There was also a role for the theories of influence by ideology and partisanship. It was difficult to implement some reforms because of the opposition from banking and contentious groups within the financial industry. The rivalry of groups positively affected regulatory outcomes, showing that such rivalry can benefit consumers because of the division in fostering self-interest. The feasibility of approving beneficial legislation was facilitated by the multiple interests of large and small banks. It is helpful to understand the interests of the various constituencies to formulate policies than can obtain final support for positive legislation.

There is significant usefulness in the political economy approach to deposit insurance because of the interplay of multiple political constituencies with conflicting interests.[161] There are many stakeholders of banks, in addition to depositors, affected by deposit insurance, such as shareholders of the banks, creditors, bank managers, agencies such as FDIC, the government, and taxpayers. There may be conflicting interests among the various groups of stakeholders as well as within groups themselves. Smaller, riskier banks may have greater interest in deposit insurance, as in the history of the United States, than larger, well-capitalized banks with enhanced credit analysis. Smaller depositors in the presence of insurance limits as in the United States may be less interested than larger depositors that would have significant funds uninsured. Deposit insurance is sold politically as protection of small depositors and against systemic runs on banks. There are major direct costs to taxpayers and indirect ones in the form of moral hazard by banks.[162] Weaker stakeholders, such as small depositors and riskier banks, may have more interest in deposit insurance.

The private interest view of regulation argues that riskier banks exert group pressure on politicians for deposit insurance to obtain benefits at the expense of safer banks. The sample used to contrast the evidence with the private interest and public interest views consists of 69 countries with deposit insurance in 1990–9.[163] Deposit insurance is measured as the ratio of coverage limit per depositor to per capita income. The econometric analysis shows that deposit insurance coverage is higher in countries where the market is dominated by banks that are poorly capitalized and in which depositors are poorly educated. The results support the proposition of the private interest view that riskier banks successfully lobby to obtain deposit insurance coverage.

The history of deposit insurance in the United States provides relevant evidence. Bank branching strengthened the stability and resilience of the system. The survey of literature concludes that unit bankers used political influence to preserve the system of unit branches, originating the need for deposit insurance, in the antebellum period and in the twentieth century.[164] The diversification and coordination of branch banking constituted an early alternative to insurance of deposits.

Summary

There is sharp distinction between the market failure approach leading to prudential and systemic regulation and the innovation approach of the FSF. The OPSR approach is far more intrusive, proposing tight regulation of financial institutions and markets. Most of the current regulatory agenda in parliaments is based on the OPSR. The FSF approach is more flexible, allowing for sufficient decisions on risks and returns in financial markets to provide for innovation that is essential to prosperity. The choice between the OPSR and the FSF depends on the interpretation of the origins and resolution of the credit/dollar crisis. The OPSR blames reckless risk decisions and leverage by financial institutions operating under lax standards. The FSF approach focuses on the shock of zero interest rates in 2003–4 on the monumental housing subsidy, the nonprime mortgages, largely promoted by Fannie Mae and Freddie Mac, and credit-risk transfer products.

3
Bank Concentration and Central Banks

Introduction

There are two general themes in this chapter. First, a group of sections focuses on the issue of monopoly in banking markets. The relaxation of entry in local markets reduced significantly the measurement and need for regulation of market power. Second, financial stabilization to prevent and resolve banking and financial crises is managed by central banks. The paradigm of modern central banking is the BOE.

Banking market organization

Free markets do not result in the outcome of the first best of efficiency and satisfaction if there are frictions that prevent perfect competition. In the ideal market organization there would be many banks with no bank large enough in terms of volume of services to determine market prices on its own. In reality, there are local markets in which there is only one bank. Even in larger markets there are not many banks engaged in effective competition. Less than perfect competition may not result in sufficient volume of lending at rates that are commensurate with the returns on projects required for economic growth and progress. Small and medium enterprises (SME) may have access only to limited credit at high interest rates, preventing sound development of business. Competition would probably increase lending volume, making credit more accessible at lower interest rates.

The application of the first-best theory to banking may not be entirely adequate because of the existence in reality of many frictions or violations of the abstract assumptions.[165] There are multiple frictions in retail banking because of various barriers to entry of new banks. Incumbent banks enjoy local reputation; their branch network may be difficult to replicate by new entrants; and there are switching costs, consisting of the reluctance of bank customers to change their accounts to another bank. Banks develop relations with their corporate customers, such as lines of credit, which prevent access to those customers by other banks. Relationship banking develops information obtained by experienced bank officers over long periods. These relations diminish the asymmetry of information between an individual bank and its clients but create a barrier of imperfect information to other banks that may not lend to those clients because of the lack of information on their creditworthiness. Thus, banks may enjoy market power, which allows them to charge higher interest rates and other fees than those that would prevail under perfect competition.

Some rivalry is desirable in banking markets.[166] Competition would encourage innovation and efficiency. Technological change and deregulation force adaptation of competition and regulation. According to a current of thought, there are dangers in excessive competition and excessive market power.[167] Banking is characterized by multiple products, such as checking accounts, CDs, collection services, fund transfers, payments, and so on. Competition occurs throughout different levels of the product structure. It is difficult to determine theoretically or empirically the optimum level of competition, which may depend on the soundness of banks and the institutional characteristics of regulation. The bank using the new technology first may gain competitive advantage over rivals, enjoying market power, which may be temporary as others acquire the new technology. Active competition policy may prevent the maintenance of these temporary advantages but there must be care in not frustrating technological progress. Multiple sophisticated banks in the segments of wholesale and investment banking engage in intensive competition, suggesting natural oligopoly as the equilibrium market structure.[168] The following subsections consider the critical issues of market structure, entry, market power, and the relation of concentration to financial stability.

Competition and productivity

Market power in banking should be analyzed in terms of the complex and prolonged evolution of US banking. Neoclassical economics would interpret the future in terms of technological progress, economies of scale and scope, and diversification of risk.[169] Technological progress increases the output that is obtained from inputs such as labor, capital, and natural resources. Economies of scale are considered extensively in the literature on bank market power. They consist of substantial fixed costs that are required for initiation of operations, such as bulky investments in branch offices and IT. Although there are huge initial investments just to start operations, the cost per unit of bank services declines with growth of banking business. That is, average cost decreases as output expands or more units of services are provided. The first entrant in a market has, after growth, the advantage of lower unit costs. Economies of scope are important in banking, consisting of lower costs of providing related services, such as underwriting and distribution of securities through the network of branch offices and clients. Diversification of risk is essential to reducing risk, allowing for stable growth of banks. Banks that entered the business early would benefit from technology, economies of scale and scope, and risk diversification by enjoying lower costs than new entrants.

The evolution of US banking reveals two important determinants of banking market organization or the existence of market power.[170] First, regulation historically created market power and its relaxation diminished it, on a national basis. The argument is related to the analysis of political economy in Chapter 2. The main problem was the restriction of competition in local deposit and loan markets typically served by one bank. The problem was compounded by restrictions of interest rates with Regulation Q that gave banks "monopsony" powers in local markets, that is, funding with low interest rates because the local bank was the only alternative for deposits. Banks enjoying market power could obtain funds at interest rates below market levels, using these funds to invest in inefficient products, with negative NPV. The appendix to Chapter 1 explains the evaluation of the NPV of a project by discounting future cash flows net of costs by riskless interest rates. Negative NPV would misallocate resources in the economy because projects would cost more in current dollars than the benefits they bring but bank officers may fund them because of reasons other than optimizing the balance sheets of their banks. The restriction of intrastate and interstate banking prevented inefficient banks from becoming acquired by more efficient banks, constraining the market for corporate control, which would have made local banks more efficient in more competitive banking markets. The crucial change toward more competitive banking markets was the erosion of geographical restrictions on establishing banking institutions.

Second, the modern industrial revolution had a profound impact on banking. Reductions in the cost and increases in the breadth and speed of processing and transmitting information are important factors of banking productivity.[171] The information technology (IT) revolution spread throughout the operations of banks. Efficient, rapid, and less costly back-office work, consisting of digitally processing and storing transactions, permitted significant increase in the business of banking. The front office, or services to clients, permitted new products, such as ATMs, online banking, and others. Credit based on standardized scores and commercial ratings became available instantaneously, allowing faster credit approvals. There had been a revolution in the analysis of financial products with the option pricing methods.[172] Risk management techniques developed to measure, analyze, forecast, and control financial risks. Securitization created risk-transfer opportunities with the development of secondary markets for mortgages, credit cards, vehicles, and others. New products cut into the competitiveness of banks with innovations such as commercial paper acquired by money-market funds and shared with many clients, also made possible by the instantaneous calculation of the value of positions and the share of clients. A virtual spiral of innovation occurred as analyzed by the FSF framework discussed in Chapter 2. Transaction costs were significantly reduced, causing shocks in institutions, market structures, and regulation. The growing world economy benefitted from the improved efficiency of financial markets and growth triggered new rounds of innovation. The innovation spiral broke the boundaries between commercial and investment banking, eventually leading to the repeal of the separation imposed by the Glass-Steagall Act.

The Bureau of Labor Statistics (BLS) measures bank productivity by the ratio of numbers of transactions, an output, to labor, an input, which may not capture many effects of technological and organizational improvement that has occurred in banking.[173] The index of the BLS does not state outputs that are intensive in the use of capital, such as those that occurred in IT improvements. Banking business consists of intermediation, but the standard measure of productivity focuses on transactions. Outsourcing to credit bureaus and other services are not included in the labor input but have become increasingly important.

Refined measurement of the reaction of banks to technology is obtained from a sample that includes virtually all banks in the United States in a period of rapid change in 1984–97, focusing on three years, 1984, 1991, and 1997.[174] The change in bank gross costs can be divided in three components. First, there are changes in the best-practice of banks or the best available knowledge and management. Second, there is dispersion or deviation of this best practice, or inefficiencies, in individual banks. Third, business conditions also affect cost changes. This analysis finds that the use of new technologies increased costs of banks but the offering of products based on the new technologies increased bank revenues. Thus, banks efficiently managed the new technology. Competition eventually reduced profits. The banks that best used technology in a given period were different. A critical finding is that merging banks successfully managed the diversification obtained from mergers, taking higher risks but experiencing the highest profits.

Restrictions on markets

Market power of banks can originate in technical factors, such as technology creating economies of scale and scope that confer cost advantages of higher volume of services to the first company to enter the market. Market power of banks can also originate in legal factors, such as regulation that protects incumbent banks by restricting the entry of new banks.

Intrastate and interstate or geographical restrictions in the United States protected incumbent banks from the entry of new banks. The movement of deregulation that lifted the restrictions of entry within and across states beginning in the 1970s provides an important sample of experience on bank market entry. There was significant improvement of bank efficiency resulting from the relaxation of geographical restrictions on new bank charters.[175] Loan losses and costs declined after the elimination of the barriers to entry. The benefits were passed on to consumers in the form of lower average loan rates. The most efficient banks grew by absorbing services from less efficient banks with high costs and low profits. That is, entry of new banks benefitted consumers of bank services and the economy as a whole. Various research studies using different samples and methods confirm the benefits of competition through relaxation of entry restrictions.[176]

Bank concentration

The first-best outcome of efficiency and satisfaction is not attained in the presence of market power. This could occur if there are a few producers in a market, which can fix prices that would be higher than those that would occur if there were many competitors with small shares in market volume. Banking in reality is characterized by a few banks that conceivably could fix prices according to criteria that are different than those followed by perfectly competitive firms.

There are four approaches to measuring the welfare losses in banking markets because of imperfect competition. First, banks enjoying market power may indulge in a "quiet life."[177] In this situation, banks would enjoy the cushion of prices higher than in competition while not minimizing costs. Bank managers would permit increases in unit costs, consuming the price difference relative to competition and passing on to consumers a part of the gain from market power.

Second, large corporations may not be managed strictly for the benefit of shareholders.[178] Managers of corporations may indulge in consuming perks, such as a larger than required computer, luxurious offices, excessive vacations, donations to favorite charities, and so on, which prevent the best possible profit for distribution to shareholders.[179] Thus, part of the excess price relative to competition would be consumed by managers. This situation is known as the principal/agent problem. The principal is the group of shareholders and the agent is the management team. Agency costs consist of excessive costs incurred by the management team that do not maximize the profits for distribution to the shareholders.

Third, monopolistic profits in excess of those that would obtain under perfect competition are called rents in economics. According to the argument of rent-seeking, firms invest the excess profits or rents in seeking higher rents or maintaining existing ones.[180] Rent-seeking occurs through lobbying efforts, an important characteristic of politics, causing the wasteful use of resources for activities that distort the efficiency of the economy.

Fourth, large corporations enjoying market power may be characterized by least-effort cultures.[181] Managers and employees may simply provide the minimum input required to avoid problems. The collection of factors that result in lax cost minimization is known as X-efficiency.

Research has measured these four types of cost laxity in 5000 US banks.[182] This research finds lower efficiency of cost minimization in banks acting in more concentrated markets. The four mechanisms of cost inefficiency reduce the pressure to control costs in banks operating in markets without competitive pressures. The implication for policy is to take into consideration cost inefficiency in market organization.

An important issue in the credit/dollar crisis is the relationship between banking concentration and the overall stability of the financial system. Theoretical considerations suggest that banking crises are more likely during inflationary episodes in both concentrated and competitive banking systems.[183] The evidence during the Great Depression considered in Chapter 6 reveals the significant exposure of banks to deflation. Bank clients have fixed nominal interest rates while deflation causes declines in the value of assets, revenue, and profits because of falling asset and product prices while costs such as labor are more rigid.

The weakness of clients erodes the balance sheets of banks. Banking panics in the United States were stronger in concentrated unit banking in states with geographical restrictions of entry. However, disruptions of economies after inflation have also caused banking stress. Central banks have focused on controlling inflation to stabilize economies and promote growth.

A study of 79 countries and 50 crises analyzes the effects of bank concentration on the fragility of bank systems.[184] There is less likelihood of banking crises in concentrated banking systems. There is less likelihood of banking crises in economics with general competition throughout the economy. Likelihood of banking crises is higher in banking systems with restrictions on entry and on banking lines of business.

Central banks

Monetary policy has become the major tool of government in controlling short-term economic adversities such as inflation and the decline in output and employment during recessions. There has been increasing emphasis on the role of nominal demand or aggregate money income in affecting prices and economic activity in the short term. Monetary policy fixes the central bank policy interest rate that in the short term affects nominal demand and general economic activity. For example, the Fed policy rate is the fed funds rate or noncollateralized loans among banks of their reserves deposited at the FRBs. The objective of this section is to provide the institutional background on the four major central banks in the world, in the United States, United Kingdom, Europe, and Japan. The institutional structure is complemented with analysis of injections and withdrawals of money by central banks to determine their policy interest rates. The following section analyzes the mechanism by which monetary policy is transmitted to income and prices. A final section discusses the critique of the effectiveness of monetary policy and countercyclical policy in general. The operations of the central banks have been entirely reshaped during the credit/dollar crisis after 2007. The types of policies used during the credit/dollar crisis are analyzed in Chapter 6 to explain the effort of central banks in recovering financial markets and the economy. Central banking is the most important tool of financial regulation, actual, and proposed.

The Federal Reserve System and US regulators and supervisors

The complex system of regulation and supervision of financial institutions in the United States is shown in Table 3.1. There are three types

Table 3.1 US Agencies of regulation and supervision of depository financial institutions

Agency	Responsibilities
Federal Reserve System	I Supervision • Supervision of state-chartered banks that are members of the FRS About 900 state member banks • Foreign operations of member banks • US operations of foreign banks • Edge Act and agreement corporations engaging in foreign banking About 5000 bank-holding companies II Regulation • Regulations applying to the entire banking industry • Regulations applying only to member banks • Regulations to implement federal laws of consumer protection Truth in Lending Equal Credit Opportunity Home Mortgage Disclosure Acts
Office of the Comptroller of the Currency	• Charter authorization, regulation, and supervision of all national banks • Supervision of the federal branches and agencies of foreign banks
Federal Deposit Insurance Corporation	• Examination and supervision of 5250 banks and savings banks • Primary federal regulator of state-charted banks that are not members of the FRS • Back-up supervisor for remaining insured banks and thrift institutions
Office of Thrift Supervision	• Examination, supervision, and regulation of 853 savings associations insured by the FDIC • Registration, examination, and regulation of 481 registered savings and loan holding companies (SLHC)
Office of Federal Housing Enterprise Oversight	• Broad-based examinations of Fannie Mae and Freddie Mac • Stress-testing Fannie Mae and Freddie Mac to develop risk-based capital standards
National Credit Union Administration	• Charter authorization and supervision of federal credit unions • Operation of National Credit Union Share Insurance Fund
New York State Banking Department	• New York State Banking Board: promulgation of general and specific regulation on banking in NYS, approve or disapprove issue of charters, licenses, and establishment of bank branches • Examination of financial entities with total assets of $1.3 trillion

Sources: FRBO, *The Federal Reserve System: purposes & functions* 9th ed. (Washington, DC: FRBO, Jun, 2005); OCC, About the OCC. http://www.occ.treas.gov/aboutocc.htm; OTS, *OMB FY 2007 budget & performance plan* (Washington, DC, OFS, Jan, 2007); OFHEO, About OFHEO. http://www.ofheo.gov/Mission.asp; NCUA, About NCUA. http://www.ncua.gov/AboutNCUA/Index.htm; NYSBD, The department. http://www.banking.state.ny.us/dep.htm; FDIC, About FDIC. http://www.fdic.gov/about/index.html

of banks in the United States according to the government agency that provided the charter and whether they are members of the FRS.[185] The banks that receive their charter from the federal government through the Office of the Comptroller of the Currency (OCC) in the US Treasury are national banks and by law must be members of the FRS. There are banks chartered by the states that are members of the FRS and others that are not members of the FRS. There is no mandatory membership requirement for state-chartered banks to become members of the FRS but they can elect for membership if they meet the requirements by the Board of Governors of the Federal Reserve System (FRBO). There were approximately 7700 commercial banks in March 2004 of which about 2900 were members of the FRS, about 2000 being national banks and 900 state banks.[186] Member banks must subscribe 6 percent of their capital and surplus as stock of the corresponding regional FRB, 3 percent as paid-in capital and the rest subject to call by the FRBO. There is no control power in this capital subscription, which is simply a legal obligation of FRS membership.

The FDIC supervises 5250 banks and is the primary federal supervisor and regulator for state-chartered banks that are not members of the FRS. The FDIC administers the $49 billion insurance fund of financial deposits. The OTS is entrusted with providing charters, supervision, and regulation to the savings and loans institutions. The OFHEO examines and determines the capital adequacy of two large public companies, Fannie Mae and Freddie Mac, which are engaged in the mortgage business. The National Credit Union Administration (NCUA) provides the charters of federal credit unions and administers the insurance of deposits in those institutions. The structure of the various supervisors and regulators is discussed below in turn.

The OCC is part of the US Treasury and was established in 1863.[187] The director of the OCC is appointed by the president for a five-year term with the advice and consent of the US Senate. The OCC charters, regulates, and supervises all US national banks and supervises the federal branches and agencies of foreign banks. There are four district offices in the United States and an office in London to supervise the international activities of national banks. The examiners of the OCC supervise domestic and international activities of national banks. These examiners also review the internal and external audits and legal compliance of banks. An important current function is the capacity of the management of banks to measure and control risk. The OCC is authorized to take supervisory measures against noncomplying banks and to issue rules and regulations on bank investments, lending, and transactions. It authorizes the application for new charters, branches, capital, and modifications of the corporate structure of banks. The objectives of the OCC are to maintain the safety and soundness of the national banking system, promote competition in banking services, improve the efficiency of its supervision, and maintain fair and equal access of the public to banking services. There are no appropriations of Congress to the OCC, which depends on the fees of its examinations and applications and the returns on the investment of its holding of US treasury securities.

The FDIC is an independent agency of the US federal government.[188] It was established in 1933 to alleviate the failure of thousands of banks. It claims that no depositor lost any funds in an insured bank since the beginning of FDIC insurance in 1934. The insurance fund of the FDIC has total resources of $49 billion that back the insurance of $3 trillion of deposits in nearly all US banks and thrifts. The failure of banks in the credit/dollar crisis requires increases in the insurance fund. The new expanded role of the FDIC in the credit/dollar crisis is discussed in Chapter 6. There are no appropriations by Congress to the FDIC. The premiums of insurance paid by banks and thrifts plus the returns of investments in US treasury securities provide for the expenses of the FDIC. In each bank insured by the FDIC, savings, deposits and other deposit accounts, when combined, are insured to the maximum of $250,000 per depositor increasing from $100,000 during the credit/dollar crisis (see Chapter 6). It also insures individual retirement accounts (IRA) and Keoghs up to $250,000. The FDIC has staff of 4500, with headquarters in Washington, DC, and six regional offices and multiple field offices throughout the United States. A five-person Board of Directors manages the FDIC. The president appoints and the Senate confirms the directors with a maximum of three originating in the same political party.

The OTS is a bureau of the US Treasury established on August 9, 1989.[189] The main statute regulating the OTS is the Home Owners' Loan Act that was originally approved by Congress in 1933. The OTS charters, examines, supervises, and regulates Federal savings associations insured by the FDIC. The OTS also examines, supervises, and regulates state-chartered savings associations that are insured by the FDIC. It also registers, examines, and regulates savings and loans holding companies (SLHC) and other affiliates. In September 2006, the OTS regulated 853 savings associations that had $1.63 trillion in assets. The OTC supervised 481 holdings company enterprises with about $7.7 trillion in assets. The holding companies regulated by the OTS own about one-half of all savings associations and 78 percent of the total assets of savings associations. The director of the OTS is appointed by the president and confirmed by the Senate for a five-year term. The main objective of the OTS is to provide for a safe and sound thrift industry. It also provides for a competitive environment in the industry, a flexible regulatory framework and excellence in its activities.

The Federal Housing Enterprise Financial Safety and Soundness Act of 1992 created the OFHEO as an independent entity within the Department of Housing and Urban Development.[190] Housing finance is discussed in Chapter 2.

The NCUA was created to charter and supervise federal credit unions and the National Credit Union Share Insurance Fund (NCUSIF) established in 1970. It is an independent federal agency.[191] The NCUSIF insures member deposits in credit unions to the federal limit of $250,000.[192] It is administered by the NCUA and is backed by the "full faith and credit" of the US government. The NCUSIF holds about 1.30 percent of the deposits of federally insured credit unions. The law requires that federally insured credit unions maintain 1 percent of their deposits in the NCUSIF and the board of the NCUA has the authority to impose a premium increase if required. There have been no losses by members of the NCUSIF. The president appoints three board members, confirmed by the Senate, of which only two can originate in the same political party. Account holders in federal and state-chartered credit unions total 80 million.

The New York State Banking Department (NYSBD) is the supervisory and regulatory body of financial institutions in New York State (NYS).[193] The NYS Banking Law of 1932 created the NYS Banking Board that is currently a quasi-legislative body issuing general and specific regulation on banking in NYS. The NYS Banking Board cooperates with the NYSBD in formulating banking standards, having the power to approve or reject banks charters, licenses and the establishment of branch banks. The NYS Banking Board has 17 members and is chaired by the Superintendent of Banks of NYS. There are eight members chosen from the public and eight members that must have experience and represent diverse areas of banking. The eight members with experience are chosen from eight different groups, including foreign bank corporations that have a license to operate a branch or agency in NYS. The NYSBD is the main regulator for state-licensed and state-chartered financial entities. The assets of the regulated institutions are about $1.3 trillion. It is the oldest regulatory agency in the United States. The NYSBD has 600 staff of which 73 percent employed as bank examiners. The fees received by the NYSBD pay for its expenses. There are multiple regulatory and supervisory institutions in the states of the United States.

The US Congress created the FRS with the Federal Reserve Act of 1913. There have been many other legislative measures since 1913.[194] The responsibilities of the FRB are in four different areas:[195]

- *Monetary policy.* The FRBO and the Federal Open Market Committee (FOMC), according to the Federal Reserve Act Section 2A: "shall maintain long run growth of the monetary and credit aggregates commensurate with the economy's long run potential to increase production, so as to promote effectively the goals of maximum employment, stable prices, and moderate long-term interest rates."
- *Supervision and regulation.* The FRS is one of the regulators and supervisors of the banking and financial system of the United States. The objective of regulation and supervision by the FRS is to maintain a sound banking and financial system, protecting consumers in their credit transactions.
- *Systemic risk.* The FRS contains systemic risks in the general effort of maintaining the stability and soundness of the US banking and financial system.
- *Financial services.* The FRS provides financial services to the US government and domestic and foreign financial institutions.

The three objectives of monetary policy—stable prices, maximum employment, and moderate long-term interest rates—may be conflicting in practice. After the second oil price increase in 1980, inflation in the United States rose to double-digit levels, prompting the FRBO to increase interest rates close to 20 percent per year. Maximum employment and moderate long-term interest rates were sacrificed to focus policy on preventing inflation from running out of control. In a way, it could be argued that inflation control was ensuring adequate employment and lower interest rates in the medium term. Central banks have traditionally been more concerned with inflation control and this emphasis has gained strength in the past 15 years with the movement toward transparency and inflation targeting.

The FRS is a federal government agency.[196] It is ruled by a seven-member FRBO; the members are appointed by the president of the United States and confirmed by the Senate. FRBO members have 14-year nonrenewable terms and are appointed in staggered fashion such as to have one term expiring on January 31 of each even-number year. The US president appoints the chairman and vice chairman of the FRBO for four-year terms. They must be members or appointed simultaneously as members and must be confirmed by the US Senate. The FRS has a staff of somewhat less than 2000.

There is significant interface and cooperation of the FRBO and other branches of the US government.[197] The chairman of the FRBO testifies every year around February 20 before the Senate Committee on Banking, Housing, and Urban Affairs and around July 20 before the House Committee on Financial Services. There is a broad range of issues discussed in these appearances, including the conduct of monetary policy, the evolution of the US economy and its prospects for the future. The FRBO provides Congress a report on these issues before testimony by the chairman. The chairman also meets periodically with the president, the secretary of the Treasury, and other members of the administration. The chairman of the FRBO has, together with other heads of central banks, a major role in the international financial system. The chairman of the FRBO is the alternate US member of the board of governors of the IMF, a member of the board of the BIS and a member of important international meetings, including representation at the Organization for Economic Cooperation and Development (OECD). The Group of Seven (G7) meeting of finance ministers and central bank governors has the participation of the chairman of the FRBO.

There are 12 regional FRBs that together with their branches conduct operations of the FRS.[198] The FRBs and their branches operate the US system of payments, distribution of currency, supervision and regulation of member banks and bank-holding companies, and banking transactions for the US Treasury. Each of the FRBs is responsible for FRS business in a specific region of the United States and receives the deposits of banks in the region. The services of the FRBs and their branches to depository institutions are under broad oversight responsibility by the FRBO. Congress also has oversight authority over the FRBs.

The FOMC of the FRS has the responsibility for US monetary policy.[199] The FOMC is legally responsible for oversight of open market operations by which the FRS affects the level of reserves of depository institutions that influence US monetary and credit conditions. It also directs foreign exchange (FX) operations of the FRS. The FOMC consists of the seven members of the FRBO and five of the 12 presidents of FRBs that serve one-year terms on a rotating basis with the exception of the president of the FRB of New York (FRBNY) who is a permanent member. The FOMC independently determines its organization as provided by the law. Traditionally, it elects the chairman of the FRBO as its chairman and the president of the FRBNY as its vice chairman. The FOMC conducts eight formal meetings every year in Washington, DC, but can hold telephone consultations or other meetings throughout the year.

US depository institutions maintain deposits in their accounts at the FRBs.[200] The accounts are used to make and receive payments for the institutions themselves or for their clients. The FRBO imposes reserve requirements on all depository institutions, including commercial banks, savings banks, savings and loan associations, credit unions and US branches and agencies of foreign banks. The FRBO has maintained a policy since the early 1990s to impose reserve requirements only on transactions deposits, or checking accounts, and interest-bearing deposits that provide unlimited checking privileges. The depository institutions maintain required reserves in the form of cash in vault and deposits in their accounts at the corresponding FRB. The required reserve balance is the excess of the required reserves over vault in cash. Deficiencies incur a charge. The depository institutions may also hold contractual balances in excess of required reserve balances to cover unexpected transactions. Excess reserves are balances that exceed reserve requirements and contractual balances and are relatively small because they do not pay interest.

The fed funds rate is the interest rate paid on unsecured or noncollateralized overnight loans of funds deposited at the accounts of depository institutions in FRBs, constituting the policy rate of the US central bank. Open market operations constitute the main instrument used by the FRBO to attain a market clearing fed funds rate that is around the desired target of monetary policy.[201] The FMOC authorizes the desk at the FRBNY to conduct open market operations to maintain the desired fed funds rate. The desk engages in transactions with primary dealers that are qualified by capital and other standards. The operations with primary dealers are conducted in the form of auctions. On the basis of information and analysis, the desk continuously assesses the level of reserves that would maintain the desired fed funds rate.

Assume that the desk decides that more reserves are needed. When significant injection is required, the desk could engage in outright purchase of authorized securities, such as US treasuries, federal agencies' securities and MBS with guarantee of federal agencies, including Fannie Mae and Freddie Mac.[202] The typical needs are not that sizeable and the desk would normally engage in financing the position in treasuries of a primary market dealer in an SRP. The dealer sells the security to the treasury in exchange for cash with the agreement to repurchase it the following day at a specified price that includes the one-day interest. There can also be an agreement for a longer term in case the desk anticipated the need for many days ahead. In both cases, the desk of the FRBNY injects money into circulation: to pay for the securities it acquires, financing the position of the dealer. The larger availability of bank reserves would tend to lower the fed funds rate. The following day or later if in a term SRP, the dealer returns the cash plus interest to the Fed and receives the securities.

Assume that the desk decides that the level of reserves is excessive, probably causing a decline in the fed funds rate below what is determined by the FOMC. The desk would then withdraw reserves by means of the sale of securities to the dealers or by financing its securities with the dealers. In the outright sale of securities, the dealers pay cash for the securities, contracting the amount of reserves. The instrument for financing positions of the FRS is to engage in a reverse sale and repurchase agreement (RSRP). The desk of the FRBNY would sell its securities to a primary dealer with the agreement to repurchase them in one day at a specified price plus one-day interest. Funds would flow from the account of the dealer to that of the FRBNY, contracting the level of reserves. The desk could also arrange a longer-term financing period for the RSRP according to the estimate of reserves in the days ahead. In both cases, funds flow into the FRS: by the payment for the purchase of the securities sold and by the financing of the securities of the FRS. The level of reserves would tend to contract, moving the fed funds rate toward the desired target.

The FRBO has been extremely active in raising and lowering interest rates in the recent past. The range is high, from a peak of 8 percent in the more inflationary period around 1990 to 1 percent during the period of fear of deflation in 2003–4. The fed funds rate then increased by 425 basis points to 5.25 percent per year, where it remained unaltered from June 29, 2006 to September 18, 2007 when the Fed began aggressive reductions culminating in the historical record low of 0 to 0.25 percent decided by the FOMC on December 16, 2008.[203] The Fed innovated with new policies to unfreeze credit markets that are analyzed in detail in Chapter 6.

The European Central Bank

The European Commission (EC) provided in the Delors Report of April 1989 three stages toward economic and monetary union.[204] The first stage would consist of the removal of all hurdles to financial integration, while reducing the differences in economies policies among member states of the European Union (EU). Economic convergence would be strengthened in the second stage while creating the basic institutions and structure of the European Monetary Union (EMU). The exchange rates would be locked in the final stage, assigning the monetary and economic duties to the institutions. The Maasstricht Treaty creating the EU was signed on February 7, 1992, and entered into force on November 1, 1993. On January 1, 1999, the conversion rates of the members of the EMU were fixed, the ECB assumed the responsibility for monetary policy in the euro area, and the euro replaced the national currencies.[205] The 11 original members of the EMU are Belgium, Germany, Spain, France, Ireland, Italy, Luxembourg, the Netherlands, Austria, Portugal, and Finland. Greece joined in 2001, raising the number of members to 12.

The European System of Central Banks (ESCB) and the European Central Bank (ECB) were established by a statute of the EU on June 1, 1998.[206] The distinction between the ESCB and the ECB will continue until there are member states of the EU that have not adopted the euro. The maintenance of price stability is the primary objective of the ESCB. Without sacrificing the objective of price stability, the ESCB would contribute to the general economic objectives of the EU. These objectives are maintaining high levels of employment, noninflationary sustainable growth and the convergence of economic performance. There is explicit emphasis on the priority to price stability based on the proposition that price stability is required for a sound economy and high employment levels. The ESCB is entrusted with four tasks for the euro area: the design and implementation of monetary policy, FX operations, management and holding of FX reserves of the member states, and promoting sound operation of the systems of payments. The ECB has exclusive authorization for the issue of banknotes within the euro area. The ECB will cooperate with the authorities that are responsible for prudential supervision of credit institutions and the stability of the financial system in the individual states. Thus, the euro area has a single authority for monetary policy but continues to have prudential supervision as a responsibility of domestic regulators and supervisors.

There are two key decision-making bodies in the ECB, the Governing Council and the Executive Board, with a third, the General Council, existing until some EU member does not adopt the euro.[207] The Governing Council is composed of the six members of the Executive Board and the governors of national central banks (NCB) that have adopted the euro. The Governing Council formulates the monetary policy of the euro area, taking the key decisions such as the determination of the key ECB interest rates, the design of the strategy of monetary policy, the guidelines for execution of operations of monetary policy and the decisions on the administration of the ECB. It has the system of equality of votes of the 18 members or the principle of one member, one vote.[208] The decisions are on the basis of majority vote except in two specific cases where a two-thirds majority is required (interference by an NCB and operational methods different than in the statutes) and unanimity for changes in the statute of the ESCB. The governing council meets twice a month, analyzing monetary and economic conditions and taking required decisions at its first monthly meeting. The operations of the ECB are conducted by the Executive Board.[209] The six members, including the president and vice president, are appointed by the heads of state or government of the euro area countries on recommendation by the EU Council (EUC). The Executive board manages the current business of the ECB, organizes the meetings of the Governing Council, implements the monetary policy of the euro area and has some powers under delegation by the Governing Council. There is a prominent statutory role for the president of the ECB. The General Council provides an institutional link with the NCBs of the members of the EU that are not in the euro area.[210]

The ECB Governing Council chose a quantitative definition of price stability in October 1998 to make monetary policy transparent, providing a yardstick for the public to evaluate the ECB and to guide price expectations.[211] Price stability, according to the ECB, is a year-on-year increase of less than 2 percent of the harmonized index of consumer prices (HICP) for the euro area. This definition was refined by the Governing Council in May 2003. The ECB intends to maintain euro area inflation below but close to 2 percent in the medium term. The HICP is a consumer price index for the euro area. The redefinition occurred in 2003 when there were fears of deflation in the United States, Germany, and China in addition to the deflation in Japan.[212] It also takes into account the known measurement errors in consumer inflation indexes that were mentioned during the fear of deflation. If there is an error of one percentage point in measuring inflation, a year-to-year increase of 1 percent measured by the price index could be a situation bordering on deflation. The medium-term horizon is consistent with the technical literature on the lags in effect of monetary policy on inflation.

Open market operations constitute the main instrument of implementation of policy by the ECB.[213] There are four types of open market operations used by the ECB. The main refinancing operations are the most important instrument of influencing liquidity and interest rates and to signal the policy direction in the euro system. Most of these refinancing operations have a one-week maturity, taking the form of standard tenders with a preannounced schedule and execution within a 24-hour period. The counterparties of the ECB must meet certain eligibility criteria and, in general, all credit institutions in the euro area could potentially qualify to be eligible counterparties. The ECB also engages in monthly refinancing operations with three-month maturity to provide longer-term funds to the euro system. There are additional fine-tuning operations to manage liquidity and influence interest rates in accordance with policy needs. The final form consists of structural operations to influence market liquidity over the long term but there has not been need yet for this instrument. There are two standing facilities. Banks can borrow from the ECB through the marginal lending facility using collateral at a rate that is set higher than the market rate. The deposit facility allows banks to deposit their excess reserves at a rate that is lower than the market rate. The lending and deposit facility trace a corridor within which the overnight money market rate fluctuates. There is a system of minimum reserves that credit institutions must hold in the corresponding NCB.

The Bank of Japan

The Institute of Monetary and Economic Studies (IMES) of the Bank of Japan (BOJ) prepared a document on the functions of the BOJ.[214] Japan established the BOJ in 1882 as a central bank. The Bank of Japan Law was promulgated in 1998 with significant revision of existing statutes. The BOJ conducts monetary policy and acts as LOLR, being the bank of banks, the bank of the government and the authority issuing banknotes. Japanese financial institutions can deposit funds in BOJ accounts called current accounts. Financial institutions can withdraw from these accounts when they require liquidity. They can also use deposits in the current accounts to settle transactions with other financial institutions by means of transferring their funds from their accounts to those of other institutions. Thus, the current accounts serve as the payments settlement mechanism of the Japanese financial institutions. The reserves of financial institutions with the BOJ are deposited as current accounts.[215] The current accounts thus act as the clearing and payments system of the financial system of Japan.

Article 2 of the 1998 law stipulates that the BOJ will use monetary policy to maintain price stability to guarantee the sound development of the economy.[216] Articles 3 and 5 provide for autonomy by the BOJ in conducting required monetary policy. The Policy Board of the BOJ, its highest decision body, is independent from the government that cannot dismiss its members or order specific policy actions or operations. The Policy Board is composed of nine members, including the governor, two deputy governors and six appointed members.[217] The cabinet of Japan appoints the nine members that have to be approved by the Diet (parliament). The members elect the chairman of the Policy Board that is currently the governor of the BOJ. The decisions are taken by a majority vote of the nine members of the Policy Board. The board has authority on monetary policy, business operations, and internal management. It meets more than twice a week because of its comprehensive agenda. The monetary policy meetings are held twice a month to decide on key issues such as the official discount rate, the guideline and framework for monetary operations and the view of the BOJ on economic and financial conditions. The headquarters of the BOJ are in Tokyo, with 33 branches and 13 local offices across the country.

Article 4 requires that the bank maintain communication with the government, allowing representatives to submit proposals and views.[218] However, government representatives do not have formal votes in decisions on monetary policy. Article 3 also provides that the BOJ should conduct its operations and policy-making process with transparency, clarifying its decisions to the public. The decisions taken by the Policy Board are revealed to the public after every meeting, including the guidelines for money market operations and the BOJ's evaluation of economic and financial conditions. The BOJ also provides the Diet two reports every year and the governor appears before relevant committees to explain policies, operations, and balance sheet conditions.

The policy rate of the BOJ is the uncollateralized overnight call rate.[219] Financial institutions make their final daily adjustment of their current account balances at the BOJ in the call market. The objective of monetary policy is to influence other interest rates and ultimately transactions in the economy. The Policy Board takes decisions on interest rates at its monetary policy meetings based on the evaluation of economic and financial conditions. The decisions and the evaluation are released to the public. Open market operations constitute the major tool of influencing the level of current account balances to attain the overnight call rate decided at the monetary policy meeting. If the BOJ desires to increase the level of current account balances, it buys securities or engages in financing SRPs. If the BOJ desires to reduce the level of current account balances, it sells securities or engages in RSRPs.

The Bank of England

There is a separation of responsibilities of the three monetary authorities in the United Kingdom: HM Treasury, the BOE, and the FSA, as shown in Table 3.2. A formal memorandum of understanding of HM Treasury with the BOE and the FSA in 2007 governs the principles and responsibilities.[220] The principles for effective financial system oversight are

Table 3.2 Framework of cooperation for financial stability of the United Kingdom

Guiding Principles
  - *Accountability.* The definition of the responsibilities must be unambiguous to show the accountability of each authority for its actions.
  - *Transparency.* Parliament, the markets and the public must know the responsibilities of each authority.
  - *Definition of responsibilities.* Proper accountability and efficiency require the avoidance of duplication.
  - *Information exchange.* Efficiency and effectiveness require provisions for sharing information.

Responsibilities of the BOE
  - Contribution to overall financial stability.
    - Stability of the monetary system, acting in the market to manage fluctuations in liquidity.
    - Overseeing the infrastructure of the financial system, helping to avoid systemic risk.
    - View of the financial system as a whole, advising on UK financial stability.
    - Limiting the risk for the financial system of problems in specific institutions.

Responsibilities of the FSA
  - Authorizing and supervising banks, investment firms, brokers, and others.
  - Supervising financial markets, securities, and clearing, and settlement systems.
  - Operations in certain cases of problem firms.
  - Regulatory policy.

Responsibilities of HM Treasury
  - Institutional structure and legislation of financial regulation.
  - Informing and accounting to Parliament for problems and measures in the financial system.
  - Accountability within government for strength of the financial sector to operational disruption.

Source: HM Treasury, Memorandum of understanding between HM Treasury, the Bank of England and the Financial Services Authority, 2007. http://www.bankofengland.co.uk/financialstability/mou.pdf.

accountability, transparency, avoidance of duplication, and the sharing of information. The Treasury is not responsible for the operations of the BOE and the FSA. However, there is an understanding of cases in which the BOE and the FSA must alert the Treasury about serious problems. In general, the framework assigns the responsibility for monetary policy to the BOE, the authorization, supervision, and regulation to the FSA and the general legal and regulatory responsibility to the Treasury.

HM Treasury chairs the Standing Committee on Financial Stability that has representatives of the Treasury, the BOE, and the FSA. This is the main forum for policy coordination and agreement among the three authorities. It provides a vehicle for sharing information on threats to the financial stability of the United Kingdom. There are regular meetings of the deputies of the institutions. In case of the need of government support operations, the meetings involve the principals: the Chancellor of the Exchequer, the Governor of the BOE and the chairman of the FSA.

The BOE was established in 1694, nationalized in 1946 and became independent in 1997. It is the central bank of the United Kingdom. The BOE Act of 1998, as in Table 3.3, consolidated the reform of the

Table 3.3 The BOE Act of 1998

Court of directors
- Composition: governor, 2 deputy governors (5-year terms) and 16 directors (3-year terms) appointed by Her Majesty
- Functions:
  - Manage bank affairs other than formulation of monetary policy.
  - Determine objectives, strategy, and effective use of BOE's resources.

Monetary Policy
- Independence from the Treasury
- Objectives:
  - Maintain price stability.
  - Support the government in the objective of growth and employment but subject to attaining price stability.
- Specification of objectives by the government
  - Once in every period of 12 months the Treasury will specify the definition of price stability and the economic policy of the government.

Monetary Policy Committee
- Responsibility: formulating the BOE monetary policy.
- Composition: the governor and deputy governors of the BOE, 2 members appointed by the governor after consultation with the Chancellor of the Exchequer (one with responsibility at the BOE with monetary policy analysis and other with BOE responsibility for monetary policy operations), and 4 members (with knowledge or experience relative to the functions of the committee) appointed by the Exchequer; terms are for 3 years.
- Publication: BOE must publish in reasonable time the decisions that require action to meet objectives with consideration if publication of decisions affects the desired outcome; minutes are published before the end of the 6 weeks beginning with the day of the meeting but not if publication of decisions affects the desired outcome; voting preferences of members are published.

Inflation Report
- Contents: review of monetary policy, assessment of inflation in the United Kingdom, and expected approach to meeting the objectives of the BOE.
- Periodicity: quarterly or other period agreed by the MPC.

Transfer of Supervisory Functions of the BOE to the FSA

Source: http://www.bankofengland.co.uk/about/legislation/1998act.pdf

financial system. This act is admirable in terms of its simplicity and proved highly effective but as all central banks was disrupted by the credit/dollar crisis. The BOE has a court of directors, with a governor, two deputy governors and 16 directors with the primary responsibility for the management and efficiency in using resources of the institution. The BOE is independent from the Treasury in its conduct of monetary policy. Its objective is to maintain price stability, supporting the government's economic policy of growth and employment but subject to attaining price stability. There is a separation of power in that every 12 months the Treasury defines price stability, in terms of a target rate of inflation, and the economic policy of the government. The BOE is independent in the policy formulation of how to attain its objectives but not in defining them. The act created the Monetary Policy Committee (MPC) that formulates the BOE's monetary policy.[221] The MPC includes the governor, deputy governors, two members from the areas of monetary policy analysis and operations of the BOE, and four outside members. The outside members have been chosen based on their knowledge and experience in economics. The act created a report that became the inflation report, an important document of disclosure in inflation targeting.[222] It also transferred the supervisory functions of the BOE to the FSA.

General principles of central banking

A general principle of central banking is derived from three historical episodes.[223] First, the Great Depression could have been only a moderate decline in economic activity if the Fed had not increased interest rates to arrest an outflow of gold. Second, the Lost Decade of Japan in the 1990s could have been shorter in duration and lower in magnitude if the monetary authorities had not increased interest rates and took earlier measures to recover economic activity. Third, the stock market decline of October 19, 1987, was better managed by the provision of liquidity by the Fed, maintaining stability in stock exchanges and futures markets. Based on these episodes Bernanke concludes that "history proves that a smart central bank can protect the economy and the financial sector from the nastier side effects of a stock market collapse."[224]

The Fed combines in the same institution supervisory and central bank responsibilities.[225] There are economies of scope in supervision and financial stability functions in the form of information, expertise, and powers. The supervisory functions of the Fed provide significant information on financial markets and institutions that is useful in design and implementation of monetary policy. The authority of bank examinations and the staff to conduct them has proved effective in taking remedial actions through the central banking function. Providing liquidity after 9/11, for example, relied on the knowledge by the Fed on the management of key institutions, funding positions, financial positions, risk management, and capacity in evaluating collateral to provide funding. There are similar examples in situations such as the Long Term Capital Management and Drexel.[226] Drexel Burham Lambert was a Wall Street investment banking firm that pioneered in the junk-bond market but faced legal inquiries in its operations, declaring bankruptcy in 1990. Because of increased perceptions of counterparty risk, Drexel experienced deterioration in its ability to finance its positions. The orderly liquidation of Drexel's positions was facilitated by the knowledge of the Fed acquired in its supervisory relationships with banks in the clearing system. Long Term Capital Management was a hedge fund that had two Nobel laureates as advisers and experienced and talented traders and partners. During the financial crisis of Russia in 1998 and the ongoing devaluation of Brazil, the positions of Long Term Capital Management deteriorated in value, triggering margin calls by its counterparties, which included major banks. The FRBNY organized an orderly liquidation of the assets of Long Term Capital Management without losses or disruption of the financial system. In this case, the supervisory relationships and knowledge of the Fed permitted an orderly resolution.

Central banking in the United Kingdom

The FSA and the BEO have been regarded as admirable financial regulation. The United Kingdom found its framework of financial system regulation after a troubled period in 1970–92. The average yearly growth rate of the United Kingdom declined from 2.8 percent in 1950–69 to 2.0 percent in 1970–92 while the average yearly rate of inflation rose from 3.9 percent in 1950–69 to 9.6 percent in 1970–92.[227] However, there was similar experience in the United States, Japan, Germany, and France of lower growth and higher inflation. The United Kingdom maintained an average yearly rate of growth of 2.8 percent in 1998–2005 and of 2.5 percent in inflation. This was performance comparable with 3.0 percent growth in the United States and inflation of 2.5 percent and better performance than 0.8 percent growth with inflation of –0.3 percent in Japan, 1.3 percent growth with inflation of 1.4 percent in Germany and growth of 2.2 percent in France with inflation of 1.5 percent. The United Kingdom experienced continuing growth during 58 consecutive quarters after 1992 before the credit/dollar crisis. The unemployment rate declined from over 10 percent in 1993 to below 5 percent in 2005, the lowest rate in about three decades. The initial target for 1992–7 was inflation of the retail price index excluding mortgage payments (RPIX) of 1 to 4 percent and a point target of 2.5 percent until the end of 2003 when it was changed to 2 percent CPI inflation, which has typically been 0.75 percentage points below RPIX inflation. Inflation did not deviate from the target by one percentage point, avoiding a letter requesting explanation from the Treasury to the BOE.

The BOE argues that the policy framework is a combination of an understanding of the functioning of the economy with lessons of experience.[228] In this analysis, the level of output and employment in the short term is affected by changes in the nominal demand for goods and services in the economy. Monetary policy operates on nominal and real interest rates that in turn change assets prices, including the exchange rate, influencing nominal demand that changes output and employment. Monetary policy is the primary tool of demand management.[229] The long-term level of output and employment depends on the capacity of the economy that is determined by productive resources such as capital, labor, land, and their use in production by applying technology. Monetary policy can have only a long-term impact on the rate of inflation. There is concern of formulating monetary policy to avoid excessive short-term fluctuations of output that can have adverse effects on investment.

The BOE finds a significant role of institutional arrangements in the stability of growth and inflation of the United Kingdom.[230] Reforms of product and labor markets were crucial.[231] The framework to anchor inflationary expectations consists of the explicit target for inflation, significant transparency and the independence of the BOE. The United Kingdom departed from anchoring to the exchange rate to floating its exchange rate and targeting domestic inflation. The EMU fixed the exchange rates of its member countries and the ECB provided common monetary policy.[232] This was a key policy choice in the international financial system, sustainable pegged exchange rates in the EMU, and sustainable floating rate with inflation targeting in the United Kingdom. The delegation of policy to the MPC withdrew political influence from the decision process, enhancing the credibility of the framework. The process of forming the view of inflation by the BOE is transparent, avoiding adverse expectations. The accountability of the members of the MPC by release of their votes and the announcement of the cycle of meetings add accountability and predictability to the system. The announcement of the target and the release of information through the inflation report make the process open, helping in the general effort of anchoring inflationary expectations.

There is a dual purpose for the BOE in preparing and publishing its inflation report.[233] It is a tool of the decision-making process by the MPC, providing a framework for discussion. In addition, the inflation report allows the sharing of the views of the MPC, explaining the reasons for monetary policy decisions. The inflation report provides the projection of GDP growth and inflation in the form of a fan chart with the probability of various trajectories. In May 2007, the best collective judgment of the MPC was for growth of GDP around the trend in the past decade of around 2.5 percent. CPI inflation was 3.1 percent in March 2007. The Governor of the BOE sent a letter of explanation on behalf of the MPC to the Chancellor of the Exchequer.[234] Increases in the prices of domestic energy and food were the main reasons for the increase of inflation by 1.3 percentage points relative to a year earlier. The best collective judgment projection of the MPC was for inflation to decline sharply below its target as a result of the processing of the energy price shocks, returning to target levels subsequently. The policy rate of the BOE is the official bank rate. This is the rate at which the BOE makes short-term loans to banks and other financial institutions. The view of the MPC was that the risks of inflation were on the upside and voted on March 10, 2007, in favor of an increase of the bank rate by 25 basis points to reach 5.5 percent. The MPC regarded this measure as necessary to meet the CPI inflation target over the medium term. Forecasting models did not anticipate the devastating credit/dollar crisis even in the central bank of the United Kingdom considered to have developed the most advanced combination of knowledge and experience.

Monetary policy, income, and prices

Monetary policy in the form of changes in interest rates is designed to have impact on output or income and prices or inflation/deflation. During inflation, the central bank increases interest rates to curb aggregate demand, reducing the rate of increase of prices. There is danger of the collateral effect of a decline in production or output, causing unemployment. Inflation is less of a concern in recessions when the central bank lowers interest rates with the objective of increasing investment and consumption that could lead to increases in output and employment. The policy of central banks during deflation is significantly less effective because the interest rate is already close to zero. The policy at low or zero interest rates characterizes the credit/dollar crisis and is discussed in Chapter 6. This section focuses on the impact of monetary policy, that is, the effects of changes of interest rates on output/employment and prices.

It is quite difficult to measure the magnitude of the effect and the time from policies of changing interest rates to actual effects on output and prices. In reality, the effects of all economic variables are observed simultaneously. With this information it is difficult to isolate the effects of interest rates on output and prices. For example, an increase in interest rates causes a decrease in aggregate demand in the economy that by itself triggers a decrease in demand for loans, exerting downward pressure on interest rates. Isolating and measuring the impact over time of interest rates on output and prices may be impossible. In addition, it is necessary to construct a uniform indicator of the rate of interest intended by the central bank over long periods. The available evidence suggests a strong and delayed effect of interest rates on output and prices.[235] To summarize, there is a strong impact of an increase in interest rates by the Fed on industrial production: an increase of one percentage point in interest rates is associated with a decline in industrial production of 4.3 percent. Moreover, industrial production begins to decline five months after the increase in interest rates and the effect continues for up to two years. The effect of increasing rates on inflation is strong but more delayed. Inflation does not change in the first 22 months after the increase in interest rates by the Fed but in 48 months inflation declines by 6 percent in response to a one-percentage point increase in interest rates.

There are theories and related empirical measurement of how monetary policy in the form of changes in interest rates by the central bank affects credit and the overall economy. An important current of thought explains the transmission of monetary policy through balance sheets of households, companies, and financial entities.[236] A key concept in this interpretation is the division of the source of finance in internal and external resources. Firms can use outside resources, such as issues of equity and debt, and internally generated resources, such as profits. Households can use outside resources, such as debt with or without collateral, and internal ones, such as savings. Because of the credit market frictions, outside finance without collateral is more expensive than internal finance. The premium on outside financing is inversely related to the quality of the balance sheets of borrowers. The higher the equity of the borrower, the lower the outside premium because the borrowing firm can provide more collateral to the lender. For example, a household with significant equity in its residence and high FICO credit score can obtain a home-equity loan at relatively low interest rates. However, a household with no equity or other collateral may only obtain a consumer loan at high interest rates. A firm with significant equity in its buildings could obtain more favorable interest rates than one without collateral to pledge in a loan. The difference between the cost of using own or internal funds and borrowed or external funds is called the premium of external finance. The fluctuations of output and investment are augmented by countercyclical movements in the premium for outside finance, which originate in the procyclical changes in the financial conditions of potential borrowers.

Suppose there is a benign "primitive" shock in the economy such as technological change, which improves fundamentals with positive effects on output and employment. In the financial accelerator model, there are indirect effects originating in increases in asset prices, which improve balance sheets, lowering the outside finance premium.[237] For example, if real estate prices improve, households can obtain favorable home-equity loans and businesses borrow using buildings as collateral. The lower premium causes further investment, which may lead to more indirect effects through improvements in balance sheets. Consider now an adverse primitive shock during the credit/dollar crisis. Sustained subsidies to residential housing over decades and a near zero interest rate in 2003–4 caused an increase in the residential equity of households of about \$4 trillion in 2000–4. The decline in the prices of houses after 2006 erased \$5 trillion of residential equity of households. Further impacts on household wealth were caused by the decline of the prices of stocks by 50 percent. The contraction of the net worth, property less debt, of households in the United States reduced the collateral that they could pledge in loans, raising the premium of external finance. External finance became unavailable to many households and businesses.

The deterioration in the conditions of the clients causes stress in the balance sheets of banks and other financial institutions. Monetary easing can improve balance sheets by increasing asset prices, thus lowering the outside financing premium because of more abundant collateral. However, during monetary tightening in the presence of weak balance sheets, there are further adverse effects on the net worth. Tightening causes a reduction in the value of collateral available for loans, squeezing households, firms, and eventually financial intermediaries. The increase in the outside financing premium may result in further decline of asset prices, weakening further the balance sheets. The effects would be different in direction of those of a benign primitive shock such as technological change. The losses with structured products, such as defaults on the underlying nonprime loans of MBS, reduced bank capital at a time when it was difficult to raise new capital from investors.

Banks maintain capital relative to assets, such as loans. The decrease of capital caused reduction of loans.

The financial accelerator is the magnification of initial shocks caused by endogenous changes in credit market conditions.[238] The borrowers that have the highest costs of borrowing may experience the highest impact of an economic downturn. These borrowers have weak balance sheets and are typically consumers and small firms. There is a flight to quality by lenders, which limits the availability of credit to units with weak balance sheets. The borrower's net worth is the sum of liquid assets and the collateral value of illiquid assets. Liquid assets for a household are cash and savings deposits and illiquid assets are the equity in residential property and other physical goods. The rise in interest rates causes a decline in the borrower's net worth, increasing the premium for outside financing.

An alternative approach is the bank lending channel.[239] Banks can experience difficulty in finding external finance, such as deposits and other funding. The effective interest rate to firms would rise because of the competition for a smaller amount of available loans. Larger firms may have access to other sources of financing, such as profits and the issue of debt, but smaller firms may not be able to replace bank loans with other sources of external financing. The unavailability of loans is sometimes called a "credit crunch," characterized by a widening differential of interest rates in bank loans and the policy rate of the central bank, which is the fed funds rate in the United States.[240] Other sources of decline of external financing by banks could occur in events such as collapse of stock markets and increasing defaults.

Summary

The United States has a complex system of banking and financial regulation at the federal and state levels. The allocation of oversight in Congress to committees and the large number and diversity of financial institutions may prevent consolidation and reform of US monetary authorities. The inflation targeting paradigm of the BOE has also succumbed to the credit/dollar crisis. Central banks could be blamed for the housing and credit events because of the lowering of interest rates that encouraged high-risk strategies and leverage. However, most reform proposals strengthen central banking powers.

4
Universal Banking, Governance, and Compensation

Introduction

The first section considers the traditional trade-off between universal banks engaged in all aspects of banking and financial markets and specialized banking focused only on taking deposits to provide loans. Two sections consider the political economy and the economic analysis of the Glass-Steagall Act, which separated investment and commercial banking in the United States. The Financial Modernization Act eliminated the final existing barriers between commercial and investment banking. Hedge funds deserve significant coverage because their regulation is included in most proposals. Corporate governance analyzes the conflicts of interest between management and shareholders. The remuneration of executives has become a critical issue in research and politics. Corporate law provides the legal framework for the market for corporate control.

Universal and specialized banking

There are advantages and disadvantages in universal banking.[241] The universal bank engages in the entire range of financial activities: taking funds from the public to lend, underwriting and brokerage of securities, and insurance. The universal bank may own equity in nonfinancial firms, voting on the shares it owns and by delegation on the shares of others and electing its employees as members of the boards on which they hold equity.[242] Financial conglomerates are financial institutions engaged in all types of financial activities: traditional banking, insurance, and securities underwriting and brokerage.[243]

The US system imposed specialized banking with the Glass-Steagall Act of 1933,[244] separating investment and commercial banking, which is discussed below. The Bank Holding Company Act and the National Banking Act prohibited US banks from engaging in insurance, real estate brokerage, and other financial services.[245] Restrictions on banking in the United States, particularly of large banks, originate in the reservations of many of the founding fathers, with the exception of Alexander Hamilton.[246] The exegesis of the first US banking reform is that:[247]

> Alexander Hamilton, US Secretary of the Treasury during 1789–1795, had absorbed important lessons of financial history during the previous decade. On the basis of what he had learned, Hamilton formulated a comprehensive plan to give the United States a modern financial system. He then executed the plan during his term of office.

The main issues relating to the benefits or disadvantages of universal banks are as follows:[248]

- *Financial stability.* Universal banks tend to be very large financial institutions, engaging in complex relations with other financial and nonfinancial entities. The failure of one or more universal banks could have systemic effects, causing the failure of other financial institutions and affecting the production side of the economy. Thus, universal banks would qualify for the doctrine of too big to fail, probably eroding their discipline in dealing with adverse selection and moral hazard. However, only 10 of the 9440 banks that failed during the Great Depression were not specialized unit banks.[249] The collapse of many savings and loans institutions after the interest rate increase of the early 1980s constitutes another fact against the view that specialized banks are less risky. Supervision of specialized, small deposit banks is more difficult both in obtaining the required information and in allowing acceptable risk. There is no reason why well-capitalized universals banks with sound culture of risk discipline can be more likely to fail than a large number of specialized deposit/lending banks.
- *Economic development.* Directed lending according to desired government objectives may be accomplished with specialized financial institutions. This has been the policy of the United States with the allocation of credit to real estate through the S&L, the FHLB system, and the GSE, such as Fannie Mae and Freddie Mac, guaranteeing mortgages. Similar directed lending has occurred in emerging countries for development purposes. Institutions for directed lending create their own political constituencies and related lobbies that perpetuate them and

erode their initial purpose and quality of management. The debate is not on prohibiting universal banking but on the economic, social, and political role of directed lending, which can also be a source of financial instability.

- *Relative efficiency.* The unique protection of minority shareholders in the United States is widely believed to influence the efficiency in allocation of capital through stock markets instead of banks. The legal environment explains the type of financial system chosen by countries.[250] The issue of whether universal banks frustrate smaller banks and are less efficient than specialized banks in promoting equity capital is difficult to resolve theoretically and empirically.

- *Crowding out.* Large universal banks benefitting from economies of scale and scope may frustrate smaller banks specialized in community lending. This issue is also not resolved.

- *Concentration and related lending.* Large universal banks could concentrate financial services and also promote concentration of nonfinancial companies that are their clients and in which they hold equity participation. Universal banks could join related nonfinancial companies in lobbying regulation favoring concentration. There are also potential harmful effects of related lending.[251] This issue also affects financial stability because the bank could provide riskier "related loans" to the nonfinancial company that has equity stake in the bank. The bank and related nonfinancial company could also influence regulation to impose concentration measures that would favor them through their joint political power.

- *Consumer choice.* There is no reason why universal banks would engage in practices that are detrimental to consumers. The combination of financial services does not suggest such discrimination in a specific line of business.

- *Conflict of interest.* Underwriting activities jointly with traditional banking could result in the issue of securities for a client likely to default to use the proceeds in redeeming the debt to the bank, effectively transferring the default risk to investors. The competing hypothesis is that with enhanced monitoring of the issuer, underwriting by universal banks could certify the quality of the issue, resulting in lower costs and higher quality. This issue is discussed below in relation to the Glass-Steagall Act and underwriting.

There has been greater acceptance of universal banking in Europe. The EU allowed member states to have financial conglomerates, or conglomeration, and universal banks.[252] The German universal bank is the criterion of definition used by the EU. There are no limits in cross-holdings of shares by financial institutions. Thus, large numbers of diversified financial conglomerates can be created because banks, investment houses, and insurance companies may own unlimited shares in each other. There are still rules limiting the participation of financial entities in nonfinancial companies because of capital requirements on financial companies. The EU implemented rules to stimulate the continuing specialization of some institutions and the diversification of others.

If the combination of diversified financial activities in a single financial entity reduces costs and increases revenues, there would be benefits to consumers, clients, and stockholders.[253] Rates and fees would be lower to consumers, clients would borrow at lower rates and stockholders would experience increases in the value of their holdings. The resulting financial conglomerate would lower costs if it realized economies of scale and scope. Economies of scale consist of lower costs because of the effect of higher output. For example, the acquisition of a computer costing $1 million would cost $1 million for the first transaction but only $1 for the one millionth transaction. Similarly, the gains from processing information in demand deposits would be realized in brokerage accounts offering investment banking products. The conglomerate would benefit from generating new revenue in diversification and cross-selling of products. Funding costs would decrease because of the reputation effects across many lines of products and rents or excess profits from market power. A critical gain would be realized in sharing initial credit evaluation and monitoring costs among activities in traditional banking and equity products of investment banking, with strong impact on profits. Universal banks could also operate in a more dynamic and competitive environment with sophisticated products and risk management. The successful investment banks in the United States, Goldman Sachs and Morgan Stanley, generated exceptionally high returns on equity and were able to survive the credit/dollar crisis. JP Morgan Chase combined commercial and investment banking, surging ahead in the crisis. The dynamic field of M&As can motivate more efficient internal structures.

An operational definition for analysis can classify banks into three categories.[254] First, specialized banks engage in the traditional activity of transforming deposits into loans. Second, financial conglomerates engage in operations in at least two of the major financial services. Third, universal banks engage in diversified financial services and also hold equity shares in nonfinancial companies, as in Japan and

Germany. The sample used for empirical research consists of 2375 banks in 17 EU countries in 1995 and 1996, accounting for over 85 percent of total bank assets in their countries.[255] The conclusions are as follows. Financial conglomerates do not enjoy greater efficiency relative to specialized banks in traditional intermediation of deposits into loans. Nontraditional banking activities are more efficient in financial conglomerates. Operational and profit efficiency is higher in financial conglomerates relative to specialized banks. Equity participation in nonfinancial companies appears to be related to the higher profit efficiency of universal banks.

The political economy of securities legislation

The Glass-Steagall Act of 1933 prohibited commercial banks to engage directly or through affiliates in underwriting, holding, or dealing in corporate securities. The motivation for this legislation was the alleged conflict of interest that would arise from the combination of lending by a commercial bank with the underwriting of securities. Legislators were also concerned with the higher risk of banking resulting from the combination of commercial and investment banking activities. There is a trade-off between the economies that banks gain by information on their clients resulting from the combination of banking and underwriting of securities and the doubts on the quality of issues originating in the suspicion of conflicts of interest.[256]

There was an effort to pursue socially useful goals in the Securities Act of 1933.[257] It provided for mandatory disclosure of the fees and stakes in companies of promoters and underwriters of new issues, correcting abuse that occurred in England and the United States since the mid 1800s. The syndicate system developed in the United States several decades before 1916. This system consisted at the top of the originating or issuing investment bank, which performed the functions of the current underwriting manager.[258] The manager advises the issuer, conducts due diligence of the company, and negotiates the terms of the deal. The compensation of the underwriters consisted of the discount in purchasing from the issuer. A fixed price for purchases by investors was fixed by the originating investment bank that consulted with the issuer. The spread between the price received by the issuer and the price paid by the investors was the compensation of the underwriters. The originating investment bank received from the syndicate the largest part of the compensation and chose the other underwriters and distributors. There were a few originating investment houses with significant political influence. Significant deterioration in the concentration of business occurred in the top five investment houses, declining from 37 percent in 1925 to 12.9 percent in 1929.[259] The war effort included the sale and distribution of government securities through a new and growing retail system. In the 1920s, this system welded into integrated originating and distributing investment houses. The integrated investment bank challenged the market power of the politically more powerful wholesale originating investment houses.

The Securities Act of 1933 and changes in 1934 included various "technical" features benefitting restrictions by wholesale and retail firms on retail competition, thus protecting their market against competition from integrated firms.[260] These features were not required to attain the goals of disclosure but benefitted high prestige investment banks, probably increasing costs to issuers and investors. The Securities Act is considered to be one of the successes of the New Deal, with no criticism of raising entry barriers or benefiting cartel agreements. The analysis of the statute in the light of competitiveness in underwriting markets in the 1920s suggests that the Securities Act likely provided rents or excess profits to the regulated firms that lobbied for the bill.[261]

Economic analysis of Glass-Steagall

Commercial banks have clients to which they provide loans on the basis of information obtained by monitoring their activities and may not approve loans to less creditworthy clients. If banks could engage in underwriting and distribution to investors of debt securities, such as bonds, and equity, such as shares in corporations, they could face conflict of interest in credit allocations. Banks could lend to the companies with best credit risk, engaging in cherry picking, keeping their loans as assets in their balance sheets. Banks could then underwrite and sell to the public the debt and equity securities of their clients with inferior creditworthiness, passing on credit risk to private investors, such as pension funds, mutual funds, and hedge funds. Asymmetric information would consist of banks knowing better the credit quality of the corporate names behind debt and equity securities than the general public of multiple investors. Combination of banking and securities underwriting and distribution could result in inferior quality of debt and equity securities in capital markets, undermining the effectiveness of intermediation in channeling resources from savers to highly productive investment projects. In addition to harms to investors from the placement of securities of inferior quality, banks could increase the risk to the financial system. The proposal of separation of commercial banking from investment banking is based on the conflict of interest of banks that leads them to underwrite and distribute securities with inferior creditworthiness, harming investors who acquired these securities, and also creating overall risks in securities markets populated by bank-originated low-quality securities.

Scholarly research has reconstructed a sample of the securities markets in the period 1921–33 before the Glass-Steagall Act of 1933 that permits profound analysis.[262] There was an innovation financial spiral in the 1920s similar to the concept of the FSF. In similarity with the introduction of commercial paper in the 1960s, competition and new market structures caused significant change in financial and capital markets. The number of national and state banks, including their affiliates, engaged in the securities business jumped from 277 in 1922 to a high of 591 in 1929, at the onset of the Great Depression. The capacity of the nationwide distribution of government securities during the effort of World War 1 was channeled toward the distribution of corporate bonds and equities.[263] In retrospect, this constituted major deepening and widening of the financial structure, bringing a new range of opportunities for savers and investors. Banks engaged in the securities business in reaction to the new opportunities for business, as is typical of spirals of innovation, and not because of the gains in issuing inferior securities. In 1921–9, the issue of all types of securities by bank affiliates was $1127 million compared with $1649 million for investment banks. The securities issued by banks and investment banks were not significantly different. In 1921–9, 54.9 percent of the bonds underwritten by bank affiliates were of investment grade level compared with 47.4 percent for investment banks; the share of issues below investment grade was 18.8 percent for bank affiliates versus 28 percent for investment banks. Nonrated bonds underwritten by affiliates of banks were 26.3 percent of the total versus 24.6 percent for investment banks. In the period 1921–33, before the Glass-Steagall Act, banks and investment banks competed on equal bases for the securities business.[264] Markets were relatively free with little regulation and common entry and exit from the business. There was also significant dynamism as characterized in financial innovation spirals.

The Glass-Steagall Act was justified by the allegation that banks exploited the good will of naïve investors, what is referred as the "naïve investor hypothesis." Banks allegedly benefitted from information on their clients, earning fees from selling to investors the securities issued by low-quality borrowers with unsound financial position. There is strong empirical evidence to refute the "naïve investor hypothesis."[265] In fact, the evidence is strongest for issues of inferior securities by financially unsound companies, or lemons, in which banks could have appropriated the largest gains from conflict of interest. Bank affiliates avoided these companies, the opposite behavior had they been interested in exploiting their information by selling low-quality securities. Credit-rating agencies correctly placed low ratings on these inferior securities.

There is a sample of 43 internal departments and 32 securities affiliates of commercial banks and trusts involved in investment banking underwriting of 906 securities.[266] There was recognition by outsiders of the potential conflict of interest of securities issued by commercial banks relative to investment banks. The prices of securities underwritten by the internal departments of banks, perceived as having higher potential conflict of interest, were discounted relative to those of securities underwritten by independent affiliates, with lower perceived conflict of interest. The internal structure of financial entities is important in the competitive edge and market perception of companies. Banks could evolve naturally on their own to the effective structure without regulatory rules.

The Gramm-Leach-Bliley Financial Modernization Act

There are three identifiable factors of the repeal of the Glass-Steagall Act.[267] First, academic research demonstrates that the combination of banking and securities underwriting in the same group did not cause the banking problems of the Great Depression. Second, the limited securities activities allowed to banks in the 1990s did not result in banking problems. Third, new technology allows the rapid use of information from one company to benefit another; there was an increase in the profitability of selling insurance and securities products to households and business. The Gramm-Leach-Bliley Financial Modernization Act (GLBA) of November 12, 1999, reformed the restrictions imposed by the Glass-Steagall Act of 1933 and the Bank Holding Company Act of 1956.[268] However, American banks still lack the full flexibility of their competitors in other advanced countries. Single holding companies can offer banking, securities, and insurance, much the same as before the Great Depression.

A critical event in the movement toward combination of financial services in traditional banks was the merger between Citicorp and Travelers Insurance Group resulting in a new financial entity, Citigroup, on April 6, 1998.[269] Progress toward combination of financial services with commercial banks was slow after the Glass-Steagall Act. The first movement was the Bank Holding Company Act of 1956 that conferred on the Fed the oversight of bank holding companies (BHC) with more than one bank. Another step was the acquisition of Charles Schwab and Company by Bank of America in 1981. However, there was no prohibition for combination of brokerage companies and banks. Three large banks, Citicorp, JP Morgan, and Bankers Trust were approved by the Fed, on April 30, 1987, to underwrite and sell stocks and bonds, decision upheld by the Supreme Court in 1988.[270] The Fed allowed BHCs to underwrite corporate bonds and equities in 1989, increasing the proportion of underwriting revenue in gross revenue to 25 percent in 1996.

The largest US banks, Citibank and Chase Manhattan Bank, engaged in overseas operations before the rise of the multinational company after World War II.[271] Branches and other operations in overseas jurisdictions permitted the large US banks to combine financial services with traditional banking. For example, Brazil authorized financial conglomerates with banks owning investment banks, companies underwriting and distributing securities, insurance distribution and underwriting and leasing entities. The largest foreign banks in Brazil were structured as financial conglomerates. The rise of the Eurodollar market in London afforded the same opportunity. The Glass-Steagall Act transferred US universal banks to overseas jurisdictions together with fixed income products, loans, FX, and derivatives.

The combination of bank and insurance services has various advantages.[272] Banks would diversify the sources of income with insurance fees, reducing their income fluctuations. Various bank and insurance services are complementary, such as mortgages with mortgage insurance and auto finance with auto insurance. The network of branches could be used for the sale of bank and insurance products. Banks could also add reputational benefits to their underwriting and distribution of insurance. Information obtained from clients could help in the risk management of the combined banking and insurance company. There would also be gains from combining securities underwriting and distribution with traditional banking. Banks could offer a complete set of investment products and benefit from lower joint IT. There would be similar gains as in insurance from the lower joint cost of branch networks as well as enhanced reputation of the products by the bank's franchise.

Before the Citigroup merger, JP Morgan had moved in the direction of combining investment banking with its Morgan Guaranty Bank. The dimensions of the new Citigroup structure were critical. Citibank, the bank of Citicorp, was the largest issuer of credit cards in the world, the second largest bank in the United States, and was engaged in banking with over a thousand branches in more than 40 countries. The Travelers Group was by itself a financial services conglomerate including operating companies with market reputation: Salomon Smith Barney, Salomon Smith Barney Asset Management, Travelers Life and Annuity, Primerica Financial Services, Travelers Property Casualty Corp., and Commercial Credit.[273] The client base of the merged Citigroup would provide a wide range of financial services including banking to over 100 million customers in 100 countries with a prestigious franchise that in fact was a collection of excellent franchises. Empirical research shows that there were significant valuation effects of the announcement of the Citigroup merger on commercial banks, insurance companies, and brokerage firms.[274] Higher valuations suggested that financial entities would derive efficiencies, or lower costs, from cross-selling diversified financial services. In particular, the valuation effects were stronger for brokerage firms than for commercial banks, suggesting that brokerage entities would benefit more from combination of banking and securities activities. As expected, valuation effects were stronger for larger than smaller banks; cost reductions and other efficiencies would have stronger impact on banks with larger assets and diversified client base.

The barriers of activities between banks and other financial entities had been eliminated by regulatory decisions and earlier legislation. Thus, GLBA can be viewed as ratifying and amplifying changes instead of as revolutionary.[275] GLBA created a new entity, the financial holding company (FHC), which is authorized to operate in activities that are "financial in nature or incidental to financial activities or even complementary to financial activities."[276] The Fed must determine if the activities are not likely to create substantial risk to the safety and soundness of banks. The structure of regulation continues, with the Fed regulating only member banks. By the principle of functional regulation accepted by GLBA similar activities are regulated by the same regulator. According to functional regulation, the regulation of federal and state banking is by federal and state banking regulators; securities activities are regulated by federal and state securities regulators; and insurance activities are regulated by state insurance regulators.

The main benefit of GLBA for banks is gains from economies of scope.[277] The costs of gathering, processing, and evaluating information can accrue once and then be distributed among many categories of financial services. There could be low marginal cost for banks in distributing securities and insurance services through already existing technology, staff, and delivery channels. The modern industrial revolution in the form of jumps in technology applicable to banking operations, such as data processing and electronic communication channels, may generate significant economies of scope. The overhead in back office, administration, and IT can be spread over a wider range of financial services. Financial theory predicts that under certain conditions diversification may reduce the volatility of returns. If there is lower correlation of returns of various bank activities, risk, or the standard deviation of returns, may decline, resulting in more stable broad banks.[278] Banks may pass on to consumers lower fees for a broader range of financial services. There are two potential adverse effects. First, there is the recurring problem of higher risk activities. Second, the combination of insured deposits with investment banking and insurance may give broader banks a strong competitive edge relative to other financial institutions. In 2008, Goldman Sachs and Morgan Stanley became depository banks.

Hedge funds

The spiral of financial innovation of the FSF triggered an institutional change with the rise of pools of capital in the form of hedge funds and private equity. Initial high returns in these activities and aggressive strategies are likely to be followed by lower abnormal returns and convergence in strategies with mutual funds and with similar regulation.[279] Pools of capital are the subject of intensive efforts of regulation. This section provides discussion of hedge funds, their role in systemic risk and proposals for regulation.

The explosive growth of assets under management in hedge funds is partly explained by financial theory and technology that allowed specialization into component parts of complex investment products.[280] These products were divided into components for trading in specialized markets. Professionals that could understand and attempt to manage the complexities of the new financial theory and technology established firms of their own. High remunerations of these professionals are similar to those in productive innovations in other activities in production of goods and services and in finance. Eventually, increasing supply of managerial talent reduces abnormal remuneration because of competition. The response of financial institutions was to create their own hedge funds. Prime brokers and investment banks derived high returns from complex trading and became important participants in the industry.

The general characteristic of a hedge fund is the flexibility of its business model and the unrestricted investment process.[281] Hedge funds choose location in unregulated and tax-free jurisdictions. Financial management is actually located in one of the financial centers such as London or New York. The clientele is typically composed of high net-worth individuals. The public participates through funds of hedge funds (FOHF) or in the third tier of funds of funds of hedge funds. The management of a hedge fund earns a small management fee and a relatively high percentage performance fee. There is asymmetry of the returns because of the lack of a penalty rate for negative returns. There is an implicit penalty because the partners may invest in the fund. Redemption may be restricted for periods of time. The participation of managers may limit risk taking. There is little regulation and disclosure of hedge funds but active proposals for disclosure and regulation. The legal structure varies, including private investment partnerships and offshore investment corporations.

The measurement of the number of hedge funds is precarious because the only available data are voluntary disclosures to data vendors. There were close to 10,000 hedge funds with $1.5 trillion of funds under management in 2006.[282] There are other estimates of about $1.125 trillion in 2006.[283] Over 70 percent of hedge funds charge a management fee of 1 to 2 percent and 80 percent charge a 20 percent performance fee.[284]

The assets under management of hedge funds increased from about $50 billion in 1990 to $200 billion in 1998 to around $1.6 trillion by May 2007 before the credit/dollar crisis.[285] The decline in equity prices at the turn of the new millennium and low interest rates motivated growth of alternative highly leveraged opportunities with enhanced yields. Institutional investor interest was important in the recent growth of the hedge fund industry.[286]

There are high rates of growth and closure of hedge funds, with 717 liquidated funds in 2006 and 1518 new funds introduced.[287] In 2006, the 100 largest hedge funds account for 65 percent of the total assets under management of the industry compared with 54 percent in 2003. The largest funds manage $20 to $30 billion or more.[288]

In 2006, the revenue of hedge funds was about 15 to 20 percent of the total industry revenue of investment banking.[289] Hedge funds assets under management were equivalent to about 4 percent of the assets of mutual funds at the end of 1993, with the share increasing to around 10 percent by 2005.[290]

The performance of hedge funds was the worst in two decades in 2008, with decline by 18.3 percent of their investment, which was still better than the performance of the markets.[291] According to some estimates hedge funds assets under management declined by about $399 billion in 2008, or by 39 percent, reaching $1.2 trillion in January 2009 compared with about $2 trillion in January 2008.[292] This was the largest loss of resources since the stock market collapse in 1987. A survey in March 2009 of investors with $1100 billion in alternative assets revealed the expectation of withdrawals from hedge funds of $200 billion and fears of the liquidation of one fifth of the hedge funds.[293]

Hedge funds do not advertise and accept investments only from large institutions and wealthy individuals to qualify for exemptions on registration, concentrating investment, leveraging trades, and short-selling financial assets.[294] However, federal securities laws prohibit fraud and insider trading by hedge funds. A recent survey finds that 86 percent of hedge funds register with a regulatory organization such as the SEC or the Commodities Futures Trading Commission (CFTC).[295] Hedge fund managers must place the interests of the funds above their personal interests because they are considered legal fiduciaries under the Investment Advisers Act of 1940. Complying with fiduciary duties requires that hedge funds make significant disclosures to potential investors. There is also indirect regulation in the form of limits on banks by federal treasury regulations on the amount of lending to hedge funds. Regulation T of the FRBO also imposes limits of lending to hedge funds by securities broker-dealers. Supervisors can inspect risk exposures of banks.

There is also a system of alignment of interests in hedge funds.[296] Managers typically invest their own resources in the hedge fund. Performance fees sometimes are only realized after recovering losses. There is monitoring by counterparties. Concerns with career preservation also add incentives.

Concentration of common strategies constitutes a major concern of policy in regards to hedge funds. The exit from similar positions triggered the near default of Long Term Capital Management. The similarity of high and low returns among hedge funds measures the similarity of hedge fund strategies and their potential for systemic disruption.[297] Hedge funds could experience losses simultaneously, causing contraction of liquidity in markets and affecting stability. It is possible that the correlation of hedge fund transactions, or similar move in direction, could increase because of the reduction of volatility, or deviation from the mean return, giving the impression that hedge fund returns have moved more closely.[298] Greater association of hedge fund returns increased their correlation in the late 1990s while the recent increase is explained by lowering volatility of returns.[299] Increasing hedge volatility and high covariance occurred before Long Term Capital Management's collapse in 1998 while the recent environment is characterized by low volatility and average covariance. Low volatility of hedge fund returns reflects the current low volatility of financial assets. Volatility could be low but there is substantial probability of loss of all assets during a market event.[300]

An analytical form of the business model of the hedge fund is to consider that the manager believes that she can earn superior returns relative to others. In this approach, all that is needed is the belief of the manager not whether she can attain those returns. If the manager has limited personal resources, the raising of external capital is the alternative to pay for the costs of the operation and a fund would be the available vehicle.[301] The issues for analysis are the strategies to generate the superior returns, the risks of these strategies and the time span that the superior returns will last. Investors are concerned about the diversification of assets provided by the hedge funds and whether the returns compensate the high fees. The counterparties of hedge funds—commercial banks, prime brokers, and investment banks—are concerned with the risks, strategies and timing together with the remuneration of the services provided. The major concern of regulators is with the crowding of highly leveraged strategies that can create systemic risk.[302] The industry is converging toward a multistrategy hedge fund, allocating capital opportunistically in global markets by means of different strategies. The objective is to maximize the enterprise value of the hedge fund management firm. These funds grow in diversity to smooth the effects on their performance caused by business cycle fluctuations.

There are four concerns of regulators with hedge funds.[303] First, the movement by the SEC to regulate hedge funds was motivated by protecting investors from losses resulting from the collapse of hedge funds or outright fraud. The investors in hedge funds are relatively wealthy and sophisticated about investment risks. Fraud has not been a common problem in hedge funds.

Second, the collapse of a large hedge fund could have impact on other financial institutions, creating systemic risk. The collapse of Long Term Capital Management was managed by the FRBNY without significant difficulty and the closure of Amaranth in 2006 had little impact on markets. Amaranth engaged in trades with high risk, involving market risk and also liquidity risk that is quite difficult to manage.[304]

Third, the simultaneous exit of hedge funds from similar positions could cause downward pressure on security prices, leading to liquidity crises. Hedge funds strategies can be classified into four different styles:[305]

- *Long-short equity.* In this style, funds search for undervalued and overvalued stocks and hedge the market risk of positions. For example, if a stock is overvalued in the analysis of the fund manager, she would take a long position in the stock, earning profits from increases in the share value, and simultaneously take a short position with derivatives, such as options and futures, earning compensatory payments in case of decline in the overall stock market. The strategy is earning the profits from an increase in the price of the overvalued stock while eliminating the effects of changes in the overall stock market. Advanced research finds that equity strategies of hedge funds have exposure to events with low probability of collapse of equity markets.[306]
- *Event positions.* The fund manager searches for corporate events, such as sale of subsidiaries, M&As, restructurings, bankruptcies, and so on. The hedge fund manager would take positions that attempt to profit from these corporate events. For example, she would take a long position in the acquired company in an acquisition to gain from the increase in price and a short position in the acquiring company to gain from the decrease in price.
- *Macro strategies.* The fund manager identifies possible changes in prices of financial assets in stock markets, interest rates, FX rates, commodities, and so on. She then takes positions on the anticipation of change in prices. A common strategy in the beginning of the credit/dollar crisis was to short the dollar, with the objective of benefitting from a flight into the euro because of decreases in interest rates more aggressively by the Fed than by the ECB, and taking a long position in commodities futures, such as gold and oil.
- *Fixed-income arbitrage.* Another strategy was the carry trade, borrowing at the low interest rate in Japan to invest in the high interest markets in Australia and New Zealand.

Empirical evidence suggests that adverse market conditions in hedge funds that follow the same strategy or style of financial management result in higher probability of adverse market conditions in other styles of hedge fund financial management.[307] Liquidity squeezes could transfer from one market segment to another, constituting systemic risk.

Fourth, hedge funds could increase market volatility or oscillation of prices. There is no conclusive evidence on this issue. In fact, hedge funds have not been conspicuous in the core events of the market turmoil of the credit/dollar crisis.

Systemic risk is difficult to specify for statistical research. A possible definition is as follows:[308]

> The term 'systemic risk' is commonly used to describe the possibility of a series of correlated defaults among financial institutions—typically banks—that occurs over a short period of time, often caused by a single major event.

The most common example is the failure of a relatively large bank or several banks after depositors withdraw their funds. The initial withdrawals in one or several institutions may spread to others. The bankruptcy of many financial institutions has magnified effects on external finance for the government, corporations, financial institutions, and individuals. There is adverse selection in finance in that banks do not finance the projects that would recover economic activity because of asymmetry of information that prevents choosing sound lending opportunities. Employment and output are adversely affected. The failure of 9440 banks during the 1930s and of financial institutions in emerging market crises are typically used as examples of systemic risk and its impact on the real economy and employment. The vast literature on contagion provides analysis of how difficulties in one or several financial institutions in one or several countries spread to other financial markets and countries. The initial financial crisis causes subsequent contraction of real economic activity and employment.

There are two important channels of potential systemic risk in analysis.[309] There is significant leverage in hedge funds, that is, loans much higher than collateral. High yields are typically found in less liquid markets or markets may become illiquid after events. The high leverage and illiquidity of markets cause sharp declines of prices of financial assets in response to a market event. The capital of hedge funds erodes. Selling positions in illiquid markets requires accepting sharply lower prices. Bid/ask spreads significantly widen during market events. Haircuts or prices lower than current market prices in SRPs and RSRPs contracts increase sharply. The second factor is possible correlation of strategies of hedge funds. The combined sharp reduction of hedge fund capital in response to decline of values of portfolios together with correlation of portfolios among hedge funds can have adverse impact on the net worth of hedge fund lenders. The initial crisis in hedge funds can thus propagate to other financial institutions, causing systemic repercussions. Thus, the two channels of propagation of crises in hedge funds, according to this analysis, are illiquidity and time-varying hedge fund correlation.[310]

There is concern by the ECB on the role of hedge funds in the credit-risk transfer markets.[311] The ECB finds a positive role in the arbitrage activities by hedge funds in enhancing efficiency of financial asset prices and liquidity. There are indications that these activities have recently increased. However, the ECB expresses concern that there is little knowledge of the activities of hedge funds in credit-risk transfer markets.[312] Because of the lack of information on strategies and volumes, it is not possible to assess the impact on financial markets of the failure of a large hedge fund or a group of hedge funds that are active in the selling side of the hedge fund market. In such an event there would not be credit hedges when they would be most needed. The evaporation of liquidity in credit-risk transfer markets could erode the hedging functions of credit risk and the syndication of leveraged buyout (LBO) loans. Improved quality of data is required to evaluate the repercussions of the collapse of hedge funds. The ECB finds risk for creditors, especially banks, in the instability of financial markets caused by collective actions of hedge funds during periods of financial stress. There was a test of such an event in 2006:[313]

> Yet when Amaranth Advisors—a multi-strategy hedge fund around twice the size of Long Term Capital Management, a fund whose near-failure in 1998 threw global financial markets into turmoil—plunged into financial distress in September 2006, this event had little discernible impact on markets.

There is an emerging consensus, according to the president of the ECB,[314] on a code of voluntary principles for hedge funds.[315] Regulatory and administrative measures would be avoided. There would be three main types of principles according to the President of the ECB:[316] optimum risk management, exchange of information with investors, and disclosure to prime brokers. The principles could follow the model used for emerging market sovereign crises. Germany and France appear more inclined to some form of regulation of hedge funds. However, the United States and the United Kingdom where managers are located did not seem as interested but changed toward regulation after the credit/dollar crisis. The *Financial Times* encourages the hedge fund industry to engage in interaction with regulators and supervisors.[317] The new regulatory paradigm to emerge from the credit/dollar crisis envisioned by the ECB centers on extending regulatory oversight to all systemically important institutions, especially hedge funds and credit rating agencies.[318] This initiative seeks to encourage international coordination of the effort to regulate hedge funds and credit rating agencies.

Table 4.1 shows the potential adverse effects of hedge funds. The major risk of hedge funds is in the form of the repercussions on other institutions in the event of unanticipated losses with high leverage. Prudential regulation of a business model such as that of hedge funds may simply lead to banning their existence. There are such risk-management controls in existence through the management of counterparty risk of the prime lenders to hedge funds such as investment banks and other prime brokers. There may be indirect effects in that a third party undermined by excessive leverage with hedge funds could affect other financial institutions. Another area of concern is the concentration of hedge funds in high-risk markets. Volatility in those markets could affect other markets, causing systemic problems. The impact of hedge funds on market volatility is still an unresolved issue of research. The superior quality of the management of Long Term Capital Management caused concentration of similar trades. It does not appear very likely that such quality of management and concentration will be repeated.

Systemic risks from hedge firms can be direct, originating in the credit exposures of core financial entities to hedge funds, which supervisors consider being limited.[319] Indirect systemic risks could result from actions by hedge funds, such as forced liquidation of positions, which could affect market liquidity and prices with stress on one or several core firms such as large banks, investment banks, and brokerages. Supervisors cannot measure the indirect effects precisely. Declining discipline in counterparties because of the competition for hedge fund

Table 4.1 Potential adverse effects of hedge funds

Counterparty Risk
    Direct risks of credit extended by prime brokers.
    Indirect risks of a third party affected by excessive lending to hedge funds.
Impact on Markets
    Frequent trading of portfolios.
    Concentrations in high-risk markets.
Volatility Benefits of hedge funds
    Inconclusive evidence.
Crowded Trades
    Hedge funds concentrate on similar strategies.

Source: Tomas Garbaravicius and Frank Dierick, *Hedge funds and their implications for financial stability* (Frankfurt am Main: ECB OPS No. 34, Aug, 2005), 35–49.

business before the credit/dollar crises could have been reflected in weakening clauses in credit contracts and exposures. A critical supervisory task with fast and robust results is strengthening counterparty risk management because of growing relative importance of counterparty financing of core firms.[320] Supervisors of core firms can create incentives for improving risk management in transactions involving complex products with potentially high risks and opaque exposures over multiple business units. There should be emphasis on monitoring, measuring, and relying on properly valued collateral in reducing tail risks, or events with low probability of occurrence but high potential losses, in counterparty transactions to ensure stable financial markets. Supervisors of core firms can also ensure prudential controls that enhance the resilience of the financial system to adverse shocks of market liquidity, that is, the evaporation of short-term financing for securitized products.[321]

There are recommendations by the Group of Thirty (G30) for the regulation of managers of private pools of capital that borrow substantial amounts.[322] These managers are hedge funds and private equity funds. The proposal would require their registration with a proper national prudential regulator. That regulator should have authority to require periodic reports and public disclosure of items such as size, investment strategy, borrowing, and performance of assets under management. There should be care in the standards not to create the impression that regulation and disclosure translate into lower investment risk. The regulator of hedge funds and private equity funds that pose significant systemic risks should have authority to determine proper standards for capital, liquidity, and risk management. The location of the fund manager should be the proper jurisdiction for prudential regulation and not the legal domicile.

Corporate governance

A critical issue in the analysis of modern corporations is the conflict of interests of owners and managers already observed by Adam Smith:[323]

> The directors of such companies, however, being the managers of other people's money than of their own, it cannot well be expected that they should watch over it with the same anxious vigilance with which the partners of a private copartney frequently watch over their own.

Another critical analysis is the consideration of transactions costs, which are quite significant in reality.[324] The combination of these two approaches ignored in neoclassical or mainstream economics leads to the contemporary analysis of corporate governance, which is essential in financial and banking regulation.

There were two observations by scholars on the nature of the modern corporation that was established by 1930.[325] First, 65 percent of the largest nonfinancial corporations, accounting for 50 percent of total assets of nonfinancial companies in the United States were controlled by managers holding small stakes in their ownership. Second, there were doubts similar to those of Adam Smith about efficient decisions by managers who did not own the corporations. That is, the separation of ownership and management of the corporations could result in decisions that benefitted the managers at the expense of shareholders. The sample originally used for 1930 was subsequently analyzed statistically in the 1980s. There were no significant differences in the compensation of executives and the use of assets to generate profits between companies controlled by management and those controlled by owners.[326] These results are surprising because there would have been superior returns in the companies controlled by owners relative to those controlled by managers. However, the depiction of the modern corporation endured with structures characterized by layers of managers and divisions in vertical integration. The modern factory system moved toward assembly lines and organizational innovations that resulted in significant economies of scale and scope. The endurance derives from the narrative of the experience of General Motors.[327] Companies became organized in pyramid regimes of command and control from top management accumulating substantial power and rents, communicating vertically through middle management. The highest rewards obtained at the top of the pyramid motivated junior and middle management to acquire the skills to climb through the organization.

The analysis of firms must take into account the inefficiencies that could result from the separation of ownership and management. The owners are considered as the *principal* and management as the *agent*. In this agency theory, the managers (agent) may promote their self-interest at the expense of the shareholders (principal). Managers derive satisfaction from perquisites such as larger offices with views, more expensive computers than those required, contributions to favorite charities, use of corporate jets for personal purposes, acquisition of inputs from friends, and the like.[328] The optimal outcome of the first-best or Pareto optimality is not realized. There are agency costs in the form of the benefits extracted by management for its personal satisfaction. Under no frictions in perfect competition and without agency costs, the firm would obtain an optimum value for shareholders after deducting the optimum investment. To deal with the agency problem, shareholders invest in monitoring the firm with the intention of limiting the "aberrant activities of the agent."[329]

The principal (owner) may require in some cases that the agent spend resources, called bonding costs, to prevent the agent (manager) of taking actions that harm the principal or to ensure that the principal is compensated in case of harmful actions. In most agency problems, the principal and the agent will incur monitoring and bonding costs. There would be also a divergence between the outcome that would be obtained in the first best of perfect competition and the actual outcome under the agency problem, which is called the residual loss. Monitoring costs include budget restrictions, operating rules, and analysis and measurement of the performance of the manager. Examples of bonding costs include "contractual guarantees to have the financial accounts audited by a public account, explicit bonding against malfeasance on the part of the manager and contractual limitations on the manager's decision-making power."[330] Agency costs are given by[331]

> Agency costs = (Optimum value of the firm less Optimum investment under perfect competition) – (Value of the firm under the principal/agency problem less Investment less Monitoring costs less Bonding costs)

There is less net value of the firm under the agency problem because of inferior outcome and the investment in monitoring and bonding management. Agency costs insert a wedge in the optimization of the firm that prevents it from attaining the first best of perfect competition.

The agency problem does not disappear with outright ownership of companies by the government or mixed public-private initiative. Fannie Mae and Freddie Mac illustrate the complex agency problem of mixed government-private enterprise. There are two principals, shareholders and the people. The OFHEO finds that in both Fannie Mae and Freddie Mac senior management falsified the earnings of the companies to obtain remuneration based on fabricated performance.[332] Fannie Mae and Freddie Mac lobbied politicians and contributed to their campaigns, creating another type of agency cost in favorable oversight by the legislature with possible regulatory capture. The legislature acted as delegated principal from the ultimate principal, the people whose taxes pay for the bailout caused by the moral hazard of the implicit guarantee of Fannie Mae and Freddie Mac by the full faith and credit of the United States. State-owned enterprises across the world are plagued by agency problem and costs.

The agency problem will exist under all regimes. The issue in an economy with market allocation is finding contractual arrangements that protect the rights of minority shareholders. Shareholders in common stock of corporations provide wealth in exchange for the residual claim on the corporation after its debts are paid. The corporation can be viewed as a set of contracts or rules of the game, written or unwritten, which establish hierarchies in the decision process, defining residual claims and creating mechanisms that control agency problems in decisions.[333] The decision process in an organization can be viewed as consisting of initiation of the decision, ratification, implementation, and monitoring.[334] The category *decision management* includes initiation and implementation while the category *decision control* consists of ratification and monitoring. Systems that separate decision management from decision control accomplish the separation of the risk of residual claims from decision management. The risk of residual claims is high in large corporations with diffuse ownership but lower in small and medium corporations with more concentrated ownership.[335]

In the framework of capital requirements of Basel II, traders can take decisions in positions based on risk guidelines proposed by a risk management area that is independent and reports to senior management. This process provides rules of the game to avoid rogue traders attempting to maximize their bonuses in conflict with the preservation of capital functions of the senior management. Monitoring is conducted by accounting and auditing areas that are also separated from traders taking risk decisions. Ratification of the key decisions and rules of the game of risk management in financial institutions is the responsibility of the board of independent directors who also exercise the monitoring or oversight of the key decisions. The discipline of this system is by stock prices in organized stock markets.[336] In addition, the market for corporate control and the job market for managers also exercise control over the agency problems of corporations. The legal system determines the overall rules of the game in the form of common law applying to governance and takeovers. Corporate law and the markets for corporate controls and managers, providing the structure for control of agency problems, are considered in the following two sections.

Remuneration

Compensation of executives became one of the emotional issues during the credit/dollar crisis. Contractual payment of bonuses by American International Group (AIG) attracted national attention at all levels up to the President and inspired a retroactive taxation bill of the bonuses passed by the House.[337] The argument in favor of the bill was that the bonuses were paid ultimately by taxpayers because of government support to prevent the failure of AIG. There are few cases in which such little value, $165 million in bonuses relative to the $180 billion bailout, created such political and emotional stress. The argument in favor of paying the bonuses was the contractual agreement with the recipients that if not honored would cause their exodus to competitors, which actually occurred, erasing the managerial talent that could recover AIG. An important issue is that the interest of the taxpayer as shareholder of AIG would be to maintain or increase the prices of the stock of the company to recover the investment and earn a profit by the sale of the public stake in AIG. The retention of the staff that had prevented further erosion of the value of the company and could increase it in the future would be part of any strategy of recovering the investment of taxpayers. This argument was hardly invoked in the rush of politicians to pass the law as defenders of the public interest.

The job market for managers is an important component of theory in reducing agency costs. Functioning of this market would require the capacity to draft and implement effective contracts that align the interest of shareholders in increasing the value of their investment with the self-interest of managers. There would be a disincentive to poor performance because managers with weak performance could be replaced with better managers. There are inadequate conditions in reality to create these contracts, which in practice differ from what would be advised by theory.[338] Managers have strong nonpecuniary disincentive to terminating employees because of loss of esteem by fellow employees, potential lawsuits and the like. Boards are reluctant to terminate CEOs for inferior performance. The pecuniary incentives such as bonuses and promotion are harder to realize, depending on the performance of the company in risky markets. The disincentives to penalize inferior performance and the difficulty in realizing incentives for superior performance combine to frustrate effective contracts reducing agency costs. In addition, compensation committees operate under uncertainty because they do not have knowledge of investment opportunities and decisions of CEOs in future alternative economic conditions; such knowledge would be required by the compensation committees to draft adequate contracts for senior management covering all situations.[339]

Agency theory suggests that CEO compensation would accompany performance as a form of aligning the interests of shareholders and managers. A sample of over 2000 CEOs in the United States over five decades before 1990 does not show remuneration by performance.[340] The change in wealth of the CEOs from total pay and stock-related ownership was $3.25 per $1000 change in shareholder wealth. There is implicit regulation of corporate remuneration by political and internal pressure to restrict compensation.

An important issue with high emotional connotations is the severance contracts popularized with the term "golden parachutes."[341] There are advantages and disadvantages in severance packages. The managers of the target companies in M&As have invested in human capital specific to their companies over a long period of time. Typically, they lose their jobs within three years of the sale of the company and incur heavy personal losses. The issue is similar to taxing heavily a few years of high income of an entertainer who may earn little in the rest of her working life. A proper incentive is to tie the severance contract to the premium of sale of the stock, creating an incentive for the managers to defend the best interest of shareholders. At the other extreme, generous severance contracts may encourage the managers to negotiate any sale price to receive the severance payment. Designing severance contracts may require focusing on the specific characteristics of the company and the type of management. In some cases, there is confusion of accumulated benefits in stock options realized at the time of severance that have nothing to do with the golden parachute clause. Managers earned the stock options and retirement benefits over a long period of service.

The most important emotional issue is the rapid increase in remuneration after the technological revolution beginning in the 1970s. There was a trebling in 1970–2005 of the inflation adjusted cash compensation of CEOs, consisting of salary and bonuses.[342] The average cash compensation increased from $900,000 in 1970 to $3,330,000 in 2005. The cash compensation of the average CEO in 1970 was 28 times that of the average production worker, jumping to 115 times in 2005. This increase in compensation was accompanied by increasing external hiring of CEOs instead of the earlier system of promoting within companies. The explanation of the growth in compensation and external hiring of CEOs is explained by the change in general managerial talents required by CEOs.[343] The management of corporations has improved because of progress in economics, management science, accounting, and finance. The credit/dollar crisis has shown in relief the need of communication skills of CEOs not only with analysts, capital markets, and shareholders but also with the media and government. The new CEO has general skills in application of complex management methods and communication skills that are not specific, as in the past, to a company in a given industry, but are valuable in many companies in diverse industries. Competition for these CEOs explains the rise in the remuneration and the search outside companies and in other industries.

The "fat cat" theory disputes the agency theory interpretation, arguing that CEOs capture board members to extract rents at the expense of shareholders.[344] In this view, CEOs exert managerial power to manipulate boards in promoting their self-interest. Multimillion remunerations cause public outrage. Companies engage in an outrage cost of inefficiency in the effort to clear their public images. Compensation consultants are hired by personnel departments controlled by management to misinform boards, shareholders, and the public. Departing managers receive loans at low rates, forbearance of loans, and special remuneration. Stock option contracts are priced to provide windfall remuneration that is unrelated to the performance of CEOs.

There is an active critique of the "fat cat" hypothesis.[345] Independent boards cannot be captured in the same way as CEO-influenced boards. There is evidence of increasing independence in corporate boards in the past 30 years.[346] SOX sanctions corporate boards. The "fat cat" theory predicts that by capturing boards internally promoted CEOs would earn more than externally hired CEOs. However, the premium for externally hired CEOs has increased over time reaching 15.3 percent. The trend of increasingly hiring external CEOs also contradicts the captive board of the "fat cat" hypothesis. Outrage costs are consistent with the adequate functioning of the control and job markets and do not prove the "fat cat" hypothesis. Companies clear their images with the public even in a situation where CEO compensation is based purely on performance. Athletes in swimming and baseball have attracted outrage because of their remuneration without any power to capture the companies that use them in advertising or the teams that hire them.

Corporate law

US investors have given trillions of dollars to corporations whose managers have discretion on their fortunes and profits. This power given to people who are not owners of the property has been studied intensely with the rise of the corporate form. The earliest warning of agency theory of managers promoting their self-interest at the expense of owners would suggest investment in bonds instead of equities.[347] However, the returns on equities have surpassed those in bonds and the system of managers of corporations with many shareholders has worked effectively. This is considered to be the "central mystery" of corporate law.[348] The traditional explanation of corporate law for the system to work rests on three types of arguments:[349]

- *Legal constraints.* The courts enforce legal prohibitions of theft, embezzlement, insider trading and others. They also enforce more vague legal constraints such as the duty of care and the duty of loyalty. Managers are caught by the courts in violation of these legal constraints, which act as deterrent of misconduct.
- *Institutional structure.* Managers are checked by boards of directors, outside directors, shareholder voting, proxy contests, and derivative suits.
- *Market monitoring.* Managers are also checked by markets in products, labor, capital, and corporate control. Ineffective or corrupt managers can lose their jobs when the companies are restructured or sold.

Checks on managers are very powerful with the exception of competitive markets in cases where they do exist.[350]

The community of the corporate system is relatively small, consisting of several thousand senior managers and directors of large, publicly held corporations.[351] There is an additional small group of lawyers, mainly in New York and Wilmington but with some in Chicago and Los Angeles. The court in charge of oversight for the most part, because of Delaware's attractive franchise of corporate form, is the Delaware Chancery Court with judicial review by the Delaware Supreme Court. Highlighting the small legal community, the decision makers responsible have close to only five members. The system is described as "how a small community imposes formal and informal, legal and nonlegal, sanctions on its members."[352]

The essence of Delaware fiduciary law is that boards have freedom of discretion as long as they follow the right procedural process and act in good faith.[353] This system can be in marked difference to other countries where protections have a stronger substantive approach. In Delaware, the courts define good faith by means of descriptions of the conduct of manager, director, and lawyer that are fact intensive and saturated with norms. Delaware fiduciary law is characterized by standards that are generated in a narrative process. The stories of this process cannot often be reduced to a rule. Instead, the Delaware courts provide parables of what are good and bad managers and lawyers to define their job descriptions. There is value in thinking "of judges more as preachers than as policemen."[354]

An excellent illustration of the operation of the review function of Delaware courts is in terms of the management buyouts (MBO) of the 1980s.[355] There were 404 MBOs in the value of $162.02 billion in 1981–90. There were only 15 cases in the Delaware courts in that period relating to MBOs even with this amount of deal activity. The MBOs are especially important because they involve the acquisition of the company by the managers from the shareholders, creating opportunities for conflict of interest. An important consideration is that the critical cases involving Macmillan, Fort Howard, and RJR Nabisco were only written in 1988 and 1989, almost a decade after the boom in MBO activity began in 1981.[356] Transactions were rapidly developing, creating pressure on business attorneys to advise their clients in an environment of vaguely defined norms on how the law would develop.

A distinguished legal scholar argues that "Delaware is a reasonably efficient system of corporate governance."[357] Opinions at this level focus primarily in granting preliminary injunctions. The common thread was that the opinions were critical of the conduct of the defendants. The deep judgments of the conduct of managers consisted of fact intensive narratives of the process by which the companies dealt with bidders and management. They marked the way for future conduct to be examined by courts and to be adhered to by companies facing such situations. These opinions contain narratives on the independence and activism of the special committees, the role of the investment banker adviser and the search for alternative bids. The Delaware courts shifted the emphasis, in opinions and extrajudicial communication, to influence the conduct and formation of the special committees tasked by the board with evaluating the proposed business transaction.[358] In deciding these cases, the Delaware court used the standard of the "business judgment rule" or alternatively the "entire fairness standard." The courts did not give rules on how MBOs should be conducted, but clear procedural steps arose as best practices which would grant and for process which would gain greater deference to managers from the courts.

A summary of the standard arises from the written opinions late in the 1990s.[359] The Delaware courts recognized the existence of an inherent conflict of interest in MBOs. In those cases, the court has favored a special independent committee to negotiate with management and third parties. Moreover, the special committee has its own independent investment banking and legal advisers. Counsel should ascertain that managers involved in the MBO do not appoint the members of the special committee and the investment banker adviser. Further procedural safeguards include an effective announcement by the special committee of the existence of a bid by management, ensuring that all material information is available to prospective bidders. The special committee should not improperly favor management over third parties that may enter the bidding. In addition, the special committee should test the market for possible alternative offers, but is not required to conduct an English style auction. There is another important norm in the Delaware courts that is relevant to M&As and buyouts developed in the so called Revlon line of cases. Management can "just say no" to an offer for the corporation if it is contrary to business plans that have been designed to optimize the corporation's long-term business model. Much like all this area of law, exceptions arise too when such situation really occurs.

The value of M&A transactions jumped from $44 billion in 1980 to $247 billion in 1988.

A significant share of these transactions consisted of hostile takeovers or defensive transactions.[360] In general, the focus of corporate legal doctrine and scholarship is on the relative power of managers and shareholders in the ultimate decision of selling or keeping the ownership structure of the company unaltered. The poison pill became the centerpiece instrument of defense because of various advantages.[361] Namely, there are no significant costs in adopting the pill and the conduct of business by the company is not altered. The most important advantage is that it gives the board time to evaluate its options as the pill substantially hinders the short-term ability of an acquirer to take over a company with a poison pill unless the target board redeems it.

One of the crucial early questions became whether a company could "just say no," using a phrase of the US First Lady of the time, choosing not to redeem the pill indefinitely on the argument that the hostile bid was not high enough. The Delaware Supreme Court provided its opinion on the subject in 1988, permitting Time to proceed with its tender offer for Warner Brothers and maintaining its poison pill. The board of Time was supported in its decision to turn down a conditional offer by Paramount of $200 per share, a premium of 58 percent over Time's pre-offer share price. This can be interpreted as the support of the decision by the board of Time given by the outside directors of its board on the basis of a fairness opinion by the investment banker advising Time.[362] A corporation need not abandon a corporate plan in exchange for short-term shareholder profits unless there is no basis for the corporate strategy. The Delaware court prefers bilateral decisions, which are those that are favored by both management and shareholders, because they are more likely to enhance welfare.[363] The "just say no" doctrine was a unilateral doctrine, favored by management. The Delaware courts may not be supportive of a "just say no" decision that does not have the support of the outside directors of the board based on the fairness opinion by an investment bank. However, this may have started to shift slightly as one of the central questions post this period was the ability of the shareholders to attain the redemption of the pill by the board.

After a brief interruption in the recession of the early 1990s, M&A activity entered into a phase of even more rapid growth, jumping from 3510 deals in 1995 with value of $356 billion to 10,883 deals in 2000 with value of $1284.8 billion.[364] During this period, the largest number of takeovers was nominally friendly in contrast with the hostile bids of the 1980s. There were also significant changes in corporate governance. Outside independent directors acquired more power than in earlier periods, increasing their share in corporate boards. An interpretation is that outside directors are more effective, in effect causing the dismissal of CEOs with poor performance.[365] Moreover, outside directors are more likely to strengthen shareholder value during tender offers and stock prices increase in response to their appointment. There are also higher premiums in MBOs of corporations with boards that have a majority of independent directors. This strengthening of outside directors has increased the monitoring function of boards. The changes in the composition and relative influence of outside directors were accompanied by a shift in compensation of managers by stock options. Stock options are often seen as the best way to tie the interest of management and the board with the performance of the company. However, managers gain in takeovers because of the bidding of stock prices but also by golden parachutes providing severance payments, benefits, early vesting in pension plans, and acceleration in vesting of unvested options.[366] The equilibrium between these devices is a fine one; while golden parachutes and other such payments have a legitimate purpose in maintaining management during the possible takeover transaction and ensuring continuation of management should it fail, there are also questions involving self-interest of management in assigning themselves such huge payoffs. Courts often follow the Delaware model of looking at the process of the implementation of such devices and often use certain limits communicated via the precedent system. The overall change in governance on the corporate form has been more in accordance with the bilateral approach of the Delaware courts, benefiting both management and shareholders.

Summary

Securities legislation provides a prime example of how regulated industries capture the regulatory process on their behalf. It also illustrates the perpetuation of regulatory errors over decades. Entry into regulation during regulatory rushes in periods of distressed economic conditions is much easier than delayed exit after substantial harm. There is no evidence that hedge funds have originated, propagated, or accentuated the credit/dollar crisis or earlier crises. Incentive remuneration is required for effective management but there is disagreement on the type and size of incentives. Corporate law has provided a flexible and effective framework for the market of corporate control, which is essential to a dynamic economy.

5
Regulation of Securities and Capital Markets

Introduction

There is a contrast between the SEC in the United States, operating with rules and self-regulatory organizations (SRO), such as securities exchanges, and the FSA in the United Kingdom, functioning under principles. There are proposals by both systems for significant regulatory change. SOX is the most drastic recent regulation of corporate governance by capital markets regulators. The choice of jurisdiction where to list securities is discussed in the final section.

Rules and principles

There was a distinction between the regulatory approaches of the United States and the United Kingdom with debate on which one was ideal for regulation of securities and capital markets. The first subsection analyzes the US approach of rulemaking by the SEC and SROs supervising markets and in turn being supervised by the SEC. During more than a decade, the UK approach was considered superior because of regulation by principles instead of rules as in the United States and significant flexibility in actual practice. The credit/dollar crisis has eroded the trust in both approaches. The US approach is considered in the first subsection followed by the UK approach. A third subsection analyzes the proposals to change the approaches.

The SEC and self-regulatory organizations

The private institutions operating in financial markets have their own regulation through SROs. The most conspicuous ones are the stock and futures exchanges shown in Table 5.1. The exchanges create governance, rules, conduct codes, and a process of investigation, discipline, prosecution, and enforcement. There are additional clearing houses that also have their own regulation. Securities regulators in turn impose supervision of the SROs. The two major systems of securities regulation are those of the United States and the United Kingdom.

Several stock and futures exchanges are listed in Table 5.1. There are also associated clearinghouses for the processing and payment of transactions. There is a global process of consolidation of exchanges. Part of the motivation for this consolidation is the loss of competitiveness of the United States, which could be viewed as the rise of the volume of exchanges in other countries. An important development is the rise of the Chinese stock market following China's accession to the World Trade Organization (WTO). China is restructuring its capital structure beginning with the opening of the financial system to foreign ownership and competition. A significant, if not the major, part of transactions in securities occurs in over-the-counter (OTC) markets. OTC transactions are between financial entities in contrast with transactions in organized exchanges. Associations of trading firms perform self-regulation in these markets. Supervisors of financial institutions also oversee these transactions. Banks also serve as custodians of securities, requiring norms of conduct and rules. There is a large sector of SROs worldwide linked online by electronic connection.

Table 5.1   Selected stock and futures exchanges

STOCK EXCHANGES
  NYSE Euronext http://www.nyse.com/ www.nyseeuronext.com
  NASDAQ http://www.nasdaq.com/
  London Stock Exchange http://www.londonstockexchange.com/en-gb/
  home.htm
  Tokyo Stock Exchange http://www.tse.or.jp/english/index.html
  Frankfurt Stock Exchange http://deutsche-boerse.com/dbag/dispatch/en/kir/
  gdb_navigation/about_us/20_FWB_Frankfurt_Stock_Exchange
  Hong Kong Stock Exchange http://www.hkex.com.hk/index.htm
  Singapore Exchange http://www.sgx.com/

FUTURES EXCHANGES
  Chicago Board of Trade Chicago Mercantile Exchange http://www.cbot.com/
  New York Mercantile Exchange http://www.nymex.com/index.aspx
  Chicago Board Options Exchange http://www.cboe.com/
  London Metal Exchange http://www.lme.co.uk/
  LIFFE http://www.euronext.com/home_derivatives-2153-EN.html
  Tokyo Commodity Exchange http://www.tocom.or.jp/

The self-regulation of the securities industry under SEC supervision was consolidated during the New Deal in the 1930s.[367] There were two factors that generated this system. It was impractical to directly supervise thousands of broker-dealers and business corporations. In addition, the industry preferred to avoid disruption of business, applying its enhanced practical knowledge of the markets. There are four alternatives to the supervision of SROs:[368]

- *Maintain the 2003 NYSE restructuring.* The NYSE reorganized by creating an independent not-for-profit company, NYSE Regulation, Inc., to conduct the self-regulation under the SEC supervision. This structure is discussed below. There are several deficiencies in this system.[369] Earlier reorganizations in 1938 and 1964 focused on preventing the conflict of interest in NYSE disciplinary mechanisms instead of on the more critical conflicts of interest of rulemaking and advocacy such as the specialist system, quote competition, and market linkages. Previous reorganizations of governance have deteriorated in periods of less concern by Congress and the SEC because conflicts of interest still remain. The 2003 reorganization did not correct the critical problem, which is the excessive concentration of power in the NYSE Chair. There still remain constitutional mechanisms that limit the authority of the Board of Directors.
- *Separation of NYSE regulation from the exchange.* The creation of NYSE Regulation, Inc. partly meets the requirements.[370] There are differences in the actual structure discussed later.
- *Establishment of an industry regulator.* The advantage of this system would be the elimination of conflicts of interest. However, there is a hurdle in conciliating diverse interests in the formation of rules.[371]
- *Regulation by the SEC.* Self-regulation is justified, as during the New Deal, by the cost and complexity of direct regulation by the SEC.

The objective of the SEC "is to protect investors, maintain fair, orderly and efficient markets and facilitate capital formation."[372] The SEC is especially concerned with investor protection to ensure that citizens have a fair chance to preserve their resources. The SEC believes that the laws and rules that govern securities in the United States derive from the simple principle that all investors, large or small, should have accessible information about an investment before buying it and during holding and selling it. This basic right is ensured by requirements of disclosure of meaningful information, financial and otherwise, to the public. Investors can make adequate investment decisions only if they have the required information.

The SEC prevents fraud and ensures disclosure by overseeing major actors in the market of securities such as securities exchanges, brokers, dealers, investment advisors, and mutual funds. The enforcement authority of the SEC empowers it to engage in civil enforcement actions for violation of securities laws, including fraud and misleading the public with erroneous information about securities and the companies issuing them. The SEC interacts with other areas of government such as Congress, federal departments and agencies, the SROs or stock exchanges, state securities regulators, and private sector organizations. The President's Working Group on Financial Markets includes the Chairs of the SEC, the FRBO, the CFTC, and the secretary of the Treasury.

Congress passed the Securities Act of 1933 and the Securities Exchange Act of 1934. In the exegesis of the SEC, the intention of Congress was to restore confidence by investors in the stock market by means of "more structure and government oversight."[373] In this view, the securities laws are based on two common sense principles. First, the issuing companies must inform the public about the securities, their business, and the risks. Second, the distributors and traders of securities—brokers, dealers, and exchanges—have to give fair and honest treatment to investors, placing the interests of investors above everything. Congress established the SEC in 1934 with the objective of enforcing the new laws, promoting market stability, and protecting investors.

There are five commissioners of the SEC appointed by the president subject to advice and consent by the Senate. The appointments are for five years and staggered in such a way that the term of one commissioner ends on June 5 of every year. There is a maximum limit of three commissioners from the same political party. The president also designates one of the commissioners as the chief executive or chairman of the SEC. In meetings open to the public, the commissioners interpret federal securities laws, amend existing rules, propose new rules and enforce rules and laws.

The objective of the Division of Market Regulation of the SEC is to establish and maintain standards "for fair, orderly and efficient markets."[374] Its main instrument to attain this objective is the regulation of broker-dealer firms, SROs and other market participants. The definition of an SRO by the SEC is as follows:[375]

A self-regulatory organization is a member organization that creates and enforces rules for its members based on the federal securities laws. SROs, which are overseen by the SEC, are the front line in regulating broker-dealers.

The SEC operates by making rules.[376] Rulemaking is the instrument for implementing legislation passed by Congress and signed into law by the president. The framework of oversight of the SEC consists of the Securities Act of 1933, the Securities Exchange Act of 1934 and the Investment Company Act of 1940. The statutes are quite broad in nature, consisting of basic principles and objectives. The evolution of securities markets requires rules "to maintain fair and orderly markets and to protect investors by altering regulations or creating new ones."[377] The process of rulemaking may start with a specific proposal or with a concept release in which the SEC requests views of the public on a given issue. The SEC then elaborates a rule proposal for the consideration of the Commission. After approval of the proposal by the Commission, the SEC presents it to the public for a period of time of 30–60 days for review and comment. The final rule takes the replies by the public as input into consideration for the final draft. The final draft is presented to the Commission; if adopted it becomes part of the official rules governing the securities markets. A major rule may require congressional review and veto consideration before it becomes effective.

The world's largest and most liquid exchange group is NYSE Euronext, which started on April 4, 2007. It is the result of the consolidation of the NYSE Group Inc. and Euronext NV. NYSE Euronext consists of six cash equities exchanges in five countries and six derivatives exchanges. It provides listings, trading in cash equities, equity, and interest rate derivatives, bonds, and distribution of market data. The listed companies had capital market value of $28.5 trillion, about twice the GDP of the United States, which has eroded in the credit/dollar crisis.

Euronext NV is a limited liability Dutch public company with registered office in Amsterdam. It has subsidiaries in Belgium, France, the Netherlands, Portugal, and the United Kingdom. The corporate governance of Euronext consists of two pillars of confidence by stakeholders and supervisors. The shareholders have approved its corporate governance structure and policy. Euronext has a Supervisory Board composed of independent members and a Managing Board. The Supervisory Board exercises power of oversight over the Managing Board and is governed by a code of rules and procedures and adopted a code of conduct. There is at least one member of the Supervisory Board that is knowledgeable on finance and at least another one that is knowledgeable on human resources.

The members of the NYSE include about 400 of the largest securities firms in the United States that service 92 million customer accounts. These firms handle 90 percent of the public customer accounts of broker-dealers with total assets of $3.28 trillion. The NYSE is an examining authority, as approved by the SEC, of its members and member firms. The merger of the NYSE and Archipelago Holdings, Inc. created a publicly traded company, NYSE Group, Inc., that is the sole owner of New York Stock Exchange LLC, a New York limited liability company. New York Stock Exchange LLC is the successor with registered securities exchange status of the NYSE. There are two subsidiaries, NYSE Market, Inc., a Delaware corporation, and NYSE Regulation, Inc., a New York Type A not-for-profit corporation.

The objective of the organizational structure of the two subsidiaries is to conform to the major changes in architecture completed in 2003. An independent commission headed by former Citigroup Chairman John Reed conducted the architecture reform. An important feature is to insulate NYSE Regulation from the potential conflicts created by public ownership.

The primary responsibility for the regulatory oversight of the exchange subsidiaries of the NYSE Group is exercised by the CEO of NYSE Regulation, reporting only to the board of directors of NYSE Regulation. The board of NYSE Regulation is composed of six independent directors with no relation to the member organizations and listed companies. It also has three directors that are simultaneously directors of the NYSE Group. The CEO of NYSE Regulation is the sole management director in the board. The CEO of NYSE Group is not a member of the board of NYSE Regulation. The management of NYSE Regulation does not report to the NYSE Group CEO.

NYSE Regulation has a major role in monitoring the activities of its member firms and listed companies and in enforcing compliance with NYSE rules and federal securities laws. The SEC oversees the self-regulatory activities of NYSE Regulation. The rules of the NYSE cover in detail the operations of its member organizations, on and off the trading floor. There are additional rules of adoption of first-class standards of financial and corporate accountability and transparency.

NYSE Regulation consists of four divisions:

- *Market surveillance.* This division conducts surveillance on real-time and after trades to detect market abuse and manipulation and insider trading. It produces rules and evaluates specialists. The staff has a presence in the trading floor and uses sophisticated electronic technology and human judgment of analysts. It recommends discipline and can refer matters to the SEC.

• *Member firm regulation.* This division engages in surveillance of NYSE members for compliance by member firms of practices of finance, operations and sales with NYSE rules and SEC regulations.

• *Enforcement.* This division investigates and prosecutes violations of NYSE rules and federal securities laws.

• *Listed company compliance.* The objective of this division is to maintain original listing standards that are of first world class.

The Financial Services Authority

The approach of the United Kingdom is a unitary authority of regulation, the FSA. According to the Director of Enforcement of the FSA, the London philosophy consists of a "light touch."[378] This flexible approach has permitted London to become a "leading center for mobile capital." The FSA does not consider itself to be a regulator driven by high-profile enforcement. The leading aspect of regulation is the use of supervision and relations with the regulated firms. It has implemented a deliberate move to principles-based regulation.

The philosophy of the FSA could be criticized by contrast with US regulation.[379] There is no evidence of high-profile prosecution of violation of securities laws in the United Kingdom. On the contrary, the approach consists of selective messages and "allows some illicit activity to go unpunished."[380] However, the FSA claims that it has created an innovative and extremely effective system.

The FSA is independent of the UK government.[381] Its origin is in the Labor administration taking office in 1997 and it was created after giving independence to the BOE in the conduct of monetary policy. The FSA was the successor organization of ten predecessor UK regulators. It is now the only regulator of financial services in the United Kingdom. The funding of the FSA originates in fees paid by large and small firms that it regulates. Its responsibility of supervision encompasses wholesale and retail markets, equities and derivatives trading, banking, and insurance. It is also the listing authority of securities in the United Kingdom. The regulation of mortgages and insurance has been recently added to the FSA. The population of the United Kingdom is about 60 million people of whom one million are in the industries regulated by the FSA that generate 7 percent of GDP. The staff of the FSA consists of 2800 employees and the current annual budget is £266 million. The FSA regulates about 30,000 firms. The objective function of the FSA is attaining maximum benefits subject to a cost restraint.

The legislation creating the system is the Financial Services and Market Act of 2000 (FSMA). The FSMA provides the FSA important powers of rulemaking, investigation, and enforcement.[382] The prevention of market abuse and the prosecution of insider trading are a key responsibility of the FSA under the FSMA. There are four statutory objectives of the FSA within the FSMA:

- Market confidence in the financial system
- Public understanding of the financial system
- Consumer protection
- Reduction of financial crime

The FSA endeavors to limit the potential for a business enterprise to be used with the objective of committing financial crime. The four objectives govern the operation of the FSA and its public, political, and legal accountability. The FSA reports yearly to Parliament and can be challenged in the courts on the interpretation or negligence of implementing the objectives.

There is significant difference in the approach of the FSA and regulation in the United States. The FSA does not target a system of perfection where there are no failures.[383] The basic principle is that "although the idea that regulation should seek to eliminate all failures may be appealing in theory, in practice it imposes prohibitive costs on the industry and on consumers."[384] The regulation by the FSA is based on "an acceptance that a regulatory system neither can nor should aim at avoiding all failures."[385] The analysis of the recent regulation of SOX is based on the proposition that eliminating all imperfections has unbearable costs relative to benefits. The costs of enforcement are minute compared with the costs of foregoing business and employment because of the heavy costs of compliance imposed on firms and markets. The approach followed by the FSA is to determine the amount of risk that the regulator is prepared to tolerate, given its objectives, and then to concentrate efforts on the risks that may be more important in terms of potential harm.[386] There is minimization of risks with respect to a constraint of four objectives provided by the FSMA. The FSA restricts "regulation to those circumstances where the market does not provide adequate answers and where regulation has the prospect of doing so at reasonable cost."[387] The objective of the FSA is of "regulation working with the grain of the market rather than against it."[388] The US approach appears not to be focused on risk but rather on the elimination of every possible form of misconduct, large or minor.

Another important contrast between the US and UK approaches is in the attitude toward "market failure." In general terms, there is market failure when the market cannot deliver the optimum welfare and maximum efficiency, which can only be provided with government intervention. Monopoly is a classic case of market failure because the market would deliver less output at a higher price than under perfect competition. The FSA reveals an interesting approach:[389]

> Even when empirical analysis shows that there has been a market failure, we are not always convinced that regulatory intervention is the most efficient and cost-effective form of correction.

In these cases, the FSA considers competition policy or the use of moral suasion with firms to change their behavior but "without reaching for the heavy-handed tool of the regulator's rule book."[390] Allegations of market failure trigger cost-benefit analysis and regulation in the United States.

The FSA enunciates principles of good regulation that orient its work:[391]

- *Efficiency and economy.* The Treasury can commission value-for-money reviews of the FSA as a form of controlling its efficiency and economy.
- *Management responsibility.* The nonexecutive committee of the Board of the FSA oversees excessive intrusion into the business of regulated firms. Senior management in firms is accountable for their risk management.
- *Proportionality.* The FSA must balance the proportionality of costs relative to benefits of regulation. It conducts professional cost-benefit analysis of measures.
- *Innovation.* The FSA considers alternative ways of compliance to avoid restricting innovation of financial products and services.
- *International view and competitiveness.* There is focus on the international nature of financial services and in maintaining the competitive position of the United Kingdom.
- *Competition.* The FSA diminishes the impact on competition of its regulatory measures and analyzes the need for competition among the regulated firms.

The outcomes-based approach of the FSA enables it to enhance its performance in improving markets.[392] The regulatory dividend of less intervention by the regulatory body is an incentive for firms to deliver compliance. The focus on compliance with rules detracts from sound judgment and enhanced knowledge of the business. The lack of flexibility and resulting opportunities causes a flight of skills out of an industry. The objective of the FSA is to maintain competent professionals in the financial services industry. Standards based on rules and authoritative enforcement do not prevent dishonesty.[393] The $65 billion worldwide Ponzi scheme over two decades originating in NY confirms this view.[394] The acceptance of risks by the regulators and the regulated firms may create a range of outcomes of judgments that can enhance market efficiency. The results of the work of the FSA are summarized as follows:[395]

> By the end of September this year [2007], companies had raised more capital on the main market of the London Stock Exchange, $26.7 billion, than the New York Stock Exchange and NASDAQ combined, $26.4 billion—and this didn't even include the $6.7 billion raised on the London Stock Exchange's alternative investment market.

International initial public offerings (IPO) even provide sharper contrast.[396] The London Stock Exchange (LSE) attracted 59 deals with combined value of $15.9 billion. In the same period, the NYSE and NASDAQ jointly had 17 deals in the combined value of $5.9 billion.

Proposals of capital market regulators

The SEC and the FSA are engaged in regulatory reform, following different approaches. The SEC is recommending to Congress that regulation of capital markets is required and should be central in the US planned regulatory overhaul.[397] There are three principles in the proposal of the SEC. First, there should be a capital markets regulator focused on investor protection. The justification for investor protection is based on the proposition that savings of the people are transferred through the capital markets to sound economic projects and financial needs that promote the growth of the economy. The focused regulator would protect savings, maintaining the "trust and confidence of investors and savers in the future."[398] There are core functions of the SEC within this principle: "regulation of market integrity, regulation of market information, regulation, and oversight of financial intermediaries and market professionals, regulation of mutual funds and other pools of funds and enforcement of the securities laws."[399]

Second, there should be an independent regulator of capital markets entrusted with investor protection. The authority and mission of the SEC are derived from Congress. The intention of Congress was to empower the SEC as the "investor's advocate."[400] The SEC builds a culture of investor protection with the objective of promoting the interest of the public and a strong economy. Investors expect the SEC to provide fair financial transactions, sound and timely disclosure of information and protection from fraud.

Third, the SEC has a role in the movement toward creating a systemic risk regulator. The argument is that "investor protection enhances the mission of controlling systemic risk."[401] Regulatory reform should include the protection of investors. The SEC can contribute to the effort of regulating major market functions and the evaluation of systemic risk.

The FSA has broader and more interconnected functions and concentrates on banking regulation. The proposed change in regulation of banks by the FSA is as follows:[402]

- *Systemic approach.* The impact of bank crises on the real economy is profound. Regulation should focus on preventing and responding to systemic risks.

- *Capital requirements, accounting and liquidity.* The quantity and quality of bank capital should be increased. In the past, trading losses, originating in the buying and selling of securities, were typically smaller in magnitude than credit losses. Basel II and other frameworks were designed without prior similar experience of major write downs in banks resulting from leveraged positions in complex instruments in banks. These positions were financed with short-term funds in SRPs in the belief that they were marketable, that is, could be easily sold at the price of acquisition or more. However, the assets in these positions became illiquid during the credit/dollar crisis. Trading book capital, or capital allocated to cushion the bank from losses in buying and selling of securities, should be increased by a multiple.[403] Basel II can accentuate the effects of business cycles. When the economy is booming, credit risks are lower resulting in lower capital requirements based on risk-weighted assets; the opposite is true during contractions when risks increase, causing increases in capital requirements. During booms the economy is encouraged to expand even more and in contractions to contract even more. Capital requirements should be based on estimates of risks during entire business cycles instead of at points in time, which was the practice and regulation before the credit/dollar crisis. The new approach intends to set capital requirements smoothing the business cycle. The FSA proposes higher capital requirements during economic expansions when banks have fewer losses from bad loans, creating a buffer that could be used during slowdowns when bad loans increase.[404] Accounting also created procyclical effects in bank balance sheets. During the sustained increase in security prices before the credit/dollar crisis, mark to market (MTM) accounting increased the values in the trading book; in the banking book loans retained their initial value because defaults were rare. The inflation of bank balance sheets provided incentives for risky behavior in leverage, credit, and remuneration. The FSA suggests a "nondistributable economic cycle reserve" that would provide for reserves in good years to offset losses in less favorable times in the future.[405] High leverage of assets to capital was a source of systemic risk when assets became illiquid. That is, banks borrowed funds to buy assets by high multiples of their capital. The FSA proposes a maximum gross leverage ratio of assets to capital.[406] Write downs of assets eroded bank capital, requiring bailouts with public funds. Liquidity regulation should be tightened with care on the trade-off that maturity transformation, or providing long-term loans for houses, automobiles and business needs, may diminish with adverse impacts on economic activity.

- *Institutions and geography.* The FSA proposes to obtain more information on hedge funds and to apply prudential regulation if they become similar to banks in systemic importance.[407] SIVs and similar vehicles should be brought on the balance sheet. Regulatory arbitrage, or creation of vehicles such as SIVs, is likely to increase in tightened regulation and should be deterred. Offshore vehicles should be subject to internationally agreed regulation.

- *Deposit insurance and bank resolution.* The FSA envisions a system of retail deposit insurance where most depositors would be protected from bank failures.[408] The Banking Act of 2009 assigned the FSA the role of deciding on bank resolution and provided Treasury, the Bank of England, and the FSA powers for orderly resolution.[409]

- *Credit ratings, remuneration, and derivatives.* Regulation can and should consider optimal governance and conduct of rating agencies, diminishing conflicts of interest. Credit ratings agencies could have provided more favorable ratings to clients. A code of remuneration is designed to prevent the increase in risk of bank operations because of inadequate compensation contracts. Clearing systems and netting of derivatives positions is also part of proposed regulation.

- *Macroprudential analysis.* Regulation will sharpen the analysis and tools of macroprudential policy. These are the methods used by central banks to smooth the fluctuations in economic activity originating in the financial system.

- *Supervisory approach*. The approach of the FSA will become more intrusive and systemic than in the earlier regime.
- *Risk management and governance*. The process of risk management and its supervision by senior management caused problems in individual banks during the credit/dollar crisis.[410] A new standard of risk management and governance is required to strengthen the financial system.
- *Large complex banks*. Increases in capital requirements for the trading book, liquidity regulation, and remuneration codes would regulate the riskier activities of broad banks without need of separation of commercial and investment banking.
- *Cross-border banks*. International cooperation through a college of international supervisors would ameliorate the problem that banks are global in their existence but may fail within the borders of their national origin.

The Sarbanes-Oxley Act of 2002

Regulation and the system of governance failed to prevent the corporate scandals of the turn of the millennium.[411] The checks and balances of the agency problem do not function perfectly in the case of overvalued equity. Equity is overvalued in the market when the company cannot produce earnings statements that support the market price of the stock. Overvaluations were significant. Enron was valued in the market at $70 billion when it was worth $30 billion.[412] Corporate cultures were redesigned to accommodate with targets the earnings required to support market valuations to prevent collapse of stock prices when announcements did not meet estimates. Decisions were distorted to maintain the overvaluations without regard to long-term economic value. M&As and LBOs could not create the profits required to be consistent with overvaluation. Governance failed in its role of preventing the agency costs of management decisions. Theory, evidence, and policy efforts are required to consider the effects of overvaluation of companies on the mechanisms of controlling agency costs.

There are numerous concerns with the consequences of SOX. The discussion below begins with an analysis of the structure of SOX. The various concerns are then discussed in turn. The SOX legislation was rushed in an election year after the WorldCom scandal. The costs of implementation are much higher in reality than anticipated and the benefits are difficult to measure. There is more emphasis in the literature on the excess of costs over benefits than the contrary view. The critical issue is whether SOX will affect governance in such a way as to create risk aversion in the management of public companies. If SOX were to affect the taking of risk by entrepreneurs it could retard the rate of economic growth of the United States, causing major damage to the country's competitiveness. There is growing literature showing that SOX can have stronger impacts on small and foreign companies. Finally, a significant part of SOX centers on gatekeepers, attorneys, and auditors, generating also differing views on the act.

The law

There were major declines of stock prices at the turn of the millennium but more pronounced in Europe than in the United States. An important approach explains the high incidence of corporate scandals in the United States relative to very few in Europe.[413] Restatements of financial statements soared in the United States in the years 1999–2002 preceding SOX. There is an explanation for the differing behavior in the concentrated ownership of companies in Europe versus the dispersed ownership prevailing in the United States.[414]

Table 5.2 has some of the elements of the theory.[415] There is much less market participation in concentrated companies, in which a few shareholders own most of the company, than in dispersed ownership companies, in which there are many shareholders owning small percentages. A key difference is that there is no incentive in equity prices in the concentrated system because controlling shareholders exercise command and control over management. Management is paid according to stock price performance in dispersed ownership systems. Thus, the type of fraud occurs in the expropriation of benefits of minority shareholders in the concentrated system versus anticipation and/or fabrication of earnings in the dispersed system. There is a revealing example of a company with price/earnings ratio of 30 to 1 paying 2 million shares to its CEO.[416] An increase in earnings by $1 causes an increase in price of $30 that can result in a payment to the CEO of $60 million. The difference in incentives explains the soaring restatement of earnings following stock market declines. The market has caused significant declines in the price of the stocks of companies engaged in this conduct. The gatekeeper failures, by auditors and boards, occur in the form of expropriation of minority shareholders in concentrated systems and in inflated earnings in the dispersed system.[417] The solution

Table 5.2   Corporate scandals according to Coffee

Ownership	Concentrated Ownership	Dispersed
Ownership	Controlling shareholders	Many shareholders
Disclosure standards	Lax	Rigorous
Transparency	Opaque	Transparent
Share turnover	Low	High
Securities markets	Weak	Strong
Management compensation	Cash	Equity options
Interest in stock market price	Low	High
Shareholder control	Command and control	Profit incentives
Disciplinary mechanisms	Banks, noncontrolling shareholders	Markets after restatements
Incidence of scandals	Low	High
Perpetrators	Controlling groups	Corporate managers
Victims	Minority shareholders	Shareholders
Type of fraud	Appropriation of benefits	Manipulation of Earnings
Examples	Parmalat	Enron, WorldCom
Gatekeeper failures	Benefit expropriation	Inflated earnings

Source: John C. Coffee, Jr., A theory of corporate scandals: why the USA and Europe differ. *Oxford Review of Economic Policy* 21 (2, 2005): 198–211.

given by SOX is to make auditing accountable to an independent auditing committee.

The US president signed SOX into law on July 30, 2002.[418] SOX created the Public Company Accounting Oversight Board (PCAOB) to oversee professional accounting in the United States. The objective of SOX was to strengthen corporate responsibility and financial disclosure, preventing corporate and accounting fraud. It was a reaction to the corporate scandals that followed the decline of the stock market after the high-tech collapse in 2000. The SEC issued numerous interpretations of rules and reports on SOX.[419]

The structure of SOX as it originally entered in force is in Table 5.3. There are 11 titles in SOX. The objective of the law is to generate rules of conduct for the principal participants in publicly issued securities. Title I is directed to the auditing and accounting profession. It creates the PCAOB as a nonprofit institution, entirely separate from the federal government. The PCAOB regulates the profession of public accounting firms to enforce compliance with SOX. Public accounting firms

Table 5.3   Structure of SOX

Established PCAOB 15 USC 7211 Title I
- Nonprofit corporation under the District of Columbia Nonprofit Corporation Act
- Not "an agency of establishment of the United States Government" Sec. 101(b)
- Duties of the PCAOB, Sec. 101(c):
  - "Register public accounting firms that prepare audit reports for issuers"
  - Determine standards of "auditing, quality control, ethics, independence and other standards relating to the preparation of audit report for issuers"
  - "Conduct inspections of registered public accounting firms"
  - "Conduct investigations and disciplinary proceedings" of registered public accounting firms and associated persons
  - Promote high professional standards by registered public accounting firms and associated persons
  - Mandatory registration of public accounting firms that prepare, issue, or participate in the preparation of any audit report to any issuer
  - Enforce compliance with SOX

Auditor Independence Title II
- Auditor reporting to audit committees, including communications with management
- Prohibited activities such as services to management
- Rotation of lead auditor after five consecutive years

Corporate Responsibility Title III
- Creation of corporate independent audit committee, Sec. 301, by amending 15 USC 78f Sec. 10A
- Objective: prevent management to mislead and influence public auditors
- Composition: entirely independent membership
- Role: hire the public auditor and communicate with it
- Complaints: procedures to receive complains of the public and anonymous complaints by employees
- Recommendation: one member should be a financial expert with knowledge of GAAP and financial statements
- Corporate responsibility for financial reports I: signing officers must certify reviewing the reports, that they do not have material misrepresentations and omissions and that they are complete
- Corporate responsibility for financial reports II: signing officers must certify their responsibility for internal controls, that such controls are adequate to ensure disclosure of all material information, that they have evaluated the effectiveness of the controls, that they have disclosed to the auditors and audit committee any deficiencies in the controls and frauds, and that all changes in the controls are disclosed
- Forfeiture of bonuses and compensation: the CEO and CFO forfeit bonuses and profits received in the 12-month period after filing of a report that requires restatement

---

Continued

Table 5.3 Continued

- Prohibition of insider trading during pension fund blackouts periods. Rules of professional conduct for attorneys: attorneys appearing before the SEC must report material violations of securities law, breach of fiduciary law or similar violation to the chief legal counsel or the CEO. If the counsel or CEO does not respond to the evidence, the attorney must report to the audit committee, another committee of the board of directors composed solely of independent directors or to the board of directors Sec. 307

Financial Disclosures Title IV
- Disclosure of all off–balance sheet transactions, arrangements, obligations, and other relationships with unconsolidated persons or entities
- Prohibition of personal loans to executives
- Disclosure of transactions of management and shareholders
- Assessment of internal controls by management
- Corporate code of ethics for senior financial officers
- Disclosure of financial expert in audit committee

Conflicts of Interests of Analysts Title V
- Objective: increase public confidence in analyst reports
- Rules of conflicts of interest by analysts
- Public disclosure of conflicts of interests by analysts

Accountability of Corporate and Criminal Fraud Title VIII
- Stiff penalties

Enhancement of White Collar Crime Penalty Title IX
- Stiff penalties

Corporate Tax Returns Title X
- Signature of corporate returns by the CEO

Corporate Fraud Accountability Title XI
- Increased criminal penalties

Source: http://www.sec.gov/about/laws/soa2002.pdf

involved in financial reports of issuers are required to register with the PCAOB, which will determine standards, conduct inspection, investigations, disciplinary processes, and issue rules, and take actions designed to promote high professional standards.

Title III introduces important measures of corporate responsibility. An important complaint that led to SOX was that management anticipated and/or fabricated earnings with the objective of receiving bonuses and higher compensation. Senior management of Fannie Mae and Freddie Mac fabricated earnings to obtain unearned performance compensation.[420] Sec. 301 created the corporate independent audit committee. Criteria have been introduced to ensure the independence of the members. The role of the audit committee is to directly hire the public auditors and to communicate with them. There is the recommendation that one member should be a financial expert with knowledge of Generally Agreed Accounting Principles (GAAP) and interpretation of financial statements. SOX enhanced corporate responsibility of financial reports by senior management signing financial reports. In addition, it made signing officers accountable for establishing and maintaining internal controls, disclosing to auditors and the public the deficiencies and fraud. SOX provided for the forfeiture of bonuses and profits from sale of corporate stock during the 12-month period following a financial report that is subsequently restated. It prohibited insider trading during pension fund blackout periods.

The disclosure requirements of financial reports are provided in Title IV. A critical provision is the disclosure of all off–balance sheet activities with unconsolidated persons or entities. In particular, this covers the SPEs that surfaced during the Enron events. SOX prohibits the loans of corporations to executives. It requires a corporate code of ethics for senior financial officers.

There were complaints about information by stock analysts after the end of the high-tech boom and during the restatements of balance sheets and the wider corporate scandals. SOX intends to improve the confidence of the public in the reports of analysts. It requires the public disclosure of potential conflicts of interests that analysts may have in their reports on stocks. Several titles of SOX provide enhanced penalties for violations and fraud.

Economic evaluation

The critical issue in the evaluation of SOX is whether the costs merit the benefits.[421] Some of the proposed benefits are questionable. The creation of a code of ethics in corporations need not deter dishonesty. Enron had a code of ethics but that did not prevent dishonesty.[422] There can also be high costs in defending the corporation from frivolous law suits based on provisions of the code of ethics. The defense and settlement costs could be quite onerous. SOX does not address another problem that is related to risk in prolonged upswings of markets that end in disappointment such as the high-tech crash. There is immense pressure on corporations and pension plans to beat the market, which leads to corporate behavior that is almost impossible to control by regulation. It is unlikely that corporate scandals were the cause of the decline in US stock prices in 2000.[423] In fact, the decline in foreign stock market prices were more pronounced.[424] It is unlikely that Enron had any impact on the decline of the US stock market. SOX was an overreaction to the corporate scandals.[425]

The costs of SOX are significant. Section 404 alone caused about $7 billion during the first year.[426] These are recurring yearly costs. AIG warned investors that the compliance costs could be as high as $300 million. The impact of the costs on smaller companies is proportionately much higher. An industrial company paid $15 million in a six-month period to comply with SOX, which represented about one-third of its profits.[427] Such a large proportionate cost could significantly reduce the market price of a company. The second impact on corporate costs derives from the time required by directors to deal with the work burden of SOX. This cost is multiplied by the consultants and attorneys required in fear of the draconian penalties of SOX. Another high expense is the opportunity cost of resources spent in complying with SOX that could otherwise be used for development of the corporation.[428]

Smaller and foreign companies bear significant indirect costs of SOX.[429] These companies chose the option of delisting to avoid the costs of SOX. Investors lose in lack of transparency of companies. The exodus of foreign companies deprives investors of attractive opportunities to diversify their portfolios. The costs of SOX reduce profits and thus returns to investors. It is an open issue if SOX produces benefits that exceed its costs.

SOX could be the "final act in regulation of corporate disclosure."[430] There is a critical issue if the costs of regulation have become sufficiently high to drive honest small and foreign companies from public registration. The costs of entirely eliminating fraud could be more expensive than allowing some fraud to exist.[431] Fraud should be prevented until the marginal cost of prevention is about equal to the returns from prevention. There is a social loss if the cost of prevention exceeds the returns. The main cost increase from SOX originates in Section 404 that is strictly confined to financial statements. The remaining aspects of corporate disclosure are left unchanged.[432] Most of the controls in SOX already existed and did not prevent episodes such as Enron and WorldCom. Concerted action by employees can defeat such controls. Section 404 is merely due diligence instead of protection against fraud. The impact of SOX is to impose procedures that would not be selected otherwise.

Section 404 is creating a cottage industry of consultants. The implementation of internal controls involves management at all levels that contract outside consultants.[433] CEOs head teams to operate these controls. Another structure of bureaucracy is being created in companies around a compliance officer. Auditing committees may retain counsel. SOX compliance also absorbs time of the CFO. The opportunity cost of compliance could be extremely high as the company abandons the focus on business development in favor of avoiding the penalties imposed by SOX. Risk aversion could have highly detrimental effects on the corporate culture of the United States, currently leading ahead of Europe and Japan in innovation. A culture of risk aversion could jeopardize the future growth of the US economy.

Some of the costs of complying with SOX will not be reported in the income statement.[434] These are the opportunity costs of complying with executive certification of financial statements, Section 302, and the certification of internal controls, Section 404. There are multiple direct costs of specialized staff required for compliance with these items. The available surveys of increases in costs caused by compliance with SOX show higher costs for every new survey.[435] Most of these surveys are for larger companies. It is difficult to find accurate estimates for smaller companies. There are about 16,000 companies requiring compliance with SOX.[436] Assuming a conservative estimate of $500,000 per company, the costs of complying with SOX are at least $8 billion per year. The estimates of losses of investors in Enron and WorldCom are about $100 billion. These were highly unusual losses and it is fair to argue that a part would not have been prevented by SOX. There is an estimate of the present value of the costs of compliance at $266 billion, using a 3 percent per year discount rate and assuming that the costs are as certain as death and taxes.[437] A study estimates the loss of $1.4 trillion in market value from the most significant rulemaking events. There is evidence of regulatory arbitrage with companies choosing other markets where to issue their stock.[438]

There are multiple advantages for a company to become private.[439] The private structure avoids numerous costs of public registration, including costs of litigation, higher directors and officers (D&O) insurance, and higher legal and accounting fees. In addition, an LBO provides the opportunity to sell large holdings that would obtain lower prices in thin markets. The total disclosed buyout transactions increased from $23.1 billion in 2001 to $136.5 billion in 2004. However, there are many factors determining LBOs that cannot be separated from the motivation of higher costs of compliance under SOX.

Corporate governance and performance

The analysis of research literature and data is used to support the view that SOX will not improve corporate governance or performance.[440] The emphasis of SOX on independent directors and independent audit committees is based on the presumption that independent directors receive fees as compensation instead of bonuses based on performance. Thus, independent directors will not feel tempted to falsify financing reporting. There is no empirical evidence in the research literature surveyed in support of the proposition that independent directors and audit committees improve corporate performance.[441] Congress did not match the problem of the corporate scandals with a solution.

Another measure of SOX is the banning of public corporations purchasing of nonaudit services from their auditors. The rationale for this measure is that management could possibly bribe the audit firms into misstatements by purchasing of nonaudit fees. Empirical research finds no relation of audit quality and the purchase of nonaudit services from the auditors.[442] The conclusion is that "SOX's prohibition of the purchase of nonaudit services from an auditor is an exercise in legislating away a nonproblem."[443] The result of no relation between audit quality and purchase of nonaudit services is the conclusion of the majority of scholarly research and the unanimous conclusion of the studies using the most advanced techniques. Moreover, the Panel on Audit Effectiveness does not find even one instance of compromise of an audit because of the purchasing of nonaudit services from the auditor by the audited company.[444]

SOX prohibits corporations, by Section 402(a), of extending loans to executive officers or directors. Corporate loans surfaced during the scandals of Enron, WorldCom, Tyco International, and Adelphia Communications. The objective of the prohibition is preventing the repetition of similar cases. The effectiveness of the measure is dubious.[445] Attempts to restrict the compensation of corporate executives typically result in different forms to maintain the compensation required to retain desired talent. SOX conflicts with the state law approach.[446] Most of the loans are used to facilitate the conversion of stock ownership provided in remuneration packages. Thus, the loans merely serve to align the interests of shareholders and managers. In this sense, the prohibition "is self-evidently a public policy error."[447] The issues have been settled for decades by means of state laws.

The difficulty in providing an optimum model of corporate governance is an important issue regarding SOX.[448] The structure of SOX favors a board of independent directors engaged in policing fraud. It is not necessarily valid that an independent board is the best model of governance. There is the competing model of board composition in which the directors are appointed on the merits of their business knowledge. The board members contribute to the development of the corporate business model in ways that are far superior to policing fraud. Moreover, it is doubtful that board members could protect shareholders from fraud by management. SOX constitutes an intrusion in the ideal corporate governance. It appears more likely that Congress and regulators will be inferior to the actual selection of work of the board and its relation to the corporate business. Contributions of the board to business development are likely to bring more returns to investors than independent boards engaged in policing misconduct by management. There is here the recurring theme with SOX that it interferes with the strengthening of US business competitiveness. In this view, "the increasing intrusion of federal law into how corporations go about their business threatens to sacrifice the prime objective of corporate productivity."[449] Federal intrusion shifts the focus of corporations away from innovation, creation of jobs, efficiency, and global competitiveness.

An important characteristic of the federalist system of corporate law is its responsiveness to changing business conditions.[450] An important example is how the Delaware courts created legal standards on takeovers, protecting the board in its oversight of control changes. Simultaneously, the courts of Delaware protect the market for corporate control. Federal intrusion in the process of state development of corporate law would restrict the process.

The focus on the internal controls provided in Section 404 of SOX has detracted attention from the burdens imposed on the CEO and CFO by Section 302: certification of the accuracy of disclosures, responsibility for internal controls, design of controls to ensure material information, evaluation of internal controls in the prior 90 days, reporting conclusions about effectiveness, changes, and corrective actions.[451] Audit Standard No. 2 (AS-2) of the PCAOB is expensive on the requirements of the audit of internal controls. It intrudes into the corporate governance process and requires "every input that goes into the process of financial reporting, as well as the mechanisms for translating those inputs into the financial reports."[452] This includes all base data originating in daily operations of a corporation. The evaluation of the control environment requires the assessment of the effectiveness of the audit committee. The ineffectiveness of the audit committee could be a failure of internal controls. The view prevailing before SOX was that the evaluation by an audit of the internal controls was not fraud prevention but rather a form of increasing confidence in the data of the company.[453]

The standard is the more than remote probability of misstatement that can be more than inconsequential. There is the issue of depth of the inquiry, double-checking, and surveillance of the control environment in the compliance with the standard of more than remote likelihood.[454] The issue of the costs and benefits of SOX centers on the need for state intervention. The two main reasons are the principal-agent problem and the aging of systems that may not work in current environments.[455] Addressing these problems requires much less effort than the instructions in AS-2, which create an extremely laborious search throughout the entire firm. The net result is an increase in personnel and paperwork.

A fundamental flaw of SOX is that it does not address the essential problem relating to episodes such as Enron, which is the complexity of transactions in the current business environment. An important consideration is the complexity of financial derivatives and the intangible nature of assets, both of which are bona fide vehicles of business.[456] Basel II was the result of almost a full decade of contributions by authorities in central banking, commercial and investment banking, the financial sector, academics, legal scholars, and critiques of every occupation. SOX will not prevent future scandals because it does not focus on the accounting failures of complex transactions.[457] It is arguable that regulators and legislators may not be more adept at the task of solving the accounting hurdles than the private sector.

Gatekeepers

On January 29, 2003, the SEC approved the final rule on implementing standards for corporate responsibility of attorneys under SOX.[458] Part 205.3(b)(1) requires reporting of evidence of a material violation for an attorney representing an issuer. The evidence on the material violation can be obtained from any officer, director, employee, or agent of the issuer. The attorney shall report the evidence to the chief legal officer (CLOF) of the issuer or to both the CLOF and the CEO. SOX requires internal reporting of the evidence of material violation but only voluntary reporting to the SEC.[459] The courts should protect unclear whistleblower rights of reporting attorneys.[460] Part 205.3(b)(2) requires that the CLOF conduct an inquiry to determine if a material violation is ongoing, has occurred, or is about to occur. The CLOF would then advise the reporting attorney of the determination reached and shall engage in all reasonable steps to have the issuer adopt a proper response. The CLOF will also advise the reporting attorney of this effort. The CLOF also has the option of referring a report of evidence of a material complaint to a qualified legal compliance committee (QLCC). Part 205.3(b)(3) provides that the reporting attorney continue reporting the evidence of material violation unless satisfied with the response of the CLOF. The secondary reporting will be to the audit committee of the issuer's board of directors, another committee of independent directors, or the board of directors. Part 205.3(c) provides that the response to the reporting attorney can be conducted by a QLCC and then is no longer required to evaluate the response of the QLCC.

The SEC encourages the use of QLCCs because they would constitute effective corporate governance.[461] An important benefit to the reporting attorney is that there is no need to evaluate the response of the QLCC as in reporting to the CLOF. The arrangement is a convenient option that benefits the companies and their attorneys.[462] If the CLO receives the complaint, it can be referred to the QLCC, which will evaluate it. The SEC has provided significant flexibility in the composition of the QLCC. It can be the audit committee or another committee composed exclusively of independent directors. The QLCC must have at least one member from the audit committee and at least two independent members of the board of directors. No member of the QLCC is required to be an attorney or have a law degree.[463] The confidentiality of the inquiry should not conflict with SOX. An attorney can provide the confidential report to the SEC to prevent unlawful activity when involved in an investigation for potential violation of reporting requirements. The QLCC has authority to notify the SEC if the issuer fails to implement a proper response recommended by the QLCC.

The main issue with the QLCC and SOX is the reconciliation of costs and benefits. The SEC believes that the costs are not significantly above the administrative expenses of establishing the committee.[464] The members of the QLCC are already members of the audit committee and the board. There are additional administrative costs. However, the costs of liability insurance of committee members may increase because of the additional service in the QLCC.[465] As in similar cases, it is easier to estimate costs than potential benefits.

Aggressive accounting consists of premature recognition of earnings in financial statements. A study by the US General Accounting Office (GAO) finds aggressive earnings management in 39 percent of the 919 financial restatements in 1997–2002.[466] SOX created the expectation that penalties will be more severe for misrepresentation of facts in financial statements, increasing to as high as $5 million and 20 years of imprisonment. The research issue is if SOX created disincentives for management to use its discretion in overstating earnings, becoming more conservative under uncertainty and increased liability. US firms are more conservative in financial reporting in the first two years after SOX than in the two years immediately preceding SOX.[467]

The objective of Section 404 of SOX is to prevent false financial reports by mandating management and independent auditors to report on the effectiveness of internal controls. There is an argument that the objective is misguided.[468] The internal controls contemplated in SOX were not designed to prevent frauds. In addition, such controls were already unsuccessfully mandated in the Foreign Corrupt Practices Act of 1976 (FCPA). There is nothing new in requiring independent auditors to evaluate internal controls. The definition of internal controls of the PCAOB can be analyzed as being centered on the objective of the reliability of financial reporting. This definition does not take into account crucial aspects of the objective and design of internal controls.[469]

The more appropriate process to internal controls is enterprise risk management (ERM).[470] This risk analysis must cover all business activities. The critical risk is that resulting from the management process. Corporate frauds originate in strategies and objectives of management that corrupt the accounting process. Another activity that requires care is information. Most internal controls are designed to prevent errors not deliberately falsifying data. The other areas of activity are operation and compliance. Errors in operation and compliance can generate data errors. Compliance is part of the operational risks of Basel II. Internal controls should not be viewed as preventing or detecting major business problems. The effectiveness of internal controls simply assures that strategies and objectives designed and directed by management are attained.

The reporting required under Section 302 of SOX of the effectiveness of internal controls on financial reporting cover two dimensions, materiality and likelihood. The deficiency or combination of deficiencies must result in material misstatement in the financial report. In addition, the likelihood that the failure of the controls is not reported must exceed a remote possibility. There is a sample using the 10–K filings from August 2002 to November 2004 of 261 companies that reported 493 distinct deficiencies of internal controls.[471] There are interesting descriptive aspects of the sample. While the segment of computers accounts for 13.7 percent of firms, it accounts for 21.4 percent of the firms with material weakness in the sample. Banks account for 22.1 percent of the firms within the industry but account for only 9.2 percent of the firms with material weakness within the industry. The explanation for the latter case is that banks must file a yearly report with supervisors on the effectiveness of their controls. There is potential for the experience of banks to be useful in compliance with Section 404.

Lack of sufficient employees and insufficient training are important deficiencies that can cause misstatement of financial reports.[472] These problems are significant in reporting complex accounts; derivatives and income taxes constitute the most important cases of complex accounts. There are major specific account deficiencies in the case of accounts receivables, accounts payable, and inventory accounts. Statistical research provides evidence of positive association between material weakness disclosures and profitability.[473] There are numerous research issues in explaining this relationship. Material weakness is positively associated with complexity of business measured by the number of operating segments and foreign currency translation. There is inverse relationship between material weakness and firm size. The audit by a large audit firm is positively related with reporting material weakness.

The market for audit reports can be analyzed by means of the information asymmetry model.[474] Public accounting firms are sellers of the audit report and investors and creditors are the buyers. The two conditions of asymmetry of information[475] are present in this market.[476] The first condition is the difference in quality of the product. There are high-quality audit reports that truly represent the financial position of the audited firm in accordance with Generally Accepted Auditing Principles (GAADP). However, there are also lemons or low-quality audit reports that do not represent the actual financial position of the audited firm. The second condition is asymmetry of information: the auditing firms may have information that the reports are substandard while the investors and creditors believe that the reports are of high quality. There is thus market failure or in this case auditing failure requiring government intervention.

The deterioration in the quality of reports by Andersen, culminating in the Enron episode, illustrates the needs for "counteracting mechanism."[477] The theoretical model of information asymmetry provides these mechanisms in the form of licensing, regulation and concerns for reputation. The licensing and regulation of the auditing profession by the states and professional institutions did not prevent the Enron episode. There are incentives for producing low quality auditing reports.[478] The remuneration of management with performance-linked stock options could have caused deterioration in the accuracy of the information provided by audited firms to their auditors with the purpose of artificially inflating stock prices. Consolidation created similar pressures in auditing firms to retain clients at all costs, lowering standards and accommodating management.

The incentives of SOX are in the form of independent auditing committees in firms, prohibition of sale of products by auditors to the audited firms and so on. SOX also created the PCAOB to oversee the auditing business. A specific proposal is that the PCAOB "include assessments of the control environment and the ethical climate as part of their annual inspections of public accounting firms."[479] There is special emphasis in this proposal on the need of reviews of the ethical climate of auditing firms.

Regulation and the choice of exchange listing

SOX, ostensive prosecution by regulatory agencies, civil litigation and similar restrictions are blamed for the exodus of finance from New York City to other locations, in particular London.[480] The exodus is compared to the permanent relocation of banking, FX and derivatives from New York City to London.[481] This section considers the disputed evidence on the exodus, the reason for a company going public or listing in an exchange and the listing in exchanges located in jurisdictions other than that of origin or cross-listing.

There are trade-offs of costs and benefits in the decision of going public.[482] The firm incurs registration costs with the regulators and exchanges and also with the underwriting investment bank. There are additional costs in meeting disclosure requirements, which could be high under regimes such as that of SOX. The public firm is typically run by hired managers that may enter into the principal/agent problem of conflict with the owners. A main benefit is the opportunity to obtain external financing in equity markets by attracting many investors who buy into the public company. The cost of capital in an equity offering may be lower than by banking relations and other forms of debt. The public company is reviewed by analysts and institutional investors, reducing the cost of monitoring to shareholders. The listing in a stock exchange increases the marketability and liquidity of the shares.

A group or party typically has control of a company. The private benefits from control of this group constitute an important determinant of the decision of going public.[483] There are numerous benefits from control such as psychic pleasure in commanding a corporation and the perquisites of the agency problem, which do not explain the premium paid for the acquisition of the company. If a manager finds an innovation in organization or technology that increases significantly the value of the company, she may find her own vehicle to realize the gains. This is especially the case in companies in which ownership is concentrated in a few owners, in privatization through public offerings and in less developed capital markets.[484]

Companies list in foreign markets outside their jurisdiction of origin because of three general reasons.[485] First, there is a set of financial incentives. Stock markets such as those in New York City and London are deeper, providing the opportunity of raising large volumes of financing. Those markets are more adequate for controlling shareholders to sell their stake in the stock of a company to realize partial or full private benefits of control. Because of a higher number and diversity of shareholders, such as institutional investors (mutual, pension, and hedge funds), stocks are more marketable or liquid. Higher liquidity means lower spread between buying and selling prices and brokerage fees. Analysts in larger markets reduce the cost of monitoring firms and disseminate information. There is less risk of mispricing stocks. Second, there is an incentive of reputation and resulting lower capital costs by cross-listing in an exchange located in the same geographical region as the market for a company's products. Third, companies may cross-list to benefit from lower costs of listing and disclosure.

Law firm calculations and academic research provide input for the calculation of costs and benefits of listing in US markets after SOX.[486] In the case of a company with small capitalization listed in the broader market covered by the Standard & Poor's 500 index, the total costs of compliance are $2.1 million per year, consisting of direct costs of $1 million and additional indirect costs of loss of productivity of $1 million. Enhanced transparency and governance reduce costs by $6.75 million. Thus, benefits exceed costs even for small-cap companies. There was a dramatic increase in the biggest awards in class action lawsuits from $150 million in 1997 to $9.7 billion in 2005. There was additional increase in litigation costs from the Attorney General of New York and lawsuits against directors. There is a proposal for a Regulation Oversight Board that could calculate the costs of compliance, benefits, and potential deadweight costs.[487]

The bonding theory explains cross-listings by the higher standards of disclosure and enforcement of US exchanges.[488] Both private and public enforcement of rules have value for cross-listing. The firms that cross-list originate in jurisdictions that have weaker protection of minority investors. Cross-listing is desired to attain higher market valuation. However, many eligible firms do not cross-list. The argument is refined by considering that firms which cross-list have higher growth potential and the willingness to sacrifice some of the private benefits of control to obtain financing required for growth.

The bonding theory is consistent with the characteristics of a comprehensive data set of the listing decisions of firms in 1990–2005.[489]

Firms listing in the LSE main market and the New York exchanges are large, with median total assets between $600 million and $700 million. These firms have low leverage below 20 percent of assets and are growing rapidly, with ownership concentrated. There is a measured premium for listing in the New York exchanges yearly and permanent over time, with no evidence that it declined after 2001. The conclusion of this research is that enhanced governance of listing in US exchanges is not available by listing in London or exchanges outside the United States.[490]

Summary

There are arguments that SOX merely imposed onerous requirements on corporations well in excess of benefits. A competing view argues that protection of shareholder rights is critical in the choice of listing in the US exchanges. There is ongoing debate on the premium of listing equities in exchanges in the United States relative to London and other markets.

6
Regulation and Policy in the Global Recession

Introduction

The forecast of the International Monetary Fund (IMF) in April 2009 is for world output declining by 1.3 percent in 2009, bouncing by 1.9 percent in 2010 after growing by 5.2 percent in 2007, and 3.2 percent in 2008.[491] Output in advanced countries is forecast to decline by 3.8 percent in 2009, growing by 0 percent in 2010. US output would decline by 2.8 percent in 2009, growing by 0 percent in 2010. The volume of world trade of goods and services is forecast to decline by 11 percent in 2009, bouncing by 0.6 percent in 2010 after growing by 7.2 percent in 2007 and by 3.3 percent in 2008. Recession in the form of contraction of output or sharp reduction in the rate of growth affects the entire world. The first section below reviews the experience and analysis of the Great Depression and the New Deal. The critical issue for the regulatory agenda is what caused the credit crisis and resulting global recession. Several sections analyze the monetary and fiscal policies. Bank nationalization is an important issue in regulatory debate. The final section outlines the heavy regulatory agenda.

The New Deal

One of the most common phrases in all types of analysis of the credit/dollar crisis is that it is the worst credit crisis and recession since the Great Depression of the 1930s. There is frequent mention of the Great Depression in analysis and policy for the credit/dollar crisis.[492] Significant part of the regulatory framework of the United States was created during the 1930s. This section provides a synthesis of the voluminous research on the Great Depression. The initial discussion presents the data on output, which is followed by consideration of the various interpretations: monetary, debt deflation, financial, gold standard, nonmonetary, wages, and employment and growth.

The Great Depression of the 1930s consisted of a unique phenomenon in terms of economic contraction worldwide. Its impact was particularly strong in the United States. Table 6.1 shows US GDP in current dollars, or without adjusting for changes in prices, and in constant dollars, or adjusting for changes in prices. The decline in real or price adjusted GDP in 1930–3 accumulated to 25.7 percent. The decline in GDP in current dollars or without adjusting for prices in 1930–3 accumulated to 44 percent. It is possible that there was recovery in employment and dynamism in the US economy only after the beginning of the effort to win World War II.

A counterfactual is the most common and difficult empirical hurdle in economics. The economist observes the data, such as output (GDP), money stock (currency plus bank deposits), and prices (consumer and wholesale price indexes), as it occurred under the influence of many factors. It is typically very difficult to isolate the causes of economic events. The counterfactual requires measuring the same data under different economic policies. Perhaps the most important counterfactual in US history is what would have happened if the Fed had followed a

Table 6.1   US GDP growth 1930–45 (in percent)

	Current Dollars	Constant Dollars
1930	−12.0	−8.6
1931	−16.1	−6.4
1932	−23.2	−13.0
1933	−4.0	−1.3
1934	17.0	10.8
1935	11.1	8.9
1936	14.3	13.0
1937	9.7	5.1
1938	−6.2	−3.4
1939	7.0	8.1
1940	10.0	8.8
1941	25.0	17.1
1942	27.7	18.5
1943	22.7	16.4
1944	10.7	8.1
1945	1.5	−1.1
1946	−0.4	−11.0

Source: US Bureau of Economic Analysis, Department of Commerce.

different policy. The original statement of this counterfactual is that the contraction of the money stock by one-third in 1929–33 resulting from failure of LOLR functions by the Fed converted what could have been a typical recession into the devastating Great Depression.[493] During the Great Depression 9440 banks failed, constituting about 40 percent of commercial banks in the United States.[494] If the Fed had followed a policy of constant increase of the money stock instead of interventions without much knowledge of future events, the counterfactual analysis argues that the failure of the banks would not have occurred and the Great Depression would have been a moderate recession.

Another strand of thought posits that excessive debt followed by deflation is the cause of depressions.[495] After excessive indebtedness, there is deflation, or decline in prices, the opposite of inflation. Deflation causes fire sales in the effort to prevent losses caused by lower prices. Bank deposits decline as loans are repaid. The public turns money into goods less frequently, causing further decline of prices. Businesses are tied to debt contracts at fixed interest rates contracted before the decline in prices. Deflation contracts profits of business as sales decline. Lower profits erode the net worth of companies that default in their loans, causing bank failures. Businesses decrease production and investment because of lower profits. Lower investment and production cause contraction of output, commerce, and employment. Pessimism or loss of confidence dominates decisions, causing further decreases of prices. Joint occurrence of deflation and depression has been extremely rare, occurring only in the Great Depression for eight countries in a sample of 17 countries over more than 100 years.[496] There is no empirical association of deflation and depression.

There is an analysis of the transmission of the Great Depression based on the breakdown of banking intermediation.[497] This view departs from the friction of asymmetry of information in the first-best model of perfect competition. Financial intermediaries provide important functions of gathering information on prospective debtors and making markets in loans and deposits. Banks have intermediation costs in transferring funds from savers and lenders to creditworthy borrowers in the form of screening, monitoring, accounting, and provisions for default. The banking panics of the 1930s raised the intermediation costs of banks. The reaction of banks was to increase their assets that could be readily converted into cash. The resulting credit crunch affected households, farmers, and small firms. Deflation eroded the collateral that could be used in obtaining loans. The output contraction resulting from the credit crunch converted a milder recession into the Great Depression.

The transmission of the Great Depression worldwide is typically attributed to the Gold Standard by which countries fixed their exchange rates. The exchange rate is the units of domestic currency per unit of foreign currency, for example the dollars required to purchase a unit of the European currency, the euro. Suppose that the exchange rate is $1.3374 per euro. An export of the United States to Europe of $10,000 would be worth 7477 euros, obtained by dividing $10,000 by $1.3374/ euro. If the dollar devalues to $1.5618/euro, that is, you pay more dollars per euro, the $10,000 export of the United States is worth 6403 euros, or $10,000 divided by $1.5618/euro. Depreciation of the dollar can make US goods cheaper in Europe, increasing exports, or sale of goods abroad by the United States, and tending to decrease imports, making the sale of foreign goods more expensive in the United States. The 1930s were characterized by competitive devaluations of countries abandoning the Gold Standard and also by tariffs and quotas to prevent the entry of goods from other countries. These protectionist policies were coined as "beggar my neighbor remedies for unemployment" by a distinguished economist of the time.[498] The current threat is a breakdown of international cooperation with regulation, trade, and devaluation wars.[499] The Group of 20 countries accounting for more than 85 percent of world output has experienced protectionist measures in 17 of its members. The countries that abandoned early by mid-1931 the fixed exchange rates of the gold standard suffered comparatively less and recovered faster than those that delayed the devaluation of their currencies.[500]

There is no evidence of substantial recovery in economic activity during the Great Depression from increasing federal government expenditures.[501] In fact, the impact of government spending on output was of smaller magnitude in the Roosevelt administration than in the preceding Hoover administration. There is no information suggesting that government spending was used during the Roosevelt administration to reverse the impact of the Depression on economic activity. However, fiscal policies may have been important in the recovery that eventually occurred with the advent of World War II.[502]

The recovery of the United States from the Great Depression was promoted by the inflow of gold after 1933. The inflow of gold increased the money supply, lowering interest rates. Lower interest rates stimulated consumption and investment expenditure. There was a negligible effect of fiscal policy.[503] The decline of the stock market caused uncertainty in the public, leading to contraction of consumer spending that accentuated the Great Depression in 1930.[504]

The rate of unemployment of the United States increased from 3.2 percent in 1929 to 22.9 percent or 23.6 percent in 1932, according to two different estimates, while real wages increased by 16.4 percent.[505] By 1940, the rate of unemployment was 17.2 percent or 9.5 percent, according to different estimates, while real wages increased by 44 percent.[506] Using disaggregated data, analysis finds that the unemployed of the 1930s were mostly workers earning low wages who remained unemployed for long periods.[507] Many of the unemployed were absorbed in sustained worker relief under the Works Progress Administration (WPA) or similar federal or state relief agencies, which provided more stable jobs than in the private sector. The increases in aggregate demand could have reduced long-term unemployment outside the worker relief programs.[508] This explains why the 1930s were characterized by increasing real wages for those employed, long period of unemployment, and high aggregate rates of unemployment. It also explains why unemployment was only reduced with the huge labor demands of the war economy.

In 1929–33, the United States experienced a decline of employment by 25 percent and of output by 30 percent.[509] In 1939, employment and output remained substantially below their levels in 1929. The severity of the Great Depression is shown by real per capita output remaining 11 percent below the 1929 level while real per capita output typically increases by 31 percent in a ten-year period. The 1930s were characterized by significant decline in employment. Total hours worked, reflecting changes in employment and in hours per worker, fell by more than total employment, with a trough only in 1934, remaining in 1939 below the 1929 level by 29 percent.[510] Private hours, excluding hours by government workers, fell more sharply than total hours because there were no losses in government hours; by 1939 private hours fell 25 percent relative to the level in 1929. The labor data suggest that the economy declined to a lower path level than the one prevailing in 1929.

There are three phases in the New Deal.[511] First, the National Industrial Recovery Act (NIRA) in 1933–5 linked collusion or high prices negotiated by monopolistic firms, suspending antitrust law enforcement if the industry accepted collective bargaining and immediately increased wages. Second, the Supreme Court declared the NIRA unconstitutional in 1935; the National Labor Relations Act (NLRA) in 1935 and the ruling of its constitutionality by the Supreme Court in 1937 strengthened collective bargaining, union representation and strikes, together with bland enforcement of antitrust prosecution by the Department of Justice. Third, toward the end of the 1930s Roosevelt became disillusioned with the recovery of the economy by high prices and wages and the war eliminated the distortion linking firm collusion with labor bargaining power.

An adviser of Roosevelt suggested a return to the policy of World War I of relaxing antitrust law enforcement to increase cooperation among firms, raising wages and output; such policies would promote growth similar to that during World War I.[512] Analysis measures the performance of the balanced growth paths of a cartel or monopolistic model similar to the phases of the New Deal and a perfectly competitive model.[513] The combination of cartels with substantial labor bargaining power depresses aggregate output and employment, explaining significant parts of the failure of the United States in fully recovering in the 1930s. The cartel model predicts output in 1939 that is 14 percent below the competitive balanced growth path and labor input 11 percent below the competitive balanced growth path, explaining 50–60 percent of the depression of output and labor input after 1933. The model also provides an explanation for the return to recession in 1937–8 and the movement toward full employment during World War II when the policies were relaxed.

What caused the credit crisis and global recession?

There are two general views on the causes, duration, and severity of the credit crisis and global recession, which are stylized below. First, the regulatory view explains the crisis and recession in terms of failures of financial markets. The FSA provides an interpretation of the origin, severity, and duration of the credit/dollar crisis.[514] Low interest rates in this view are explained by the savings imbalances in the world. High savings rates in countries such as China and Japan resulted in investment in government securities in countries such as the United States, causing a decline in real interest rates (adjusted for inflation) from levels around 3 percent in the 1990s to about 1.5 percent in the beginning years of the new millennium. Investors facing low returns on financial assets generated demand for higher yielding alternatives. There is no magic in higher yields other than increasing leverage and risk in mismatches such as borrowing on overnight SRPs to finance pools of 30-year mortgages in MBS. Financial innovations developed to cater for this voracious risk appetite of investors. Structured credit products accommodated the increase in credit demand propelled by low interest rates. Securitization grew at extremely high rates after 1995 in a system of "originate to distribute," with financial institutions originating credit to all sectors but primarily to households and the financial system, distributing in the form of securities backed by the pools of credit. Financial institutions did not transfer risk completely but kept on and off balance sheets part of the new riskier products. There is a contemporary approach to "animal spirits":[515]

> The term 'animal spirits,' popularized by John Maynard Keynes is related to consumer or business confidence, but it means more than that. It refers also to the sense of trust we have in each other, our sense of fairness in economic dealings and our sense of the extent of corruption and bad faith. When animal spirits are on ebb, consumers do not want to spend and businesses do not want to make capital expenditures or hire people.

The resolution of the crisis and global recession requires the taming of these animal spirits by regulation and prudential macroeconomic policies, such as fiscal stimulus.

Second, an alternative view posits that the crisis and the recession were caused by regulatory failure.[516] The essential calculus of risk and return in financial decisions and productive investment was distorted. The first lowering of interest rates toward zero propagated through the financial structure of securitization, causing mispricing of risk, low volatility, and high leverage. The prolonged and substantial subsidy of housing in the United States, calculated at $221 billion per year,[517] and the entry of Fannie Mae and Freddie Mac in subprime and Alt-A mortgages[518] were key contributors to the erosion of the calculus of risk and the magnitude, propagation and duration of the recession. The timing of entry of Fannie Mae and Freddie Mac in subprime and Alt-A mortgages coincided with the acceleration of that market from $395 billion in 2003 to $715 billion in 2004, reaching $1005 billion in 2005.[519] In addition, the GSE remained in the market after the interruption in the rise of house prices in 2006. The combined acquisition or guaranteeing of subprime and Alt-A mortgages by Fannie Mae and Freddie Mac reached $1.6 trillion, accounting for one half of the total outside the FHA.[520] Interest rates at or near zero indefinitely were part of the subsidy to housing. Families and financial institutions acted on the belief that there was no risk in the price of houses and financial assets such as mortgages because the central banks would maintain low interest rates forever. The Fannie Mae and Freddie Mac disaster casts doubts on public-private partnerships.

The maximum perceived risk to the debtors was to live in a better house until the teaser rates converted into onerous payments when the house could be sold at a profit. The creditors would never lose even in foreclosure because the house could be sold to recover at least the principal and perhaps a profit. There was no collective irresponsibility of families and financial institutions that were actually misled by housing and interest rate policies. The other possible causes of the credit/dollar crisis could have been the new financial structure, lack of regulation of derivatives, mortgage origination, systemic risk, failure of risk management models, and others. The use of Fannie Mae and Freddie Mac to broaden house ownership together with the elimination of the 30-year Treasury bond may have contributed more to real estate exuberance than the separation of mortgage origination, distribution, and short-term financing. None of these probable causes could have created the severe credit/dollar crisis without interest rates close to zero. The lowering of interest rates is the prime suspect of the necessary condition for the credit crisis. This is not a criticism of the intentions of central banking but rather of the almost impossible task of lowering and increasing interest rates without more precise knowledge of the future and of the impact of policy instruments on the financial and real sectors of the economy. It is simplistic to argue that only markets failed when government also failed.

The focus of policy should be in balancing regulation with market allocation. The crisis was prolonged and deepened by the confusion by the central banks of a liquidity problem with deterioration of the perception of counterparty risk. Credit was paralyzed because ABS could not be financed in short-term markets as prospective providers of finance were uncertain on the credit quality of the pools of assets bundled in securities. Credit originates in the financing of ABS securities backed by pools of credit such as mortgages, credit cards, vehicle loans, and student loans. The fed lowered interest rates too fast and by too much after August 2007 and injected massive liquidity that fueled increases in oil prices while counterparty risk uncertainties continued constraining credit. A balanced approach needs to include the possibility that both markets and governments fail to guide the search for balanced policy options.

The instruments of monetary policy

The strategy of the Fed is self-described as "credit easing."[521] It is predicated on a congressional mandate to promote full, sustained employment with stable prices. Simultaneously, the Fed seeks congressional authority for resolution of "systemically critical nonbank financial institutions" such as AIG.[522] There are restrictions in the design of policy. The Fed will refrain from taking credit risk or channeling credit to narrow classes of sectors and borrowers. Monetary policy should not be compromised by the easing of credit.

The policy followed by the Fed resembles the "quantitative easing" by the Bank of Japan to recover the economy from prolonged deflation. The Fed has lowered the fed funds rate to 0 to 0.25 percent per year. In quantitative easing, the central bank injects more liquidity than what is required to maintain the fed funds rate at 0 percent. The objective of policy is to cause reductions in long-term interest rates that could stimulate investment and economic recovery.[523] Quantitative easing is implemented by expanding and changing the composition of the Fed's balance sheet.

Table 6.2 provides a simplified Fed balance sheet in February 2008 and a year later in February 2009. The data are available weekly at the Web site of the Fed. The assets held by the Fed increased substantially, from $855 billion in 2008 to $1844 billion in 2009. Moreover, they are programed to increase by $1.25 trillion with a new facility of purchasing long-term securities. The Fed used to hold most of its assets in

Table 6.2   Federal Reserve System simplified balance sheet (in billions of dollars and percent)

	Feb 13, 2008	Feb 11, 2009	Percent change
Assets	855.1	1844.9	115.7
Securities and Loans	801.4	1079.1	34.7
Treasury Securities	713.4	524.1	−26.5
Central Bank Swaps	n.a.	390.9	–
Holding Commercial Paper	n.a.	251.2	–
Other	53.7	123.7	–
Liabilities and Capital	855.1	1844.9	115.7
Net FRS Notes	778.9	856.0	9.9
Deposits	23.4	862.3	36.9*
Depositary Institutions	18.0	600.1	33.3*
Treasury Supplementary	n.a.	199.9	–
Capital	37.8	41.4	9.5
Other	38.4	85.2	121.8

*Multiples
Source: FRBO http://www.federalreserve.gov/releases/h41/
Ben S. Bernanke, The crisis and the policy response. London, Stamp Lecture, London School of Economics, Jan 13, 2009. http://www.federalreserve.gov/newsevents/speech/bernanke20090113a.htm

Treasury securities, $801 billion in 2008, but declining significantly to $524 billion in 2009. The holdings of Treasury securities were used in the open market operations of monetary policy. The liabilities of the Fed provide the source of growth of the balance sheet. There was a monumental increase in idle reserves deposited by banks at the Fed, from $18 billion in February 2008 to $600.1 billion in February 2009. The lack of investment and lending opportunities of banks and the increase in demand deposits were important causes of this unprecedented high level of idle reserves of banks at the Fed.[524] However, the Fed motivated the increase by paying interest on required and excess reserve balances with a decision on October 8, 2008, to anticipate the Financial Services Regulatory Relief Act of 2006, which provided for interest payments as of October 1, 2011.[525] The Fed intended to maintain the fed funds rate at target levels by paying interest on excess and required reserve balances.

The supplementary Treasury account of $199.9 billion also contributed to funding the Fed.[526] The supplementary Treasury account consists of the issue of Treasury bills by Treasury with proceeds deposited in an account of the FRS, resulting in draining of bank reserve balances.[527] This account peaked at $559 billion in 2008, declining to $259 billion by year end.

The combined resources allowed the Fed to increase its balance sheet by 115.7 percent, from $855.1 billion in February 2008 to $1844.9 billion in February 2009. Table 6.3 provides the new facilities created by the Fed. The most important initial facility was the provision of liquidity through the Term Auction Facility (TAF) because the Fed reacted to the crisis as in most similar cases as if it were a liquidity problem. The TAF assured financial institutions that there would be sufficient liquidity to meet runs. Subsequent facilities were created to meet squeezes in various parts of the financial system: securities dealers, financing of ABS, money market funds, mortgage securities, consumer loans, and small business loans. The Fed also faced credit squeezes in dollars in foreign markets, providing currency swaps to key central banks. There were also needs to prevent the failure of AIG and Bear Stearns. The Fed is also buying $300 billion in Treasury securities in a sort of quantitative easing program, which is dwarfed by government expenditures of $3.6 trillion and a deficit close to $2 trillion.

The Fed is facing a difficult exit strategy from the bloated balance sheet. There could be losses from the loans extended by the Fed.[528] The Fed argues that the losses could be minimal.[529] If the economy recovers, banks would have better opportunities, withdrawing their deposits at

Table 6.3   United States monetary policy

Facility	Description and objectives
TAF	The Term Asset Facility (TAF) provides fully collateralized term funds to qualifying depository institutions under primary credit program in minimum bid rate TAF auctions. The 02/09/09 auction was $150 billion for 28-day terms with auction results: 02/09/09: 117 bidders for $142.5 billion at stop-out rate of 0.250 percent; 02/11/09: 66 bidders for $30 billion at stop-out rate of 3.01 percent. The TAF offerings were $900 billion in 2008 but because of under subscribing had outstanding credit of $450 billion at year-end 2008.
PCDF	The Primary Dealer Credit Facility (PDCF) provides overnight loans to primary dealers backed by specific, eligible collateral to promote effective functioning of money markets. On September 14, 2008, all eligible tri-party repo collateral was accepted to maintain the confidence of investors on the tri-party repo framework. On September 21, the FRBO extended the PDCF to Goldman Sachs and Morgan Stanley and subsequently to Merrill Lynch as they transitioned to banking charters. The rate is the primary credit rate of the NYFRB. PDCF is available only to New York dealers through their clearing banks. The borrowing peaked at $155.9 billion on September 29, 2008, declining to $40 billion at year end.
TSLF	The Term Securities Lending Facility (TSLF) lends primary dealers treasury securities from the System Open Market Account (SOMA) in exchange for all eligible securities for tri-party repos (Schedule 1) in addition to investment grade, corporate, mortgage-backed and asset-backed securities (Schedule 2). The terms are for 28 days with the minimum fee of 10 basis points for Schedule 1 collateral and 25 basis points for Schedule 2 collateral and are determined in a competitive single-price auction. At year-end 2008, the balance reached $165 billion relative to the $200 billion initial allocation. The facility was expanded by $50 billion on August 8 to include options.
AMLF	The Asset-Backed Money Market Mutual Fund Liquidity Facility (AMLF) provides financing to US depository institutions to purchase ABCP from money market mutual funds. The objective is to enhance liquidity in the ABCP market and meeting redemptions by investors in money market mutual funds. Loans in the AMLF peaked at $152 billion in 2008, declining to $24 billion by year end.
CPFF	The Commercial Paper Funding Facility (CPFF) provides loans to special purpose vehicles (SPV) that acquire three-month ABCP from FRBNY primary dealers. The objective is improving credit availability for business and households by enhanced liquidity in short-term funding markets. The CPFF increased to $334 billion by year-end 2008 with limited daily borrowing at the end of 2008

Continued

Table 6.3   Continued

Facility	Description and objectives
MMIFF	The Money Market Investor Funding Facility (MMIFF) provides. loans to SPVs to purchase money market instruments and ABCP from eligible investors. The objective is providing liquidity to money market investors but no investors used the MMIFF in 2008. The AMLF, CPFF, and MMIFF were created to reduce aversion to counterparty risk that clogged securitization of credit.
TALF	The Term Asset-Backed Securities Loan Facility (TALF) intends to improve credit for households and small businesses by lending to holders of AAA-rated ABS originating in consumer loans and Small Business Administration (SBA) guaranteed loans to small businesses. TALF loans are for three-year terms secured by eligible collateral. The initial line was $200 billion but may be expanded to $1 trillion by the Financial Stability Plan (FSP). TARP would provide $20 billion of credit protection to a SPV created by the FRBNY but this protection may increase to $100 billion under the FSP resulting in a $1 trillion TALF. The TALF was delayed until 2009.
Securities	The FOMC decided to purchase $1.25 trillion of agency MBS and $200 billion of agency debt by the end of 2009 and $300 billion of long-term Treasury securities. The intention of the purchases is to lower long-term interest rates to stimulate consumption and investment.
Dollar Swaps	The initial Reciprocal Currency Arrangements or dollar swaps in 2007 included only the European Central Bank and the Swiss National Bank but were extended to include central banks in Australia, Brazil, Canada, Denmark, England, Japan, Korea, Mexico, New Zealand, Singapore, and Sweden. Worsening world markets resulted in an increase of the dollars swaps by the Fed to other central banks in 2008 from $14 billion to $554 billion.
Maiden Lane LLC	On March 24, 2008, the FRBNY created a limited liability company, Maiden Lane LLC, to control $30 billion of assets of Bear Stearns, with $29 billion provided by the FRBNY and $1 billion by JP Morgan Chase. The available estimated fair value of the portfolio toward the end of 2008 was $27 billion.
AIG	In September 2008, the FRBO provided AIG a secured loan of up to $85 billion, reduced after the purchase by Treasury of $40 billion of preferred shares of AIG under TARP on November 10. On October 8, the FRBO provided AIG $37.8 billion collateralized by investment grade, fixed-income securities. Maiden Lane LLC II funded the purchase of residential MBS from AIG, with $19.5 billion provided by the FRS and $1 billion from AIG. Maiden Lane III purchased CDOs on which AIG had written CDS, with FRS funding $23.4 billion and AIG funding $5 billion. The fair value of the assets toward the end of 2008 was $20 billion for Maiden Lane LLC II and $27 billion for Maiden Lane LLC III.

Source: FRBO http://www.federalreserve.gov/monetarypolicy/default.htm
Ben S. Bernanke, The Federal Reserve's balance sheet. Charlotte, NC, Federal Reserve Bank of Richmond Symposium, Apr 3, 2009; FSOB, First quarterly report to Congress pursuant to section 104(g) of the Emergency Economic Stabilization Act of 2008. Washington, DC, US Treasury, Jan 2009 http://www.financialstability.gov/docs/FSOB/FINSOB-Qrtly-Rpt-123108.pdf; FOMC, Domestic open market operations during 2008. New York, FRBNY, Jan, 2009.

the Fed to lend to their customers, causing an increase in the money stock and inflationary pressure.[530] The Fed would be committed to three-year loans to consumer financing and small businesses, facing difficulty in preventing an increase in the money stock in an expansion.[531] The Fed appears to act under the "unusual and exigent" clause of section 13(3) of the Federal Reserve Act assisting firms and people who can obtain credit but at high interest rates.[532] There is danger in the exit from this strategy. It could also be used to fuel expansions of the economy. It can be partly characterized as an industrial policy and not merely monetary policy.[533]

The Troubled Assets Relief Program

The Emergency Economic Stabilization Act of 2008 (EESA) created the Troubled Assets Relief Program (TARP). The initial intention of the TARP was the removal of troubled assets from the balance sheet of financial institutions. A general definition of a trouble asset is one that cannot be financed, which is equivalent to the absence of a generally agreed and observable price. The initial troubled assets in the credit crisis were CDOs and credit default swaps (CDS), with the range rapidly growing into MBS, ABS, ABCP, and nearly every securitized structure and corporate debt securities. There are two interrelated problems with withdrawal of troubled assets from balance sheets of financial institutions. First, the lack of financing for the troubled asset is equivalent to the lack of a price, which may be closer to zero than to the original acquisition price. Second, the purchase of the troubled asset at the distressed price causes a loss to the financial institutions by the difference between the selling and acquisition price, eroding the capital base that could worsen its risk as counterparty in financial transactions. In the absence of undesirable changes in accounting practices and/or losses to taxpayers the removal of troubled assets presents difficult hurdles.

Because of these hurdles, the Treasury moved the implementation of the TARP toward capital injections in financial institutions and asset guarantees. The correct conception of equity injections is to prevent erosion of the capital base of financial institutions resulting from the deductions in the value of assets. Unfortunately, the public perception is different in that the equity injections of the TARP would immediately result in more credit instead of the primary objective of stabilizing financial markets with credit returning subsequently.

There are evaluations of the TARP by the Financial Stability Oversight Board (FSOB), the Congressional Oversight Board (COP), and Duff &

Phelps.[534] As in all economics, these evaluations encounter the difficulty of specifying and measuring the counterfactual of what would have happened without TARP, in the case of the FSOB, and with a different TARP, as in the case of the COP. Table 6.4 shows the different programs implemented under TARP that changed, as Fed policy, when new problems developed. The Capital Asset Program (CPP) injected preferred stock with warrants in financial institutions in the value of

Table 6.4   The Troubled Assets Relief Program

Facility	Description and Objectives
CPP	The Capital Purchase Program (CPP) was created in October 2008. The objective is to stabilize financial markets and recover confidence in financial institutions. UST acquires preferred shares of qualifying financial institutions (QFI) paying 5 percent interest during the first five years and 9 percent after five years. US Treasury also receives warrants to purchase common equity in participating companies. Eligibility of institutions is recommended by the primary federal regulator. As of February 17, 2009, the CPP reached $195.9 billion.
SSFI	The Systemically Significant Failing Institutions Program (SSFI) consisted of the acquisition of $40 billion of senior preferred stock of AIG on November 25, 2008, with the objective of preventing systemic disruption to financial markets. The eligibility and allocations are managed by the TARP on a-case-by-case basis.
TALF	The TARP will provide credit protection to the Fed to support the TALF. The initial credit support was set at $20 billion in November 2008 but is programed to increase to $100 billion under the FSP.
TIP	The Targeted Investment Program (TIP) consisted of two additional injections of capital in the form of preferred stock with warrants in Citigroup Inc. of $20 billion on December 31, 2008, and Bank of America Corporation of $20 billion on January 16, 2009.
AGP	The Asset Guarantee Program (AGP), jointly by the US Treasury, Fed, and FDIC, provided credit protection of $5 billion for a pool of assets of Citigroup valued at $360 billion.
AIFP	The Automotive Industry Financing Program (AIFP) provided capital injections, in the form of preferred stock with warrants, to GMAC, General Motors and Chrysler in the amount of $24.8 billion in the last days of 2008 and the first days of 2009. A presidential task force on the auto industry was appointed by the President at the cabinet level and began deliberations on February 20, 2009.

Sources: FSOB, First quarterly report to Congress pursuant to section 104(g) of the Emergency Economics Stabilization Act of 2008. Washington, DC, US Treasury, Jan 2009 http://www.financialstability.gov/docs/FSOB/FINSOB-Qrtly-Rpt-123108.pdf; http://www.ustreas.gov/initiatives/eesa/docs/transaction_report_02–17-09.pdf

$195.9 billion. The TALF is being reformulated under the FSP. The other programs assisted in the resolution of problems in AIG, Citigroup, Bank of America, and the automotive industry.

Financial Stability Plan

On February 10, 2009, the US Treasury announced the replacement of the TARP with the Financial Stability Plan (FSP).[535] The FSP consists of comprehensive stress tests for major banks, increased balance sheet transparency and disclosure, Capital Assistance Program (CAP), Public-Private Investment Program (PPIP) of $500 billion to $1 trillion to remove illiquid financial assets, increase of the TALF to $1 trillion, agenda of transparency and affordable housing and foreclosure prevention.[536]

The CAP consists of two elements.[537] First, supervisory agencies conduct an exercise of stress testing the balance sheets of 19 financial institutions with more than $100 billion of assets.[538] The objective is to determine a "forward-looking capital assessment" of the major bank holding companies (BHC) under a baseline scenario using the average of professional forecasting models and a worse adverse scenario. The exercise would provide information on the need for additional capital under stressful conditions. The major federal supervisory agencies jointly determined interagency the FSP forward-looking economic assessments to be completed no later than the end of April 2009.[539] Second, the BHCs would apply for capital injection by the government by May 25, 2009, but will have six months to raise capital privately. Government capital injection would consist of preferred shares that could be converted into common equity if required to strengthen confidence on the financial institution. The objective of the CAP is not permanent government ownership but rather the return of the financial institution to private capital after recovery of confidence. The capital investments by Treasury will be held by a separate trust that would be managed to protect and create value for shareholders.

In March 2009, Treasury announced the creation of the PPIP.[540] The objective of the PPIP is to remove legacy loans and legacy assets from the balance sheets of banks. Legacy loans are loans with uncertain future performance and legacy securities do not have liquidity and, thus, a ready market. Legacy loans and securities in the balance sheets prevent banks from raising additional capital because of the fear of potential investors of further write downs. Banks could restrict lending because of the uncertainty of the performance of legacy loans and securities, which could result in reduction of capital. The original intention of TARP was to remove legacy loans and securities from bank balance sheets. The fundamental obstacle is that the banks would have substantial losses if they sell the loans and securities at less than the value in the balance sheets. Treasury would establish Public-Private Investment Program Funds (PPIPF). In the legacy loan program, PPIPFs would be created with capital from the TARP/FSP and private investors, obtaining financing by issuing FDIC-guaranteed debt up to leverage of six to one. In the legacy securities program, PPIPFs would be created with TARP/FSP and private capital with financing by the TALF of the Fed. The initial program consists of a TARP/FSP capital contribution of $75 to $100 billion that would provide $500 billion with FDIC-guaranteed debt and TALF financing.

Treasury estimates that the PPIP could increase from the initial $500 billion to $1 trillion. Those values would be the prices actually paid by the PPIPFs to purchase the legacy loans and securities. Table 6.5 provides the data of the Fed on US banks assets and liabilities, which permit some rough calculations. The credit of US banks, $9676.3 billion, less holdings of Treasury and agency securities, $1275 billion, is $8401.3 billion. Assuming a very conservative discount of 30 percent of the value of the loans and securities in the balance sheet of the banks, the $1 trillion acquired by PPIP would be equivalent to value in the books of the banks of $1428 billion ($1 trillion divided by 0.7). The write down of the banks would amount to $428 billion. The residual of assets and liabilities in the Fed statistics shown in Table 6.5 is $1225 billion, which is a rough approximation of bank capital. The highly conservative discount of 30 percent could reduce bank capital by 34.9 percent. If banks could continue carrying legacy loans and securities in their balance sheets without write downs, it would be tempting to wait for

Table 6.5   US Banks assets and liabilities

Billions of Dollars on March 25, 2009	
Assets	12,035.6
Credit	9676.3
Securities	2698.8
Treasury and Agency	1275.0
Loans	6986.5
Liabilities	10,810.1
Residual*	1,225.5

*Assets less liabilities
Source: http://www.federalreserve.gov/releases/h8/Current/

recovery of the economy. There are no data for precise calculations of the impact of legacy loans and securities on bank capital. The value of legacy loans and securities could be much higher than $1 trillion and the discount in the market could be 70 percent. The price of an illiquid good is close to zero because it is not marketable.

Mortgage modification

The Housing and Economic Recovery Act of 2008 provides through the FHA, as of October 1, 2008, government insurance to lenders who voluntarily reduce the value of mortgages to at least 90 percent of the current value of the property.[541] The objective was to support about 400,000 homeowners at risk affordable mortgage rates to avoid foreclosure. An eligible homeowner must have a mortgage payment exceeding at least 31 percent of the borrower's total monthly income. It provides first-time homebuyers an interest-free loan not to exceed $7500 to be repaid in 15 years. It also allocated $11 billion to states for use in refinancing subprime loans and assisting with loans first-time homebuyers and builders of rental housing. The law raised conforming loan limits for the FHA, Fannie Mae and Freddie Mac to $625,000.

On February 18, 2009, the US government announced the Homeowner Affordability and Stability Plan.[542] The objective of the plan is to provide assistance to seven to nine million homeowners in avoiding foreclosure, which lowers residential prices and tightens credit. Treasury subsequently released the guidelines of the plan.[543] There are two parts to the homeowner plan. First, the affordability part facilitates refinancing of mortgages by four to five million "responsible" homeowners who have conforming mortgages purchased or insured by Fannie Mae and Freddie Mac. Because of the decline in residential prices, these homeowners cannot qualify for refinancing criteria with the requirement that the value of the mortgage balance be lower than 80 percent of the home price. Refinancing at a lower rate would reduce the monthly payment, reducing the risk of foreclosure.

Second, the stability part of the law provides $75 billion to assist three to four million homeowners who struggle to meet mortgage payments but cannot sell their homes because of the fall in price. The law provides for a shared effort in reducing monthly payments. The lender would reduce the rates on the mortgage to decrease the monthly mortgage payment to 38 percent or less than the homeowner's income. The government would then match equally further reduction in the monthly payment down to 31 percent of the homeowner's monthly income. Simultaneously,

Treasury increased the preferred stock purchase agreements with Fannie Mae and Freddie Mac to $100 billion for each company, for a total $200 billion.[544] Treasury also increased the size of the retained mortgage portfolios of the GSE by $50 billion to total $900 billion.

A hurdle of the home ownership program is that 55 percent of modified mortgage loans are characterized by a re-default rate of 55 percent after six months.[545] Thus, the new plan could simply prolong the real estate and credit crisis. It is conceivable that the re-default rate may increase for longer periods after modification. MBS markets and even the entire ABCP market could paralyze by a threat in the homeownership plan that considers another measure to "allow judicial modifications of home mortgages during bankruptcy for borrowers who have run out of option."[546] Bloomberg informs that Asian investors require guarantee of the debt of Fannie Mae and Freddie Mac similar to that of debt by US banks under the Temporary Liquidity Guarantee Program (TLGP) of the FDIC to continue purchasing the debt and securities of the GSE.[547] The continuing placement of Fannie Mae and Freddie Mac debt and securities in Asia is critical to financing the US external deficit.

Fiscal policy

The President signed the American Recovery and Reinvestment Act of 2009 on February 17. The objective of the act is to turn around the recession affecting the United States since December 2007.[548] In addition, the act intends to double production of alternative energy in three years, modernize federal buildings, improve the efficiency of American homes, computerizing medical records, investing in science and technology, and increasing the access of broadband. The act is expected to increase jobs in the US economy by three to four million by 2010.[549] However, there is controversy on the potential job increases by the fiscal stimulus.[550] In testimony to Congress, the Chairman of the Board of Governors of the Federal Reserve System alerted that:[551]

> One risk arises from the so-called adverse feedback loop, in which weakening economic and financial conditions become mutually reinforcing. To break the adverse feedback loop, it is essential that we continue to complement fiscal stimulus with strong government action to stabilize financial institutions and financial markets.

Apparently, this loop is processed through the credit channel by which weakening household and business balance sheets weaken balance sheets of financial institutions, which in turn diminish credit or external financing to households and businesses in a loop-type process. The calculation of job creation resulting from the fiscal stimulus would require a more complex model incorporating the interactions of the real and financial sectors.

The actual expenditure task is an important hurdle of the fiscal stimulus. For example, the Department of Energy's annual budget is $25 billion but its portion of the fiscal stimulus is $40 billion.[552] The current funding for efficient electricity grids would jump from $140 million to $11 billion. The size of the deficit is a major concern. The deficit after the fiscal stimulus could reach $1.75 trillion, which would be equivalent to 12.3 percent of GDP,[553]declining to 8 percent of GDP in 2010.[554] There could be rigidity in expenditures in the future as it has occurred in other episodes of high deficits, requiring painful adjustment and tax increases. Heavy borrowing by the budget proposal of the White House[555] could increase the debt held by the public from 40 percent of GDP before the credit/dollar crisis to 60 percent of GDP, the highest level since the early 1950s after the effort of World War II.[556] The budget proposal would reduce the deficit to $533 billion in 2013 but the assumptions on GDP growth, inflation, and unemployment may be excessively optimistic.[557] Even conjectures on the impact of such large government expenditure of 27.6 percent of GDP[558] are not reliable because of the impossibility of assessing how economic agents will react to significant wealth transfers and changes in the structure of the economy. There would be significant pain in rebalancing expenditures of 27.6 percent of GDP relative to revenue of 15.3 percent of GDP in 2009 as programed in the budget proposal.[559] The Congressional Budget Office provides a much less optimistic projection of the deficit in 2009–19 that could sum to $9.3 trillion.[560] The tax increase to pay for this fiscal exuberance[561]

> If spread evenly over all those paying income taxes (which under Mr. Obama's plan would shrink to a little over 50 percent of the population), every income-tax paying family could get a tax bill for $163,000.

Liquidity guarantee

The TARP and other programs of the Fed were complemented with deposit insurance and the TLGP of the FDIC. The TLGP consists of two programs: (1) the Transactions Account Guarantee Program (TAGP) and

(2) the Debt Guarantee Program (DGP). The FDIC requires that participating institutions must post after December 19, 2008, a notice in their lobbies and in their Web site if they offer online services showing in clear terms their participation in the TLGP.[562] The FDIC provides a list of the institutions that opted out of the programs.[563]

The FDIC provides under the TAGP temporary full guarantee by the FDIC of[564]

All funds in noninterest-bearing transaction deposit accounts held in domestic offices and insured branches in Puerto Rico and US territories and possessions of FDIC-insured institutions. A 'noninterest-bearing transaction account' is defined as a transaction account with respect to which interest is neither accrued nor paid and on which the insured depository institution does not reserve the right to require advance notice of an intended withdrawal.

The definition includes demand deposit checking accounts permitting unlimited number of deposits and withdrawals at any time but does not include interest-bearing money market deposit accounts. The FDIC includes accounts known as interest on lawyers trust accounts (IOLTA) and negotiable order of withdrawal accounts (NOW). The TAGP is intended to last until December 31, 2009. It is possible that it could be extended depending on conditions in financial markets. The TAGP is above the deposit insurance limit of $250,000, increased from $100,000 by the FDIC in 2008. For example, a depositor could have $1million in a transactions account and $250,000 in a time CD and would be fully covered by the FDIC.[565]

The FDIC provides under the DGP temporary guarantee of timely payment of interest and principal to newly issued unsecured debt up to 125 percent of the par or face value of senior unsecured debt outstanding on September 30, 2008, net of debt to affiliates, scheduled to mature on or before June 30, 2009. The TLGP considers a variety of senior unsecured debt: fed funds purchased, promissory notes, commercial paper, unsubordinated unsecured notes, US dollar-denominated CDs owed to an insured depository institution, credit union or foreign bank, US dollar-denominated deposits in an international banking facility (IBF) of an insured depository institution, and US dollar-denominated deposits on the books and records of foreign branches of US-insured depository institutions. The fees are annualized in basis points (BP): 50 BPs for terms of 180 days or less, 75 BPs for terms of 181–364 days, and 100 BPs for terms of 365 days or greater. In

November, 2008, Goldman Sachs issued $3 billion in bonds under the TLGP.[566] Issuing debt under the TLGP is attractive to financial institutions because they have the guarantee of the US government and provide higher yields than treasuries. TLGP bonds can provide fresh source of funds for financial institutions and contribute to orderly refinancing of maturing debts.

The Swedish bank workout

The management of the banking crisis by Sweden in 1992–3 is considered as rich in lessons of how to manage a situation similar to the current credit crisis. In the second half of the 1980s the ratio of private-sector debt to GDP of Sweden increased from 85 percent to 135 percent and real aggregate asset prices by 125 percent.[567] Swedish GDP decreased by 6 percent between the summers of 1990 and 1993 while the rate of unemployment increased from 3 to 12 percent and the public deficit deteriorated to 12 percent of GDP. Sweden was experiencing a currency crisis resulting from overvaluation and loss of external confidence together with domestic banking crisis. Bankruptcies caused loan-loss provisions in Swedish banks accumulating to the equivalent of 12 percent of GDP.[568] In 1996, the Financial Supervisory Authority of Sweden, in charge of supervising banks, concluded after careful evaluation that the 114 banks and other credit institutions that had received government guarantees since December 1992 were financially strong and the guarantees could be lifted without risk to the financial system.[569]

Many of the bank recovery policies of Sweden were similar to some adopted by central banks during the credit/dollar crisis after 2007. In December 1992, the Swedish parliament, Riksdag, approved a bank support guarantee, extended to all creditors but excluding shareholders.[570] There was no upper limit in this guarantee. There is resemblance in this program with the TLGP guaranteeing transaction deposits and debts discussed before. The guarantee was followed by a decline in the spreads paid for credit by Swedish banks, stabilizing the inflow of credit. The reduction in the ratings did not prevent the banks from obtaining required financing.

The Swedish government established a Bank Support Authority at the Ministry of Finance to supervise the resolution of banks. The Bank Support Authority established a Valuation Board that had experts in real estate. The Swedish valuation approach was to report all expected losses instead of deferring losses.[571] The FSP consists of stress tests of banks to determine government support. The earlier Swedish program determined the size and forms of support of scenarios of possible future development based on forecasts of bank balance sheets and the economic environment.[572] Banks were classified in three categories: (1) an A bank would experience decline in its capital ratio to 8 percent but remain solvent; (2) a B bank would experience deterioration of the capital ratio to less than 8 percent but would recover capital adequacy subsequently; and (3) a C bank would eventually experience negative capital and would not return to profitability. The approach for resolving the C bank was the separation of good and bad assets with subsequent sale or merger of the remaining bank. This process is similar to the disposition of bad assets of banks mentioned in the analysis of the FSP. The Swedish approach recognized the existence of the losses and the impossibility of recovering the bank if the government imposed excessively stringent requirements.[573]

The Swedish approach relied also on expert knowledge about the workout of bad loans by creating asset management companies.[574] Securum and Retriva were two asset management companies created to work out the massive bad loans in banks.[575] The government transferred SEK 50 billion (after write downs) to Securum and a contribution of capital of SEK 24 billion to cover its costs during the workout. The nonperforming loans in Gota bank were more than 45 percent of total assets and the scenario analysis showed the bank was not viable in the long term. The approach was to separate the bad loans and subsequently sell the remaining good bank. Retriva was created for this purpose and received SEK 16 billion (after write downs) and a capital contribution of SEK 4 billion.[576] An essential characteristic of the Swedish workout was[577]

> Right from the start it was stated explicitly, for instance in the Riksdag's decision in 1992, that the bank support was not to result in the State becoming a long-term owner of banks. In so far as state ownership of a bank was necessary as a temporary measure, the aim should be to privatize the ownership as soon as this is feasible in a manner that is economically sound (as in the case of the plans for Nordbanken).

It appears prudent to include such commitment in Congressional and executive decisions in the recovery of financial institutions.

Regulation

There are numerous proposals for banking and financial regulation. The proposals can be grouped in common areas: systemic regulation, changes by the BCBS, hedge funds, compensation, derivatives, Fannie Mae and Freddie Mac, and money market funds. Each of these groups is considered later.

Regulatory authorities and parliaments believe that the credit/dollar crisis was propagated through financial institutions and across borders. The US Treasury is proposing a single, independent regulator of systemic risk. In addition, there would be regulation of payment and settlement systems.[578] The United Kingdom intends to create regulation of prevention and resolution of systemic crises.[579] The effects on financial markets of the collapse of Bear Stearns and Lehman Brothers and the rescue of AIG motivate regulation on large, complex systemic financial institutions. It is difficult to define systemic risk in a form that can be measured.[580] The United States intends to increase higher capital requirements and enhanced risk management for systemically important financial institutions.[581] Treasury and the Fed are seeking authority for resolution of complex systemic institutions. The resolution would be paid by an insurance fee deposited by the institutions perhaps at the FDIC. An important issue related to systemic risk is the behavior of banks during the economic cycle. The regulatory argument is that banks lend excessively during periods of expansion in the economy and reduce credit during the periods of contraction, accentuating the downturn of the entire economy. There is significant international support for capital buffers: banks would increase their capital during expansion to create a cushion to face defaults during adverse economic conditions.[582] Systemic risk could affect large, complex financial institutions operating worldwide. There is regulatory effort in cooperation of preventing and resolving international financial crises by means of enhanced international cooperation.[583]

An important principle of the Basel II framework of capital requirements is the effort to maintain competition of financial institutions worldwide, or a level playing field. The high quality of the consultations with all sectors enhances the credibility and wide adoption of the proposals of the BCBS. The BCBS has issued a consultative package with proposals to amend the Basel II framework.[584] The reform of Basel II is prudently delayed for implementation after the global recession. The focus is to increase capital requirements in the exposure that was most affected during the crisis, trading of securities. The proposals also provide for oversight and capital requirements of structured products and special purpose entities such as the SIVs and liquidity guarantees by banks. Banks will also be required to conduct their own analysis and not simply rely on that of credit agencies. Measurement, management, and oversight of liquidity are an important part of the regulatory effort because of deficiencies found during the crisis.[585] Another area of regulatory enhancement is the oversight of risk management by supervisors.[586] Deposit insurance systems should be managed to maintain financial stability and avoid moral hazard under sound internationally designed principles.[587]

Hedge funds were not evident in the credit/dollar crisis or even in other episodes. However, there are proposals for regulations in Europe and the United States. Under the US proposal, hedge funds above certain size would be required to register with the SEC, providing information and reports to the systemic regulator.[588] Prudential regulation of hedge funds is also proposed in Europe and international forums.[589]

There are several other proposed regulatory reforms. Compensation in financial institutions would be aligned with risk management and long-term results.[590] The United States is proposing strict regulation for OTC derivatives.[591] There are proposals to separate the guarantee function of Fannie Mae and Freddie Mac in a government agency with the sale of the retained portfolio.[592] The United States is also considering reduction in the withdrawal risk of money market funds that caused concern during the crisis.

Summary

The reduction of fed funds rates by the Fed to nearly zero in 2003–4, followed by other central banks, is the prime suspect of the origin of the credit/dollar crisis. The low interest rate motivated overproduction of houses in the United States. Fannie Mae and Freddie Mac guaranteed and acquired nonprime mortgages. Because of the implicit guarantee of the solvency of Fannie Mae and Freddie Mac by the full faith and credit of the US government, their endorsement of nonprime mortgages granted them the status of riskless. The large share of Fannie and Freddie of 43 percent of the mortgage market, the largest credit debt in the United States, and their similar share in nonprime mortgages, motivated the growth of mortgage securities based on pools of mortgages with high probability of default. The structured products were simply vehicles for the policies of the Fed and Fannie and Freddie. The stimulus of the Fed and Treasury on the reduction of US output of –2.8 percent for 2009, as forecast by the IMF, is far larger than any program during the contraction of 25.7 percent of US output in 1930–3. The ad hoc nature of the policy and the role of the current LOLR in initiating the credit/dollar crisis raise significant doubts on the agenda of creating a systemic regulator. There is more regulation in the agenda than the available knowledge on its implementation.

Conclusion

There are two main views on the origin of the credit/dollar crisis and
the new measures for regulatory reform. The first view is based on the
public interest or official regulatory view proposing tight regulation
to avoid financial instability and resulting loss of output and employment. The second view is based on the finance view or FSF approach.[593]
These two approaches are discussed in turn.

First, the official regulatory view argues that banks used financial
innovation to arbitrage regulatory capital. The SIVs were off–balance
sheet to avoid regulatory capital charges. The system of "originate to
distribute" created incentives to lax standards in documentation and
verification of mortgages because the originating party did not bear
the risks of default. Mortgages were bundled in securities and sold to
ultimate investors but banks retained part of the risk to improve their
earnings not only with high-return but also with high-risk assets. Risk-
management measurement, analysis and control lagged innovations in
structured products. Banks and other financial institutions engaged in
imprudent risk-taking by financing excessive volumes of assets in short-
term SRPs without consideration of liquidity risk. The careless credit
decisions at origination magnified through the securitization chain
to investors with imprudent leverage in complex CDOs, which proved
impossible to MTM. The uncertainty of the default risk of underlying
mortgages in structured products increased the perception of counterparty credit risk. The financing of most financial assets paralyzed
because of fear of losses of principal if the financed counterparty did
not repurchase the financed security. Higher margins and haircuts
in counterparty transactions reduced capital of financial institutions,
causing fire sales in a collective movement of reducing leverage. The
credit/dollar crisis was characterized by large, complex, and systemically

important institutions with cross-border effects. The core of regulatory proposals consists of the creation of a systemic regulator with the powers to intervene in systemically important institutions. There are subsidiary proposals to tighten capital for trading and controls on leverage and liquidity exposures. The regulatory reform would be incomplete without tighter standards for credit contracts. Limits and regulation of executive compensation are contemplated to prevent excessive risks on short-term transactions.

The alternative approach claims that the credit/dollar crisis was caused by government intervention.[594] The critical policy impulse was the reduction of the fed funds rate to 1 percent in 2003–4 with the expressed intention that it would be maintained at that level or lower until required to prevent deflation.[595] The interest-rate "subsidy" by the central banks processed through the gigantic housing subsidy of the United States, amounting to $221 billion per year. The housing GSE, Fannie Mae and Freddie Mac, guaranteed or acquired $1.6 trillion of nonprime mortgages. The crucial entry of Fannie Mae and Freddie Mac in the nonprime market, staying until the peak in 2006, provided an implicit seal of approval by the full faith and credit of the US government. The discipline of calculating risks and rewards was eroded not only for financial institutions but also for the public. The low interest rate maintained by the Fed and the approval of the government through Fannie and Freddie created the impression that housing prices would increase forever. The only perceived risk to the mortgagor was to live in a better house for some time and then sell it for a higher price to pay the mortgage. The lender believed that the only risk was to sell the house in foreclosure to recover at least the principal and owed interest. An affordable house is a subsidized house in the presence of perennial scarcity of resources relative to unlimited wants by economic agents. Eventually, the Fed raised interest rates from 1 percent to 5.25 percent, almost as rapidly. The increase in interest rates triggered the nonprime crisis as the reset of adjustable rate mortgages and the end of teaser rates with no principal increased monthly mortgages payments beyond what the debtor could pay. The innovation in securitization had worked throughout decades and the problems were exacerbated in mortgages because of the housing subsidy and the unsound credit decisions of Fannie and Freddie.

The finance view or FSF does not propose entirely unregulated markets. The proposal is rather for balanced regulation that allows for innovation of financial products, risk management[596], and the efficient functions of banks and financial institutions. Economic prosperity has been created in economies with some market allocation by taking entrepreneurial decisions that require successful ex ante calculation of risk and returns. Regulation preventing or limiting entrepreneurial initiative are as damaging as restrictions on health care innovation that have increased our life expectancy and participation in the labor force. Regulation needs sound weights for prosperity and stability. Excessive regulation and restrictions of financial innovation can limit future economic growth and employment.

Notes

1. Richard A. Posner, Re-regulating the banking industry. Apr 4, 2009 www. becker–posner–blog.com. The calculation of citations is by Fred R. Shapiro, The most-cited legal scholars. *Journal of Legal Studies* 29 (1, 2000): 409–26. See also Posner, An economic analysis of the use of citations in the law. *American Law and Economics Review* 2 (2, 2000): 381–406.
2. Adam Smith, *The wealth of nations* (Chicago: University of Chicago, 1976 reprinted from 1776), 477.
3. Mark Blaug, The fundamental theorems of modern welfare economics, historically contemplated. *History of Political Economy* 32 (2, 2007): 186–207.
4. Kenneth Arrow, An extension of the basic theorems of classical welfare economics. In Jerzy Neyman, ed. *Proceedings of the second Berkeley symposium on mathematical statistics and probability* (Berkeley: University of California Press, 1951); Gerard Debreu, The coefficient of resource allocation. *Econometrica* 19 (3, 1951): 273–92.
5. Richard G. Lipsey and Kelvin Lancaster, The general theory of second best. *Review of Economic Studies* 24 (1956): 11–32.
6. Arthur C. Pigou, *The economics of welfare 4th ed.* (London: Macmillan & Co., 1932).
7. George A. Akerlof, The market for 'lemons': quality uncertainty and the market mechanism. *Quarterly Journal of Economics* 84 (3, 1970): 488–500; Michael A. Spence, Job market signaling. *Quarterly Journal of Economics* 87 (3, 1973): 434–59; Joseph E. Stiglitz, Information and the change in the paradigm in economics. *American Economic Review* 92 (3, 2002): 460–501.
8. George A. Akerlof, Writing 'The market for lemons': a personal and interpretive essay (Berkeley, University of California, 2003).
9. Stiglitz, Information, 469.
10. Ibid, 469.
11. Joseph E. Stiglitz, The role of the state in financial markets. *Proceedings of the World Bank Annual Conference on Development Economics 1993* (Washington, DC: World Bank, 1994).
12. Harold Demsetz, Information and efficiency, another viewpoint. *Journal of Law and Economics* 12 (1969): 1–21.
13. Clifford Winston, *Government failure versus market failure* (Washington, DC: Brookings, 2006), 73–4.
14. Ronald H. Coase, The problem of social cost. *Journal of Law and Economics* 3 (1, 1960): 1–40.
15. Ibid.
16. Ibid.
17. Ibid.
18. John J. Wallis and Douglass C. North, Measuring the transactions sector in the American economy. In Stanley L. Engerman and Robert E. Gallman, eds. *Long–term factors in American economic growth* (Chicago: University of Chicago Press, 1986).

19. Oliver E. Williamson, The new institutional economics: taking stock, looking ahead. *Journal of Economic Literature* 38 (3, 2000): 595–613.
20. Ibid, 596–8.
21. Coase, The problem.
22. Ibid; Demsetz, Information.
23. For a comparison of the new world see Stephen H. Haber, Political institutions and financial development: evidence from new world economies (Cambridge, MA, NBER, Jul 11, 2007).
24. Ronald H. Coase, The nature of the firm. *Economica* 4 (16, Nov 1937): 386–405.
25. Oliver E. Williamson, The institutions of governance. *American Economic Review* 88 (2, 1998): 75–9.
26. Sam Peltzman, *Regulation and the natural process of opulence* (Washington, DC: AEI–Brookings, 2004).
27. George R. Stigler, The theory of economic regulation. *The Bell Journal of Economics and Management Science* 2 (1, 1973): 3–21. The term of economic theory of regulation was introduced by Richard Posner, Theories of economic regulation. *Bell Journal of Economics and Management Science* 5 (2, 1974): 335–58.
28. Stigler, The theory, 4–5.
29. Ibid, 4–6.
30. Sam Peltzman, The economic theory of regulation after a decade of deregulation. *Brookings Papers on Economic Activity* (1989), 6–7.
31. For extensions see Gary S. Becker, A theory of competition among pressure groups for political influence. *Quarterly Journal of Economics* 98 (3, 1983): 371–400.
32. Stigler, The theory .
33. Posner, Theories of economic regulation.
34. Ibid, 339–40.
35. Ibid, 339.
36. Ibid, 339–40.
37. Ibid, 340.
38. Sam Peltzman, Toward a more general theory of regulation. *Journal of Law and Economics* 19 (Aug, 1976): 211–40.
39. Ernesto Dal Bó, Regulatory capture: a review. *Oxford Review of Economic Policy* 22 (2, 2006): 203–25.
40. Becker, Theory of competition.
41. Anne O. Krueger, The political economy of the rent–seeking society. *American Economic Review* 64 (1974): 291–303; Gordon Tullock, The welfare costs of tariffs, monopolies and theft. *Western Economic Journal* 5 (1967): 224–32.
42. Mark J. Roe, Rents and their consequences. New York, Columbia Law School, WP, Apr 10, 2001, 3.
43. Andrei Shleifer, Understanding regulation. *European Financial Management* 11 (4, 2005): 439–51.
44. Ibid, 442.
45. Ibid, 442–3.
46. For a critique of capital requirements in Basel II see James R. Barth, Gerard Caprio, Jr. and Ross Levine, *Rethinking bank regulation* (Cambridge: Cambridge University Press, 2006). With a worldwide sample, they conclude

that the evidence supports more the private interest view than the public interest view.

47. Edward L. Glaeser and Andrei Shleifer, The rise of the regulatory state. *Journal of Economic Literature* 41 (Jun 2, 2003): 401–25. The approach of transaction costs is by Coase, The problem.

48. Glaeser and Shleifer, The rise of the regulatory state.

49. Ibid, 411.

50. Dal Bó, Regulatory capture: a review; Jean-Jacques Laffont, The new economics of regulation ten years after. *Econometrica* 62 (May 3, 1994): 507–37.

51. Efraim Benmelech and Tobias Moskowitz, The political economy of financial regulation: evidence from the US state usury laws in the nineteenth century. Washington, DC, Conference on the Causes and Consequences of Structural Reforms, Feb 28–9, 2008 http://www.imf.org/external/np/seminars/eng/2008/strureform/pdf/poleco.pdf

52. Thomas F. Hellmann, Kevin C. Murdock and Joseph E. Stiglitz, Liberalization, moral hazard in banking and prudential regulation: are capital requirements enough? *American Economic Review* 90 (1, 2000): 147–65.

53. Ibid, 148.

54. Ibid.

55. Arnold C. Harberger, Three postulates for applied welfare economics: an interpretive essay. *Journal of Economic Literature* 9 (3, 1971): 785–97.

56. Harberger and Glenn P. Jenkins, Introduction. In *Cost-benefit analysis* (Cheltenham, UK: Edward Elgar, 2002).

57. Harberger, Three postulates, 795.

58. Ross Levine, Financial development and economic growth: views and agenda. *Journal of Economic Literature* 35 (2, 1997): 688–726.

59. Ibid.

60. Ibid.

61. Arrow, An extension; Debreu, The coefficient; Kenneth J. Arrow and Gerard Debreu, Existence of an equilibrium for a competitive economy. *Econometrica* 22 (3, 1954): 265–90.

62. Levine, Financial development, 691.

63. Zsolt Becsi and Ping Wang, Financial development and growth. *Economic Review—Federal Reserve Bank of Atlanta* 82 (4, 1997): 46–62.

64. John G. Gurley and Edward S. Shaw, Financial aspects of economic development. *American Economic Review* 45 (4, 1955): 515–38; Gurley and Shaw, *Money in a theory of finance* (Washington, DC: Brookings Institution, 1960); Rondo Cameron, *France and the economic development of Europe, 1800–1914: conquests of peace and seeds of war* (Princeton: Princeton University Press, 1961); Cameron, *Banking in the early stages of industrialization* (Oxford: Oxford University Press, 1967); Cameron, *Banking and economic development* (Oxford: Oxford University Press, 1972); Cameron *et al. International banking 1870–1914* (Oxford: Oxford University Press, 1992); Raymond Goldsmith, *Financial structure and development* (New Haven: Yale University Press, 1969).

65. William J. Baumol, John C. Panzar and Robert D. Willig, *Contestable markets and the theory of industry structure* (New York: Harcourt, Brace, Jovonovich, 1982).

66. Douglas W. Diamond, Financial intermediation and delegated monitoring. *Review of Economic Studies* 51 (1984): 393–414; Diamond, Financial

intermediation as delegated monitoring: a simple example. *Economic Quarterly Federal Reserve Bank of Richmond* 82 (3, 1996): 51–66.

67. Diamond, Financial intermediation, 65.

68. Ross Levine, Finance and growth: theory and evidence. In Philippe Aghion and Steven N. Durlauf, eds. *Handbook of economic growth, 1A* (Amsterdam: North–Holland Elsevier, 2005).

69. Ibid.

70. Robin Boadway, Principles of cost-benefit analysis. *Public Policy Review* 2 (1, 2006): 1–43.

71. Ibid, 12.

72. Ross Levine, Bank–based or market–based financial systems: which is better? *Journal of Financial Intermediation* 11 (4, 2002): 398–428.

73. Ibid. See Jean Tirole, *The theory of corporate finance* (Princeton: Princeton University Press, 2005).

74. Levine, Bank-based.

75. Cameron, *France and economic development*; Cameron, *Banking in the early stages*; Alexander Gerschenkron, *Economic backwardness in historical perspective, a book of essays* (Cambridge, MA: Harvard University Press, 1962); Raghuram Rajan and Luigi Zingales, Financial dependence and Growth. *American Economic Review* 88 (3, 1998): 559–86; Joseph A. Schumpeter, *The theory of economic development: an inquiry into profits, capital, credit, interest, and the business cycle.* Translated by Redvers Opie (Cambridge, MA: Harvard University Press, 1942 reprinted from 1911).

76. Levine, Bank-based.

77. Michael C. Jensen, Takeovers: their causes and consequences. *Journal of Economic Perspectives* 2 (1, Winter, 1988): 21–48; Jensen, The modern industrial revolution, exit and the failure of internal control systems. *Journal of Finance* 48 (Jul 3, 1993): 831–80.

78. Levine, Bank-based.

79. Ben S. Bernanke, Financial reform to address systemic risk. Washington, DC, Speech delivered at the Council on Foreign Relations, Mar 10, 2009.

80. Levine, Bank-based.

81. The distinction between an economic and a finance view is analyzed by Larry Summers, On economics and finance. *Journal of Finance* 40 (3, 1985): 633–35; the sharp differentiation of the economic and finance view is analyzed by Fischer Black, Comment. In *NBER Macroeconomics Annual* 8 (1993): 368–71. Black disputes the economic view that banks create crises.

82. Robert C. Merton and Zvi Bodie, Design of financial systems: towards a synthesis of function and structure. *Journal of Investment Management* 3 (1, 2005): 1–23. The direct quote is in page 1.

83. Ibid; Merton and Bodie, A conceptual framework for analyzing the financial environment. In Dwight B. Crane et al., eds. *The global financial system: a functional perspective* (Cambridge, MA: Harvard University Press, 1995).

84. This section is based on the manuscript of Magnolia M. Peláez, Primary health care in the United States. Atlantic City, Jun, 2008.

85. Congressional Budget Office, Technological change and the growth of health care spending. Washington, DC, CBO, Jan, 2008.

86. David M. Cutler and Mark McClellan, Is technological change in medicine worth it? *Health Affairs* 20 (5, 2001): 11–29.

87. Merton and Bodie, Design.

88. Merton and Bodie, A conceptual.

89. Merton and Bodie, Design.

90. A partial list includes Fischer Black and Myron Scholes, The pricing of options and corporate liabilities. *Journal of Political Economy* 81 (May/June, 1973): 637–54; Robert C. Merton, Theory of rational option pricing. *Bell Journal of Economics and Management Science* 4 (1, Spring, 1973): 141–83; Franco Modigliani and Merton Miller, The cost of capital, corporation finance and the theory of investment. *American Economic Review* 48 (2, 1958): 261–97; Miller and Modigliani, Dividend policy, growth and the valuation of shares. *Journal of Business* 34 (1961): 411–33. See Miller, The Modigliani-Miller propositions after thirty years. *Journal of Economic Perspectives* 2 (4, 1988): 99–120; Merton, Applications of option–pricing theory: twenty–five years later. *American Economic Review* 88 (3, 1998): 323–49; Merton, Paul Samuelson and financial economics. *American Economist* 50 (2, Fall 2006): 9–30.

91. Coase, The nature; Coase, The problem, 1–44; Coase, The new institutional economics. *American Economic Review* 88 (2, 1998): 72–4; Douglass C. North, Economic performance through time. *American Economic Review* 84 (3, 1994): 359–68; Williamson, New institutional economics; Williamson, *Markets and hierarchies* (New York: Free Press, 1975); Williamson, *The economic institutions of capitalism* (New York: Free Press, 1985).

92. Coase, The nature; Coase, The problem.

93. Merton and Bodie, Design, 13.

94. Ibid, 14.

95. Ibid, 18.

96. Rafael La Porta, Florencio Lopez-de-Silanes and Andrei Shleifer, Law and finance. *Journal of Political Economy* 106 (6, 1998): 1113–55.

97. Ibid.

98. Rafael La Porta, Florencio Lopez-de-Silanes and Andrei Shleifer, What works in securities laws? *Journal of Finance* 61 (1, 2006): 1–32.

99. Rafael La Porta, Florencio Lopez-de-Silanes, Andrei Shleifer and Robert W. Vishny, Legal determinants of external finance. *Journal of Finance* 52 (3, 1997): 1131–50.

100. Diamond, Delegated monitoring; Diamond, Financial intermediation.

101. Ibid.

102. Diamond, Financial intermediation.

103. Diamond, Delegated monitoring, 401.

104. Ibid.

105. Douglas W. Diamond and Philip H. Dybvig, Banking theory, deposit insurance and bank regulation. *Journal of Business* 59 (Jan 1, 1986): 55–68.

106. Ibid.

107. Robert A. Eisenbeis, Scott Frame and Larry D. Wall, An analysis of the systemic risks posed by Fannie Mae and Freddie Mac and an evaluation of the policy options for reducing those risks. *Journal of Financial Services Research* 31 (2007): 75–99; Fannie Mae, An introduction to Fannie Mae. http://www.fanniemae.com/media/pdf/fannie_mae_introduction.pdf; W. Scott Frame and Lawrence J. White, Fusing and fuming over Fannie and Freddie: how much smoke, how much fire? *Journal of Economic Perspectives*

19 (2, Spring, 2005): 159–84; Dwight M. Jaffee and John M. Quigley, Housing subsidies and homeowners: what role for government–sponsored enterprises? *Bookings–Wharton Papers on Urban Affairs* (2007): 103–49.

108. Jaffee and Quigley, Housing subsidies, 108. See http://www.fhlbanks.com/

109. FHA, The Federal Housing Administration, http://www.hud.gov/offices/hsg/fhahistory.cfm

110. Jaffee and Quigley, Housing subsidies, 108. See http://www.homeloans.va.gov/veteran.htm

111. Fannie Mae, An introduction, 3.

112. http://www.ginniemae.gov/

113. Gordon H. Sellon and Deana VanNahmen, The securitization of housing finance. *Economic Review—Federal Reserve Bank of Kansas City* 73 (7, Jul/Aug, 1988): 3–20.

114. http://www.ofheo.gov/about.aspx?Nav=55

115. Jaffee and Quigley, Housing subsidies, 120–2.

116. Ibid, 123.

117. Jaffee and Quigley, Housing subsidies, 109.

118. Ibid, 111.

119. Ibid, 111; Xudong An, Raphael W. Bostic, Yonghen Deng and Stuart A. Gabriel, GSE loan purchases, the FHA and housing outcomes in targeted, low–income neighborhoods. *Brookings-Wharton Papers on Urban Affairs* (2007): 205–56.

120. Franklin D. Raines, Testimony. Washington, DC, US House Committee on Oversight and Government Reform, Dec 9, 2008.

121. Edward J. Pinto, Statement. Washington, DC, US House of Representatives, Committee on Oversight and Government Reform, Dec 9, 2008.

122. Office of Federal Housing Enterprise Oversight, *Report of the special examination of Fannie Mae* (Washington, DC: OFHEO, May, 2006).

123. Ibid, Dec 2003.

124. Lucian A. Bebchuk and Jesse M. Fried, Executive compensation at Fannie Mae: a case study of perverse incentives, nonperformance pay and camouflage. *Journal of Corporation Law* 30 (4, 2005): 807–22.

125. Dwight M. Jaffee, Reforming Fannie and Freddie. *Regulation* 31 (4, Winter, 2009): 52–7.

126. The Joint Forum, Credit risk transfer: developments from 2005 to 2007. Basel, BIS, Apr 2008; The Joint Forum, Credit risk transfer. Basel, BIS, Mar 2005.

127. Ibid.

128. Financial Stability Forum, Report of the Financial Stability Forum on enhancing market and institutional resilience: follow-up on implementation. Basel, BIS, Oct 10, 2008.

129. Carlos M. Peláez and Carlos A. Peláez, *International financial architecture: G7, BIS, debtors and creditors* (Basingstoke: Palgrave Macmillan, 2005).

130. Peláez and Peláez, *Globalization and the State: Volume II* (Basingstoke: Palgrave Macmillan 2008), Chapter 4, International Law; Peláez and Peláez, *Government intervention in globalization: regulation, trade and devaluation wars* (Basingstoke: Palgrave Macmillan, 2008), Chapter 10, International Law.

131. Douglas W. Diamond and Raghuram G. Rajan, A theory of bank capital. *Journal of Finance* 55 (6, Dec, 2000): 2431–65; Diamond and Rajan,

Liquidity risk, liquidity creation and financial fragility: a theory of banking. *Journal of Political Economy* 109 (Apr 2, 2001): 287–327; Diamond and Rajan, Banks and liquidity. *American Economic Review* 91 (May 2, 2001): 422–5.

132. Diamond and Philip H. Dybvig, Bank runs, deposit insurance and liquidity. *Journal of Political Economy* 91 (Jun 3, 1983): 401–49.
133. Diamond and Rajan, A Theory, 2432.
134. Diamond and Rajan, Liquidity theory, 317.
135. Diamond and Dybvig, Bank runs.
136. Sam Peltzman, Capital investment in commercial banking and its relationship to portfolio regulation. *Journal of Political Economy* 78 (Jan 1, 1970): 1–26.
137. John J. Mingo, Regulatory influence on bank capital investment. *Journal of Finance* 30 (Sep 4, 1975): 1111–21.
138. BCBS, *Basel II: international convergence of capital measurement and capital standards: a revised framework* (Basel: BCBS Publications No. 107, BIS, Jun, 2004).
139. BCBS, *International convergence of capital measurement and capital standards* (Basel: BIS, Jul 1988).
140. BCBS, Initiatives on capital announced by the Basel Committee, Mar 12, 2009, http://www.bis.org/press/p090312.htm
141. George J. Benston and George G. Kaufman, The FDICA after five years *Journal of Economic Perspectives* 11 (3, Summer, 1997): 139–58.
142. Ibid, 146; Benston and Kaufman, The appropriate role of bank regulation. *Economic Journal* 106 (436, May, 1996): 688–97. See Frederic S. Mishkin, An evaluation of the Treasury plan of banking reform. *Journal of Economic Perspectives* 6 (1, Winter, 1992): 133–53; Lawrence J. White, The reform of federal deposit insurance. *Journal of Economic Perspectives* 3 (4, Autumn, 1989): 11–29.
143. Milton Friedman, Controls on interest rates paid by banks. *Journal of Money, Credit and Banking* 2 (Feb 1, 1970): 15–32.
144. Ibid, 18.
145. Ibid, 24.
146. Ibid, 25.
147. Friedman, The euro-dollar market: some first principles. Chicago, University of Chicago Graduate School of Business, Selected Papers No. 34, 1969.
148. Friedman, Controls, 26–7.
149. Ibid, 27.
150. Ben S. Bernanke and Cara S. Lown, The credit crunch. *Brookings Papers on Economic Activity* 1991 (2, 1991): 205–47.
151. Joe Peek and Eric Rosengren, The capital crunch: neither a borrower nor a lender be. *Journal of Money, Credit and Banking* 27 (Aug 3, 1995): 625–38.
152. Randall S. Kroszner and Philip E. Strahan, What drives deregulation? Economics and politics of the relaxation of bank branching restrictions. *Quarterly Journal of Economics* 114 (4, 1999): 1437–67.
153. Charles W. Calomiris, Banking approaches the modern era. *Regulation* 25 (2, Summer, 2002): 14–20.

154. Nicholas R. Economides, R. Glenn Hubbard and Darius Palia, The political economy of branching restrictions and deposit insurance: a model of monopolistic competition among small and large banks. *Journal of Law and Economics* 39 (Oct 2, 1996): 667–704.
155. Kroszner and Strahan, What drives, 1443.
156. Ibid, 1453.
157. Ibid, 1454.
158. Ibid, 1458.
159. Ibid, 1461–2.
160. Kroszner and Strahan, Obstacles to optimal policy: the interplay of politics and economics in shaping bank supervision and regulation reform. In Frederic S. Mishkin, ed. *Prudential supervision. What works and what doesn't* (Chicago: University of Chicago Press, 2001).
161. Luc Laeven, 2004. The political economy of deposit insurance. *Journal of Financial Services Research* 26 (3, 2004): 201–24.
162. Ibid.
163. Ibid.
164. Calomiris, Is deposit insurance necessary? A historical perspective. *Journal of Economic History* 50 (2, Jun, 1990): 283–95.
165. Xavier Vives, Competition in the changing world of banking. *Oxford Review of Economic Policy* 17 (4, 2001): 535–48.
166. Ibid.
167. Ibid.
168. Ibid.
169. Allen N. Berger, Anil K. Kashyap and Joseph M. Scalise, The transformation of the US banking industry. *Brookings Papers on Economic Activity* 1995 (2): 55–218.
170. Ibid.
171. Ibid.
172. See note 19 in Chapter 2.
173. Allen N. Berger and Loretta J. Mester, Explaining the dramatic changes in the performance of US banks: technological change, deregulation and dynamic changes in competition. *Journal of Financial Intermediation* 12 (1, 2003): 57–95.
174. Ibid.
175. Jith Jayaratne and Philip E. Strahan, Entry restrictions, industry evolution and dynamic efficiency: evidence from commercial banking. *Journal of Law and Economics* 41 (Apr 1, 1988): 239–73.
176. Alan S. McCall and Manferd O. Peterson, The impact of de novo commercial bank entry. *Journal of Finance* 32 (Dec 5, 1977): 1587–1604; Peter S. Rose, Agency theory and entry barriers in banking. *Financial Review* 27 (Aug 3, 1992): 323–53; Robert DeYoung, De novo bank exit. *Journal of Money, Credit and Banking* 35 (Oct 5, 2003): 711–28; Nicola Cetorelli and Philip E. Strahan, Finance as a barrier to entry: bank competition and industry structure in local US markets. Chicago, FRBC, WP, 2003; Allen N. Berger and Astrid A. Dick, Entry into banking markets and the early-mover advantage. *Journal of Money, Credit and Banking* 39 (Jun 4, 2007): 775–807.
177. John R. Hicks, Annual survey of economic theory: the theory of monopoly. *Econometrica* 3 (1, 1935): 1–20.

178. Adolf Berle and Gardiner Means, *The modern corporation and private property* (New York: Macmillan, 1932).
179. Michael C. Jensen and William H. Meckling, Theory of the firm: managerial behavior, agency costs and ownership structure. *Journal of Financial Economics* 3 (4, 1976): 305–60.
180. Gordon Tullock, The welfare costs of tariffs, monopolies and theft. *Western Economic Journal* 5 (3, 1967): 224–32; Krueger, Political economy; Jagdish N. Bhagwati, Directly unproductive, profit-seeking (DUP) activities. *Journal of Political Economy* 90 (5, 1982): 998–1002.
181. Harvey Leibenstein, Allocative efficiency vs. 'X-efficiency.' *American Economic Review* 56 (June 2, 1966): 392–415.
182. Allen N. Berger and Timothy H. Hannan, The efficiency cost of market power in the banking industry: a test of the "quiet life" and related hypotheses. *Review of Economics and Statistics* 80 (Aug 3, 1998): 454–65.
183. John Boyd, Gianni De Nicoló and Bruce Smith, Crises in competitive versus monopolistic banking systems. *Journal of Money, Credit and Banking* 36 (3, 2004): 487–506.
184. Asli Demirgüç-Kunt and Vojislav Maksimovic, Law, finance and firm growth. *Journal of Finance* 53 (6, 1998): 2107–39.
185. FRBO, *The Federal Reserve System: purposes & functions* 9th ed. (Washington, DC: FRBO, Jun, 2005).
186. Ibid, 12.
187. OCC, About the OCC. http://www.occ.treas.gov/aboutocc.htm.
188. FDIC. 2007. About FDIC. http://www.fdic.gov/about/index.html
189. OTS, *OMB FY 2007 budget & performance plan* (Washington, DC, OFS, Jan, 2007).
190. OFHEO, About OFHEO. http://www.ofheo.gov/Mission.asp
191. NCUA, About NCUA. http://www.ncua.gov/AboutNCUA/Index.htm
192. NCUA, Your insured funds, February 2009. http://www.ncua.gov/Publications/brochures/insured_funds/YourInsuredFundsYIF_English.pdf
193. NYSBD, The department. http://www.banking.state.ny.us/dep.htm
194. FRBO, *The Federal*, 2. See Allan H. Meltzer, *History of the Federal Reserve, Volume 1: 1913–1951* (Chicago: University of Chicago Press, 2004); Milton Friedman and Anna Jacobson Schwartz, *A monetary history of the United States 1867–1960* (Princeton: Princeton University Press, 1963).
195. FRBO, *The Federal*, 1.
196. Ibid, 4.
197. Ibid, 5.
198. Ibid, 6.
199. Ibid, 11.
200. Ibid, 27.
201. Ibid, 34.
202. Ibid, 40.
203. http://www.federalreserve.gov/fomc/fundsrate.htm
204. Hanspeter K. Scheller, *History, role and functions* 2nd rev. ed. (Franfurt am Main: European Central Bank, 2006), 21.
205. Ibid, 25.
206. ECB, *The monetary policy of the ECB.* (Frankfurt am Main: European Central Bank, 2004), 9.

207. Scheller, History, 51.
208. Ibid, 53.
209. Ibid, 59.
210. Ibid, 61.
211. Ibid, 80.
212. Peláez and Peláez, *International financial architecture*, 18–27.
213. Scheller, History, 87–9.
214. IMES, *Functions and operations of the Bank of Japan* (Tokyo: IMES/BOJ, 2004)
215. Ibid, 55–78.
216. Ibid, 16–8.
217. Ibid, 21–2.
218. Ibid, 17–8.
219. Ibid, 126.
220. HM Treasury, Memorandum of understanding between HM Treasury, the Bank of England and the Financial Services Authority, 2007 http://www.bankofengland.co.uk/financialstability/mou.pdf
221. For an evaluation see Charles Bean, Is there a new consensus in monetary policy? In Philip Arestis, ed. *Is there a new consensus in macroeconomics* (Basingstoke, UK, and New York: Palgrave Macmillan, 2007).
222. BOE, The monetary policy committee of the Bank of England: ten years on. *Quarterly Bulletin 2007 Q1*: 24–38.
223. Ben S. Bernanke, A crash course for central bankers. *Foreign Policy* 120 (Sep/Oct, 2000): 49.
224. Ibid.
225. Ben S. Bernanke, Bank supervision in the United States. *Vital Speeches of the Day* 73 (2, 2007): 61–5.
226. Ibid.
227. BOE, The monetary, 26.
228. Ibid, 25.
229. Bean, Is there.
230. BOE, The monetary, 27.
231. Charles Bean, Inflation targeting: the UK experience. *Bank of England Quarterly Bulletin* 43 (4, Winter, 2003): 479–94.
232. Barry Eichengreen, The EMS crisis in retrospect. Berkeley, University of California, Nov 2000.
233. BOE, *Inflation report May 2007* (London: Bank of England, May, 2007).
234. Ibid, 6–7.
235. Christina D. Romer and David H. Romer, A new measure of monetary shocks: derivation and implications. *American Economic Review* 94 (Sep 4, 2004): 1055–84.
236. Ben S. Bernanke and Mark Gertler, Inside the black box: the credit channel of monetary policy transmission. *Journal of Economic Perspectives* 9 (4, Fall, 1995): 27–48.
237. Ben S. Bernanke, Mark Gertler and Simon Gilchrist, The financial accelerator in a quantitative business cycle framework. In John B. Taylor and Michael Woodford, eds. *Handbook of macroeconomics, Volume 1C* (Amsterdam: Elsevier North Holland, 1999).
238. Bernanke, Gertler and Gilchrist, The financial accelerator and the flight to quality. Cambridge, MA, NBER, Jul 1994.

239. Simon Hall, Credit channel effects in the monetary transmission mechanism. *Bank of England Quarterly Bulletin* 41 (4, Winter, 2001): 442–8.
240. Ibid, 445.
241. George J. Benston, Universal banking. *Journal of Economic Perspectives* 8 (3, Summer, 1994): 121–43; Anthony Saunders and Ingo Walter, *Universal banking in the United States: what could we gain? What could we lose?* (New York: Oxford University Press, 1994).
242. Benston, Universal banking, 124.
243. Rudi Vander Vennet, Cost and profit efficiency of financial conglomerates and universal banks in Europe. *Journal of Money, Credit and Banking* 34 (Feb 1, 2002): 254–82.
244. George J. Benston, *The separation of commercial and investment banking: the Glass-Steagall Act revisited and reconsidered* (New York: Oxford University Press, 1990).
245. Benston, Universal banking, 122.
246. Alexander Hamilton, National bank (1780). In Henry Cabot Lodge, ed. *The works of Alexander Hamilton.* New York and London: G. P. Putnam & Son, 1904: 319–45, http://files.libertyfund.org/files/1380/0249–03_Bk.pdf; David J. Cowen, Richard Sylla and Robert E. Wright, Alexander Hamilton central banker. Helsinski, XIV International Economic History Congress, Aug, 2006; Carlos A. Peláez, The reform of Alexander Hamilton. Philadelphia, University of Pennsylvania Law School, unpublished manuscript, Jan 2008.
247. Cowen et al., Alexander Hamilton.
248. Benston, Universal banking.
249. Ibid, 124.
250. Rafael La Porta et al.,Legal determinants.
251. Rafael La Porta, Florencio López de Silanes and Guillermo Zamarripa, Related lending. *Quarterly Journal of Economics* 118 (1, 2003): 231–68; Noel Maurer and Stephen Haber, Related lending and economic performance: evidence from Mexico. Stanford, Hoover Institute, Nov, 2005; Maurer and Haber, Related lending: manifest looting or good governance: lessons from the economic history of Mexico. In Sebastian Edwards, Gerardo Esquivel and Graciela Márquez, eds. *The decline of Latin American economies: growth, institutions and crises* (Chicago: University of Chicago, 2007).
252. Vennet, Cost and profit .
253. Ibid, 256.
254. Ibid, 260.
255. Ibid, 261.
256. Randall S. Kroszner and Raghuram G. Rajan, Is the Glass-Stegall Act justified? A study of the US experience with universal banking before 1933. *American Economic Review* 84 (4, 1994): 810–32.
257. Paul G. Mahoney, The political economy of the Securities Act of 1933. *Journal of Legal Studies* 30 (1, Jan, 2001): 1–31.
258. Ibid, 4.
259. Ibid, 13.
260. Ibid.
261. Ibid, 31.
262. Kroszner and Rajan, Is the Glass-Steagall Act, 813.
263. Mahoney, The political.

264. Kroszner and Rajan, Is the Glass-Stegall Act.
265. Ibid.
266. Randall S. Kroszner and Raghuram G. Rajan, Evidence from commercial bank securities activities in the Glass-Steagall Act. *Journal of Monetary Economics* 39 (Aug, 1997): 475–516.
267. James R. Barth , Dan Brumbaugh, Jr. and James A. Wilcox, The repeal of Glass-Steagall and the advent of broad banking. *Journal of Economic Perspectives* 14 (2, Spring, 2000): 191–204.
268. Ibid.
269. Jarrod Johnston and Jeff Madura, Valuing the potential transformation of banks into financial service conglomerates: evidence from the Citigroup merger. *The Financial Review* 35 (2, 2000): 17–36.
270. Ibid, 19.
271. Harold van B. Cleveland and Thomas F. Huertas, *Citibank 1812–1970* (Cambridge, MA: Harvard University Press, 1985); Srinivas B. Prasad, The metamorphosis of City and Chase as multinational banks. *Business and Economic History* 28 (2, 1999): 201–11; John Donald Wilson, *The Chase: the Chase Manhattan Bank, N.A., 1945–85* (Cambridge, MA: Harvard Business School Press, 1986); Phillip L. Zweig, *Wriston: Walter Wriston, Citibank and the rise and fall of American financial supremacy* (New York: Crown, 1996).
272. Johnston and Madura, Valuing.
273. Ibid, 22.
274. Ibid.
275. Barth et al., The repeal, 196; Harvard Law Review, The new American universal bank. *Harvard Law Review* 110 (Apr 6, 1997): 1310–27.
276. Barth et al., The repeal, 194.
277. Ibid, 198.
278. Ibid, 198.
279. René Stulz, Hedge funds: past, present and future. *Journal of Economic Perspectives* 21 (2, Spring, 2007): 175–94.
280. John Gieve, Hedge funds and financial stability. *Bank of England Quarterly Bulletin* 46 (4, 2006): 447–51.
281. Tomas Garbaravicius and Frank Dierick, *Hedge funds and their implications for financial stability* (Frankfurt am Main: ECB OPS No. 34, Aug, 2005), 7.
282. Houman B. Shadab, The challenge of hedge fund regulation. *Regulation* 30 (1, 2007): 36–41; Tobias Adrian, Measuring risk in the hedge fund sector. *Current Issues in Economics and Finance FRB of New York* 13 (3, 2007): 1–7.
283. Gieve, Hedge funds, 447.
284. William K. H. Fung and David Hsieh, Hedge funds: an industry in its adolescence. *Federal Reserve Bank of Atlanta Economic Review* Fourth Quarter (2006): 1–34.
285. Financial Stability Forum, Update of the FSF report on highly leveraged institutions. Basel, BIS, May 19, 2007; Stulz, Hedge funds, 176.
286. Financial Stability Forum, Update, 8.
287. Ibid, 8.
288. Ibid, 8.
289. Ibid, 8.
290. Stulz, Hedge funds, 176.

291. David Walker, Hedge-fund redemptions were $328 billion in 2008. *Wall Street Journal*, Jan 21, 2009.
292. Ibid.
293. James Mackintosh, Fears of record hedge fund withdrawals. *Financial Times*, Mar 23, 2009.
294. Shadab, The challenge, 36.
295. Ibid, 36–7.
296. Ibid, 37–8.
297. Adrian, Measuring, 1.
298. The covariance of returns between two funds measures the extent to which their losses can simultaneously occur. The appropriate measure requires normalizing the covariance of hedge fund returns, dividing it by the total variability of returns. The normalized covariance provides a measure of the association of HF returns relative to their overall volatility.
299. Ibid, 2.
300. Stulz, Hedge funds.
301. Fung and Hsieh, Hedge funds, 2.
302. Ibid, 2. The hedge fund decides on leverage and the allocation of risk capital to factor-bets versus the delivery of alpha or excess risk-adjusted return.
303. Stulz, Hedge funds, 187–8.
304. Ludwig Chincarini, A case study on risk management: lessons from the collapse of Amaranth Advisors L.L.C. *Journal of Applied Finance* 18 (1, Spring, 2008): 152–174.
305. Stulz, Hedge funds, 182. See Garbaravicius and Dierick, *Hedge funds* and Fung and Hsieh, Empirical characteristics of dynamic trading strategies: the case of hedge funds. *Review of Financial Studies* 10 (2, Summer, 1997): 275–302.
306. Vikas Agarwal and Narayan Y. Naik, Multi-period performance persistence analysis of hedge funds. *Journal of Financial and Quantitative Analysis* 35 (Sep 3, 2000): 327–42.
307. Nicole M. Boyson, Christof W. Stahel and René M. Stulz, Is there hedge fund contagion? Cambridge, MA, NBER WP 12090, Mar, 2006.
308. Nicholas Chan, Mila Getmansky, Shane M. Haas and Andrew W. Lo, Do hedge funds increase systemic risk? *Federal Reserve Bank of Atlanta Economic Review* Fourth Quarter (2006): 49–80. See International Monetary Fund, *Global financial stability report: responding to the financial crisis and measuring systemic risks* (Washington, DC, IMF, Apr 2009), Chapter 3, Detecting systemic risk. www.imf.org
309. Ibid, 50–1.
310. Ibid, 50.
311. European Central bank, *Financial stability review December 2006* (Frankfurt am Main: ECB, Dec 2006), 12.
312. Ibid, 12.
313. Ibid, 9.
314. Jean-Claude Trichet, Interview. *Financial Times*, May 17, 2007.
315. Ralph Atkins and Lionel Barber, Trichet sees support for hedge fund code. *Financial Times*, May 17, 2007; Atkins and Barber, A vindicated Trichet continues to press for reform. *Financial Times*, May 17, 2007; Financial Times,

Hedge fund industry could do more to engage its critics. *Financial Times*, May 17, 2007.
316. Trichet, Interview.
317. Financial Times, Hedge fund industry.
318. Jean-Claude Trichet, Keynote address. Paris, Committee of European Securities Regulators, Feb 23, 2009.
319. Financial Stability Forum, Update, 2.
320. Ibid, 5.
321. Ibid, 6.
322. G30 Working Group, *Financial reform: a framework for financial stability* (Washington, DC: G30, 2009), 30–1.
323. Adam Smith, *An inquiry into the nature and causes of the wealth of nations*, 1776, V.1.107 *65, http://www.econlib.org/library/Smith/smWN.html
324. Coase, The nature.
325. Berle and Means, *The modern corporation* ; Patrick Bolton and David S. Scharfstein, Corporate finance, the theory of the firm and organization. *Journal of Economic Perspectives* 12 (4, Autumn, 1998): 95–114.
326. George J. Stigler and Claire Friedland, The literature of economics: the case of Berle and Means. *Journal of Law and Economics* 26 (Jun 2, 1983): 237–268.
327. Alfred P. Sloan, Jr., *My years with General Motors* (New York: Doubleday & Company, 1963); Raghuram G. Rajan and Luigi Zingales, The governance of the new enterprise. In Xavier Vives, ed. *Corporate governance, theoretical and empirical perspectives* (Cambridge, UK: Cambridge University Press, 2000).
328. Jensen and Meckling, Theory of the firm.
329. Ibid.
330. Ibid.
331. Ibid.
332. See the special examination reports by the OFHEO, http://www.ofheo. gov/Regulations.aspx?Nav=199
333. Eugene F. Fama and Michael C. Jensen, Agency problems and residual claims. *Journal of Law and Economics* 26 (Jun 2, 1983): 327–49.
334. Ibid, 321–2.
335. Ibid; Fama and Jensen, Separation of ownership and control. *Journal of Law and Economics* 26 (Jun 2, 1983): 301–25.
336. Fama and Jensen, Separation.
337. Edward M. Liddy, Testimony. Washington, DC, House Financial Services Subcommittee on Capital Markets, Insurance and Government–Sponsored Enterprises, Mar 18, 2009; 111th Congress, 1st Session, To impose an additional tax on bonuses received from certain TARP recipients. Washington, DC, US House of Representatives, Mar 18, 2009.
338. George P. Baker, Michael C. Jensen and Kevin J. Murphy, Compensation and incentives. *Journal of Finance* 43 (Jul 3, 1988): 593–616.
339. Michael C. Jensen and Kevin J. Murphy, Performance pay and top–management incentives. *Journal of Political Economy* 98 (Apr 2, 1990): 225–64.
340. Ibid, Table 11, 260.
341. Jensen, Takeovers: 21–48.

342. Kevin J. Murphy and Ján Zábojník, Managerial capital and the market for CEOs. Los Angeles, USC Working Paper, Apr, 2007.

343. Ibid.

344. Lucian Arye Bebchuk, Jesse M. Fried and David I. Walker, Managerial power and rent extraction in the design of executive compensation. *University of Chicago Law Review* 69 (3, Summer, 2002): 751–846; Bebchuk and Jesse M. Fried, Executive compensation as an agency problem. *Journal of Economic Perspectives* 17 (3, Summer, 2003): 71–92; Bebchuk and Fried, *Pay without performance: the unfulfilled promise of executive compensation* (Cambridge, MA: Harvard University Press, 2004).

345. Murphy and Zábojník, CEO pay and appointments: a market-based explanation for recent trends. *American Economic Review* 94 (May 2, 2004): 192–6.

346. Brian J. Hall and Murphy, The trouble with stock options. *Journal of Economic Perspectives* 17 (3 Summer, 2003): 49–70.

347. Adam Smith, *An inquiry*; Berle and Means, *The modern corporation*.

348. Edward B. Rock, Saints and sinners: how does Delaware corporate law work? *UCLA Law Review* 44 (1997):1009–1107.

349. Ibid, 1011.

350. Ibid, 1011.

351. Ibid, 1013.

352. Ibid, 1014.

353. Ibid, 1015.

354. Ibid, 1015.

355. Ibid.

356. Ibid, 1095.

357. Ibid, 1099.

358. Ibid, 1104.

359. Ibid, 1062.

360. Marcel Kahan and Edward B. Rock, How I learned to stop worrying and love the pill: adaptive responses to takeover law. Philadelphia and New York, Institute for Law and Economics and Center for Law and Business, Apr, 2002.

361. Ibid.

362. Ibid.

363. Ibid.

364. Ibid, 10.

365. Ibid.

366. Ibid, 14.

367. Joel Seligman, Cautious evolution or perennial irresolution: stock market self-regulation during the first seventy years of the Securities and Exchange Commission. *The Business Lawyer* 59 (Aug, 2004): 1347–87.

368. Ibid, 1377–84.

369. Ibid, 1378–9.

370. Ibid.

371. Ibid.

372. SEC, The investor's advocate: how the SEC protects investors, maintains market integrity and facilitates capital formation, 2006 http://www.sec.gov/about/whatwedo.shtml

373. Ibid.
374. Ibid.
375. Ibid.
376. Ibid.
377. Ibid.
378. Margaret Cole, The UK FSA: nobody does it better? *Fordham Journal of Corporate and Financial Law* 12 (2, 2007): 259–83.
379. Ibid, 267.
380. Ibid, 267.
381. Ibid, 267.
382. Ibid, 268.
383. Ibid, 269–70.
384. Ibid, 269.
385. FSA, About the FSA. http://www.fsa.gov.uk/Pages/About/index.shtml
386. Cole, The UK FSA, 270; FSA, About the FSA.
387. FSA, About the FSA.
388. Ibid.
389. Cole, The UK FSA.
390. Ibid, 270.
391. FSA, About the FSA.
392. Cole, The UK FSA, 270–1.
393. Ibid, 271.
394. Robert Frank, Amir Efrati, Aaron Luccheti and Chad Bray, Madoff jailed after admitting epic scam. *Wall Street Journal*, Mar 13, 2009.
395. Cole, The UK FSA, 271.
396. Ibid, 272.
397. Mary L. Schapiro, Testimony concerning enhancing investor protection and regulation of the securities markets. Washington, DC, US Senate Committee on Banking, Housing and Urban Affairs, Mar 26, 2009.
398. Ibid.
399. Ibid.
400. Ibid.
401. Ibid.
402. FSA, The Turner review: a regulatory response to the global banking crisis (London: FSA, Mar, 2009). http://www.fsa.gov.uk/pages/Library/Corporate/turner/index.shtml
403. See Christopher C. Finger, IRC comments. *RiskMetrics Group Research Monthly*, Feb 2009; Finger, VaR is from Mars, capital is from Venus. *RiskMetrics Group Research Monthly*, Apr 2009, www.riskmetrics.com
404. FSA, The Turner, 61.
405. Ibid, 66.
406. Ibid, 67.
407. Ibid, 73.
408. Ibid, 75.
409. Ibid.
410. See the evaluation by Finger, VaR is from Mars.
411. Michael C. Jensen, Agency costs of overvalued equity. *Financial Management* 34 (1, Spring, 2005): 5–19.
412. Ibid, 10–1.

413. John C. Coffee, Jr., A theory of corporate scandals: why the USA and Europe differ. *Oxford Review of Economic Policy* 21 (2, 2005): 198–211.
414. Ibid.
415. Ibid.
416. Ibid, 202.
417. Ibid.
418. US 107th Congress, Public Law 107–204. Sarbanes–Oxley Act of 2002. http://www.sec.gov/about/laws/soa2002.pdf
419. SEC, Sarbanes-Oxley rulemaking and reports. http://www.sec.gov/spotlight/sarbanes–oxley.htm
420. http://www.ofheo.gov/Regulations.aspx?Nav=199
421. Cory L. Braddock, Penny wise, pound foolish: why investors would be foolish to pay a penny or a pound for the protections provided by Sarbanes-Oxley. *Brigham Young University Law Review* (2006): 175–210.
422. Ibid, 175.
423. Ibid.
424. Coffee, A theory.
425. Braddock, Penny wise, 174.
426. Ibid, 175.
427. Ibid, 175.
428. Ibid.
429. Ibid.
430. William J. Carney, The costs of being public after Sarbanes-Oxley: the irony of "going private." *Emory Law Journal* 55 (1, 2006): 141–60.
431. Ibid, 141.
432. Ibid, 142.
433. Ibid, 145.
434. Ibid, 147.
435. Ibid, 148.
436. Ibid, 151.
437. Ibid.
438. Ibid, 152–3.
439. Ibid, 154–5.
440. Roberta Romano, The Sarbanes-Oxley act and the making of quack corporate governance. *Yale Law Journal* 114 (7, 2005): 1521–1611.
441. Ibid, 1529–33.
442. Ibid, 1536.
443. Ibid.
444. Ibid, 1537.
445. Ibid, 1538–9.
446. Ibid.
447. Ibid.
448. Jill E. Fisch, The new federal regulation on corporate governance. *Harvard Journal of Law and Public Policy* 28 (1, 2004): 39–49.
449. Ibid, 49.
450. Ibid, 47–8.
451. Donald C. Langevoort, Internal controls after Sarbanes-Oxley: revisiting corporate law's "duty of care as responsibility for systems." *Journal of Corporation Law* 31 (3, 2006): 949–73.

452. Ibid, 956.

453. Ibid.

454. Ibid, 957.

455. Ibid.

456. Roberta Romano, Is regulatory competition a problem or irrelevant for corporate governance? *Oxford Review of Economic Policy* 21 (2, 2005): 212–31.

457. Ibid, 214.

458. SEC, Final rule: implementation of standards of professional conduct for attorneys. 17 CFR Part 205. January 29, 2003 http://www.sec.gov/rules/final/33-8185.htm

459. Kim T. Vu, Conscripting attorneys to battle corporate fraud without shields or armor? Reconsidering retaliatory discharge in light of Sarbanes-Oxley. *Michigan Law Review* 105 (1, 2006): 209–39.

460. Ibid.

461. William H. Volz and Vahe Tazian, The role of attorneys under Sarbanes-Oxley: the qualified legal compliance committee as facilitator of corporate integrity. *American Business Law Journal* 43 (3, 2006): 439–65.

462. Ibid, 450.

463. Ibid, 451.

464. Ibid, 460–1.

465. Ibid, 461.

466. Gerald J. Lobo and Jian Zhou, Did conservatism in financial reporting increase after the Sarbanes-Oxley Act? Initial evidence. *Accounting Horizons* 20 (1, 2006): 57–73.

467. Ibid.

468. Heng Hsieu Lin and Frederick H. Wu, Limitations of Section 404 of the Sarbanes-Oxley Act. *CPA Journal* 76 (3, 2006): 48–53.

469. Ibid, 52.

470. Ibid.

471. Weili Ge and Sarah McVay, The disclosure of material weakness in internal control after the Sarbanes-Oxley Act. *Accounting Horizons* 19 (3, 2005): 137–58.

472. Ibid, 143.

473. Ibid.

474. Steven E. Kaplan, Pamela B. Roush and Linda Thorne, Andersen and the market for lemons in audit reports. *Journal of Business Ethics* 70 (2006): 363–73.

475. Akerlof, Market for 'lemons'.

476. Kaplan, Roush and Thorne, Andersen.

477. Ibid, 366–8.

478. Ibid.

479. Ibid, 370.

480. Committee on Capital Markets Regulation, Interim report of the committee on capital markets regulation. Nov 30, 2006 http://www.capmktsreg.org/index.html ; Committee on Capital Markets Regulation, 2007 http://www.capmktsreg.org/index.html; Committee, Update. Mar 13, 2007 http://www.capmktsreg.org/index.html ; McKinsey & Co, *Sustaining New York's and the US' global financial services leadership* (New York: McKinsey & Co., 2007); US Chamber of Commerce, *Commission on the regulation of the*

US capital markets in the 21st century: report and recommendation. Executive Summary (Washington, DC: National Chamber Foundation, Mar, 2007) www.uschamber.com/ncf; US Chamber of Commerce, *Commission on the regulation of the US capital markets in the 21st century: report and recommendation* (Washington, DC: National Chamber Foundation, Mar, 2007) www.uschamber.com/ncf; US Chamber of Commerce *Capital markets, corporate governance and the future of the US economy* (Washington, DC: National Chamber Foundation, Feb, 2006) www.uschamber.com/ncf

481. R. Glenn Hubbard and John L. Thornton, Is the US losing ground? Oct 30, 2006. http://www.capmktsreg.org/index.html ; Hubbard and Thornton, Action plan for capital markets. *Wall Street Journal*, Nov 30, 2006 http://www.capmktsreg.org/index.html

482. Luigi Zingales, Insider ownership and the decision to go public. *Review of Economic Studies* 62 (Jul 3, 1995): 425–48; Marco Pagano, Fabio Panetta and Luigi Zingales, Why do companies go public? An empirical analysis. *Journal of Finance* 53 (Feb 1, 1998): 27–64.

483. Alexander Dyck and Luigi Zingales, Private benefits of control: an international comparison. *Journal of Finance* 59 (Apr 2, 2004): 537–600.

484. Ibid.

485. Marco Pagano, Ailsa A. Roell and Josef Zechner, The geography of equity listing: why do companies list abroad. *Journal of Finance* 57 (Dec 6, 2002): 2651–94.

486. Luigi Zingales, Is the US capital market losing its competitive edge? Bruxelles, European Corporate Governance Institute, Finance WP 192, Nov, 2007.

487. Ibid.

488. John C. Coffee, Jr., Racing toward the top? The impact of cross-listings and stock market competition on international corporate governance. *Columbia Law Review* 102 (7, 2002): 1757–1831; Coffee, Privatization and corporate governance: the lessons from securities market failure. *Journal of Corporation Law* 25 (1, Fall, 1999): 1–39; René Stulz, Globalization, corporate finance and the cost of capital. *Journal of Applied Corporate Finance* 12 (3, Fall, 1999): 8–25.

489. Craig G. Doidge, Andrew Karolyi and René M. Stulz, Has New York become less competitive in global markets? Evaluating foreign listing choices over time. Columbus, OH, Dice Center WP 2007-9, Jul, 2007.

490. Ibid.

491. International Monetary Fund, *World economic outlook: crisis and recovery* (Washington, DC: IMF, Apr 2009), 10.

492. Christina D. Romer, Lessons from the Great Depression for economic recovery in 2009. Washington, DC, Brookings Institution, Mar 9, 2009; Romer, Lessons from the New Deal. Washington, DC, Senate Committee on Banking, Housing and Urban Affairs, Mar 31, 2009.

493. Friedman and Schwartz, *A monetary history* .

494. Kris James Mitchener, Bank supervision, regulation and instability during the Great Depression. *Journal of Economic History* 65 (Mar 1, 2005): 152–85.

495. Irving Fisher, The debt-deflation theory of great depressions. *Econometrica* 1 (Oct 4, 1933): 337–57.

496. Andre Atkeson and Patrick J. Kehoe, Deflation and depression: is there an empirical link. *American Economic Review* 94 (May 2, 2004): 99–103.

497. Ben S. Bernanke, Nonmonetary effects of the financial crisis in propagation of the Great Depression. *American Economic Review* 73 (Jun 3, 1983): 257–76.

498. Joan Robinson, Beggar-my-neighbor remedies for unemployment. In Robinson, ed. *Essays in the theory of employment* (London: Macmillan, 1937); Robinson, The pure theory of international trade. *The Review of Economic Studies* 14 (2, 1946–1947): 98–112.

499. Peláez and Peláez, *Globalization and the state: Volume I* (Basingstoke, UK: Palgrave Macmillan, 2008); Peláez and Peláez, *Globalization and the state: Volume II*; Peláez and Peláez, *Government intervention*.

500. Barry Eichengreen, The origins and nature of the great slump revisited. *Economic History Review* 45 (May 2, 1992): 213–39. Brazil was among the countries that abandoned the gold standard: Carlos Manuel Peláez, A balança commercial, a Grande Depressão e a industrialização brasileira. *Revista Brasileira de Economia* 22 (1, Jan/Mar, 1968): 15–47; Peláez, The state, the Great Depression and the industrialization of Brazil. New York, unpublished PhD dissertation, Columbia University, 1968; Peláez, *História da industrializaçao brasileira* (Rio de Janeiro: APEC, 1972).

501. Prosper Raynold, W. Douglas McMillin and Thomas R. Beard, The impact of federal government expenditures in the 1930s. *Southern Economic Journal* 58 (Jul 1, 1991): 15–28.

502. J. R. Vernon, World War II fiscal policies and the end of the Great Depression. *Journal of Economic History* 54 (Dec 4, 1994): 850–68.

503. Christina D. Romer, What ended the Great Depression? *Journal of Economic History* 52 (Dec 4, 1992): 757–84.

504. Ibid.

505. Robert A. Margo, Employment and unemployment in the 1930s. *Journal of Economic Perspectives* 7 (2, Spring, 1993): 41–59.

506. Ibid.

507. Margo, The microeconomics of depression unemployment. *Journal of Economic History* 51 (Jun 2, 1991): 333–41.

508. Ibid.

509. Harold L. Cole and Lee E. Ohanian, The Great Depression in the United States from a neoclassical perspective. *Federal Reserve Bank of Minneapolis Quarterly Review* 23 (1, Winter, 1999): 2–24.

510. Ibid.

511. Cole and Ohanian, New Deal policies and the persistence of the Great Depression: a general equilibrium analysis. Minneapolis, Federal Reserve Bank of Minneapolis, WP 957, May, 2001.

512. Ibid.

513. Ibid.

514. FSA, The Turner.

515. Robert J. Shiller, Animal spirits depend on trust. *Wall Street Journal*, Jan 27, 2009.

516. John B. Taylor, The financial crisis and the policy responses: an empirical analysis of what went wrong. Palo Alto, CA, Stanford University, Nov, 2008. http://www.hoover.org/research/globalmarkets?section=publications;

Taylor, Housing and monetary policy. In Housing, housing finance and monetary policy. Jackson Hole, WY: Symposium by the Federal Reserve Bank of Kansas City, 2007. http://www.kc.frb.org/home/subwebnav.cfm?level=3&theID=10982&SubWeb=10658; Taylor, *Getting off track: how government actions and interventions caused, prolonged and worsened the crisis* (Stanford: Hoover Institution Press, 2009); Taylor, How government created the financial crisis. *Wall Street Journal*, Feb 9, 2009; Taylor and John C. Williams, A black swan in the money market. *American Economic Journal Macroeconomics* 1 (Jan 1, 2009): 58–83; Charles W. Calomiris, The subprime turmoil: what's old, what's new and what's next. New York, Columbia University, Oct 2, 2008; Calomiris, Financial innovation, regulation and reform. New York, Columbia University, Feb, 2009. Critique of the dangers of the low fed funds rates leading to recession are in Peláez and Peláez, *International financial architecture*; Peláez and Peláez, *The global recession risk* (Basingstoke, UK: Palgrave Macmillan, 2007); Peláez and Peláez, *Globalization and the State, Volume I and Volume II*; Peláez and Peláez, *Government intervention*.

517. Jaffee and Quigley, Housing subsidies.
518. Pinto, Statement.; Raines, Testimony; Calomiris, The subprime; Calomiris, Financial.
519. Calomiris, The subprime; Calomiris, Financial.
520. Ibid; Pinto, Statement.
521. Ben S. Bernanke, The Federal Reserve's balance sheet. Charlotte, NC, Federal Reserve Bank of Richmond Symposium, Apr 3, 2009.
522. Ibid.
523. Ben S. Bernanke and Vincent R. Reinhart, Conducting monetary policy at very low short-term interest rates. *American Economic Review* 92 (May 2, 2004): 85–90.
524. FOMC, Domestic open market operations during 2008. New York, FRBNY, Jan, 2009.
525. Ibid, 4.
526. Treasury, Treasury announces supplementary financing program, Sep 17, 2008. http://www.ustreas.gov/press/releases/hp1144.htm
527. FOMC, Domestic, 28.
528. James D. Hamilton, Federal Reserve balance sheet, Dec 22, 2008. http://www.mrswing.com/articles/Federal_Reserve_balance_sheet.html
529. Bernanke, The Federal Reserve's balance sheet.
530. Hamilton, Federal Reserve.
531. Jon Hilsenrath, Fed faces constraints in market-revival role. *Wall Street Journal* Feb 12, 2009.
532. John B. Taylor, The need to return to a monetary framework. Palo Alto, CA, Hoover Institution, Jan 2009.
533. Ibid.
534. FSOB, First quarterly report to Congress pursuant to section 104(g) of the Emergency Economic Stabilization Act of 2008. Washington, DC, US Treasury, Jan 2009. http://www.financialstability.gov/docs/FSOB/FINSOB–Qrtly–Rpt–123108.pdf; COP, February oversight report. Washington, DC, US Congress. Feb , 2009. http://cop.senate.gov/documents/cop–020609–report.pdf; Duff & Phelps. 2009. Valuation report. Washington, DC, Congressional Oversight Panel, Feb 4, 2009 http://cop.senate.gov

535. Timothy Geithner, Remarks introducing the Financial Stability Plan. Washington, DC, US Treasury, Feb 10, 2009. http://www.treas.gov/initiatives/eesa/; Treasury, Financial Stability Plan fact sheet. Washington, DC, US Treasury, Feb 10, 2009 http://www.treas.gov/initiatives/eesa/

536. Ibid.

537. Treasury, Treasury white paper. Washington, DC, US Treasury Department, Feb 25, 2009. http://www.financialstability.gov/

538. Board of Governors of the Federal Reserve System, The supervisory capital assessment program: design and implementation. Washington, DC, FRBO, Apr 24, 2009.

539. Ibid.

540. Treasury, Public–Private Investment Program. Washington, DC, UST, Mar 30, 2009. http://www.financialstability.gov/roadtostability/publicprivatefund.html

541. HUD, Public Law 110–289 of July 30, 2008, Housing and Economic Recovery Act, Jul 30, 2008 http://www.hud.gov/offices/cpd/community development/programs/neighborhoodspg/hera2008.pdf HUD, Housing and Economic Recovery Act of 2008 FAQ, Feb 2009 http://www.hud.gov/news/recoveryactfaq.cfm

542. Treasury, Homeowner affordability and stability executive summary, Feb 18, 2009 http://www.ustreas.gov/news/index2.html; Geithner, Statement by Secretary Tim Geithner on Treasury's commitment to Fannie Mae and Freddie Mac, Feb 18, 2009 http://www.ustreas.gov/press/releases/tg32.htm

543. Treasury, Home affordable modification program guidelines. Washington, DC, US Treasury, Mar 4, 2009. http://www.ustreas.gov/press/releases/reports/modification_program_guidelines.pdf

544. Geithner, Statement.

545. WSJ Forum, Dukes of moral hazard. *Wall Street Journal* Feb 18, 2009.

546. Tresury, Homeowner.

547. Wes Goodman and Jody Shenn, Fannie Mae rescue hindered as Asians seek guarantee. Bloomberg, Feb 20, 2009.

548. White House, The President's American recovery and reinvestment plan, Feb 2009. http://www.whitehouse.gov/agenda/economy/

549. Romer and Jared Bernstein, The job impact of the American recovery and reinvestment plan. Jan 9, 2009. http://otrans.3cdn.net/45593e8ecbd339d074_l3m6bt1te.pdf

550. Curtis Dubay, Karen Campbell and Paul Winfree, Economic stimulus pushed by flawed jobs analysis. *Web Memo* No. 2252, Washington DC, The Heritage Foundation, Jan 28, 2009.

551. Bernanke, Semiannual monetary policy report to the Congress. Washington, DC, Committee on Banking, Housing and Urban Affairs, US Senate, Feb 24, 2009.

552. Stephen Power and Neil King, Jr., Next challenge on stimulus: spending all that money. *Wall Street Journal*, Feb 13, 2009.

553. Jonathan Weisman, Obama to shift focus to budget deficit. *Wall Street Journal*, Feb 14, 2009; Weisman, Obama delivers $3.6 trillion budget blueprint. *Wall Street Journal*, Feb 26, 2009.

554. White House, The President's.

555. Ibid.

556. Bernanke, Current economic and financial conditions and the federal budget. Washington, DC, Committee on the Budget, US Senate, Mar 3, 2009.

557. Sudeep Reddy, Rosy assumptions hold down deficit. *Wall Street Journal*, Feb 27, 2009.

558. White House, The President's.

559. Ibid.

560. Congressional Budget Office, The budget and economic outlook: fiscal years 2009–2019. Washington, DC: US Congress, Jan 2009. http://www.cbo.gov/ftpdocs/99xx/doc9957/01–07–Outlook.pdf

561. Michael J. Boskin, Obama's $163,000 tax bomb. *Wall Street Journal*, Apr 2, 2009.

562. FDIC, Temporary Liquidity Guarantee Program Frequently Asked Questions, Jan 12, 2009. http://www.fdic.gov/regulations/resources/TLGP/faq.html

563. http://www.fdic.gov/regulations/resources/TLGP/optout.html

564. FDIC, Temporary; FDIC, Temporary Liquidity Guarantee Program. 12 CFR Part 370. *Federal Register* 72 (229), Nov 26, 2008.

565. FDIC, Temporary.

566. Liz Rappaport and Kellie Geressy, Goldman's massive bond sale goes well. *Wall Street Journal*, Nov 25, 2008.

567. Urban Bäckström, What lessons can be learned from recent financial crises? The Swedish experience. Jackson Hole, WY, Federal Reserve Bank of Kansas City, 1997.

568. Ibid, 132.

569. Stefan Ingves and Göran Lind, The management of the bank crisis—in retrospect. Sveriges Riksbank *Quarterly Review* 1 (1996): 5–18.

570. Ibid, 8.

571. Ibid, 9.

572. Ibid, 11.

573. Ibid, 13.

574. Ibid; Bäckström, What lessons; O. Emre Ergungor. On the resolution of financial crises: the Swedish experience. Cleveland, PDP No. 21, Federal Reserve Bank of Cleveland, Jun, 2007; Ergungor and Kent Cherny, Effective practices in crisis resolution and the case of Sweden. Cleveland, Federal Reserve Bank of Cleveland, Feb 12, 2009. http://www.clevelandfed.org/Research/commentary/2009/0209.cfm?DCS.pr=20090212

575. Ingves and Lind, The management, 13–4.

576. Ibid, 14.

577. Ibid, 15.

578. US Treasury, Treasury proposes legislation for resolution authority. Washington, DC, US Treasury Mar 25, 2009; US Treasury, Treasury outline framework for regulatory reform. Washington, DC, US Treasury, Mar 26, 2009; Tim Geithner, Remarks. New York, Council on Foreign Relations, Mar 25, 2009; Geithner, Written Testimony. Washington, DC, House Financial Services Committee, Mar 26, 2009.

579. FSA, The Turner.

580. G30, *Financial reform: a framework for financial stability* (Washington, DC: G30, 2009).

581. See note 95.
582. FSF, Report of the Financial Stability Forum on addressing procyclicality in the financial system. Basel, BIS, Apr 2, 2009; BIS, Addressing financial system procyclicality: a possible framework. Basel, BIS, Sep 1, 2009; FSF–BCBS, Reducing procyclicality arising from the bank capital framework. Basel, BIS, Mar, 2009; FSF, Report of the FSF Working Group on Provisioning. Basel, BIS, Mar, 2009; FSF–CGFS, The role of valuation and leverage in procyclicality. Basel, BIS, Mar, 2009; FSA, The Turner.
583. FSF, FSF principles for cross-border cooperation on crisis management. Basel, BIS, Apr 2, 2009.
584. BCBS, Proposed enhancements to the Basel II framework. Basel, BIS, Jan, 2009; Nout Wellink, Basel Committee initiatives in response to the financial crisis. Brussels, Remarks before the Committee on Economic and Monetary Affairs of the European Parliament (ECON), Mar, 2009; FSF, Report of the Financial Stability Forum on enhancing market and institutional resilience. Basel, BIS, Apr 7, 2008; FSF, Report of the Financial Stability Forum on enhancing market and institutional resilience. Update on implementation. Basel, BIS, Apr 2, 2009. See Finger, IRC comments.
585. BCBS, Principles for sound liquidity risk management and supervision. Basel, BIS, Sep, 2009.
586. BCB, Enhancements.
587. BCBS, Consultative document for core principles for effective deposit insurance systems. Basel, BIS, Mar, 2009.
588. See note 95.
589. G30, Financial; FSA, The Turner.
590. FSF, FSF principles for sound compensation practices. Basel, BIS, Apr 2, 2009.
591. See note 95.
592. G30, Financial.
593. Fischer Black, US commercial banking: trends, cycles and policy: comment. *NBER Macroeconomics Annual* 8 (1993): 368–71; Black, Merton H. Miller and Richard A. Posner, An approach to the regulation of bank holding companies. *Journal of Business* 51 (Jul 3, 1978): 379–412; Merton and Bodie, Design; Merton and Bodie, A conceptual; Levine, Bank-based.
594. Taylor, The financial crisis ; Calomiris, Financial.
595. Peláez and Peláez, *International financial architecture*; Peláez and Peláez, *The global recession risk*; Peláez and Peláez, *Globalization and the State Volume I and Volume II*; Peláez and Peláez, *Government intervention*.
596. Finger, VaR is from Mars.

Index